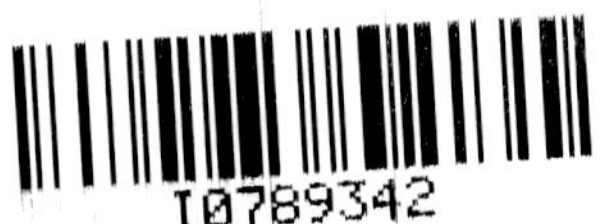

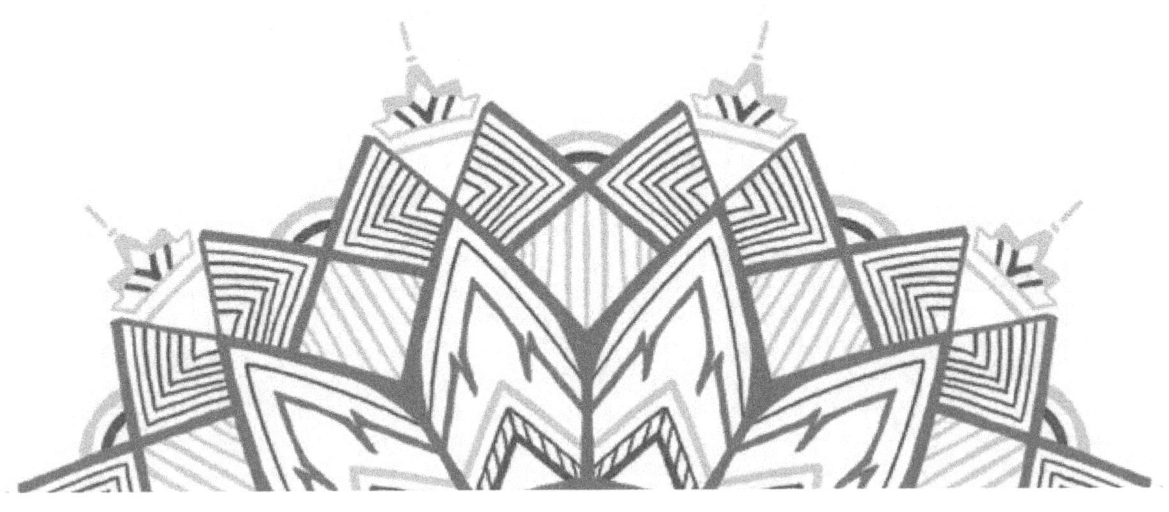

Beautiful Mandalas
Coloring Book

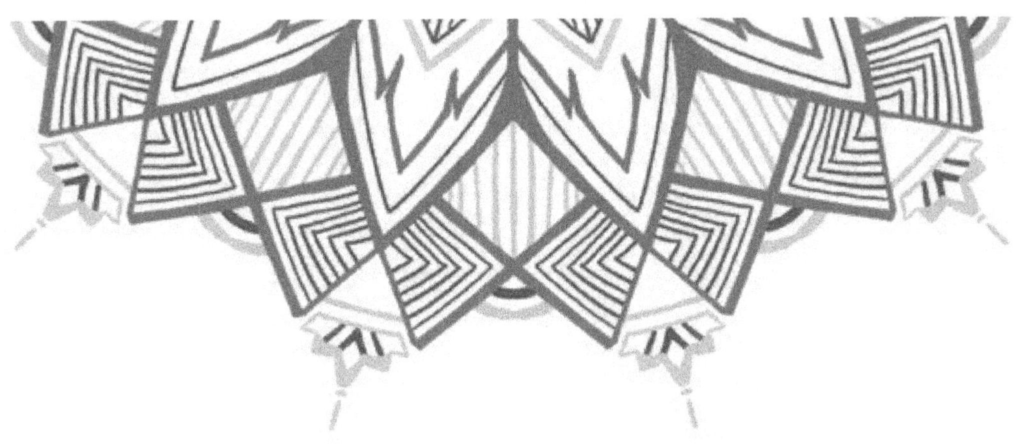

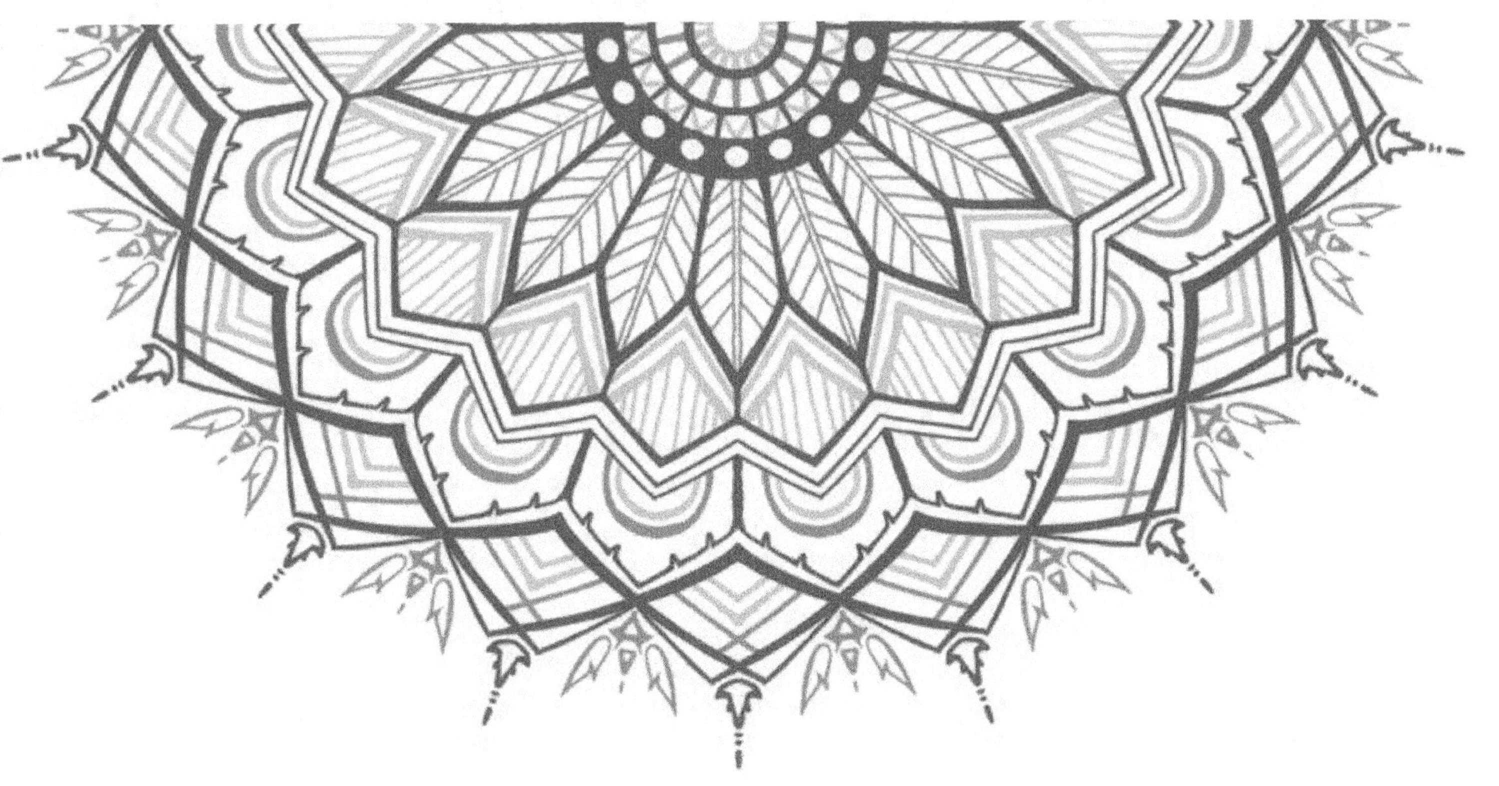

This book belong to

____

____

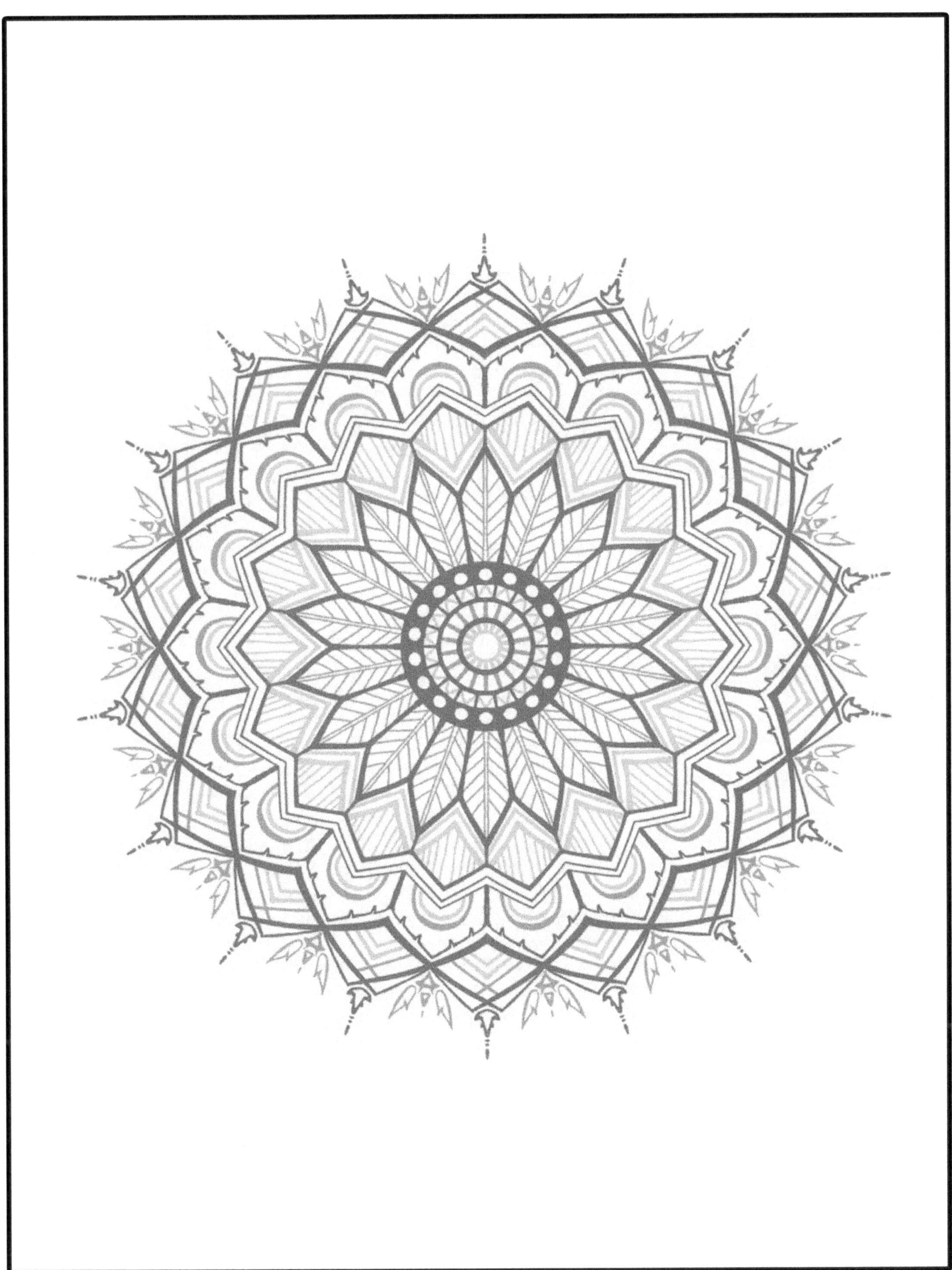

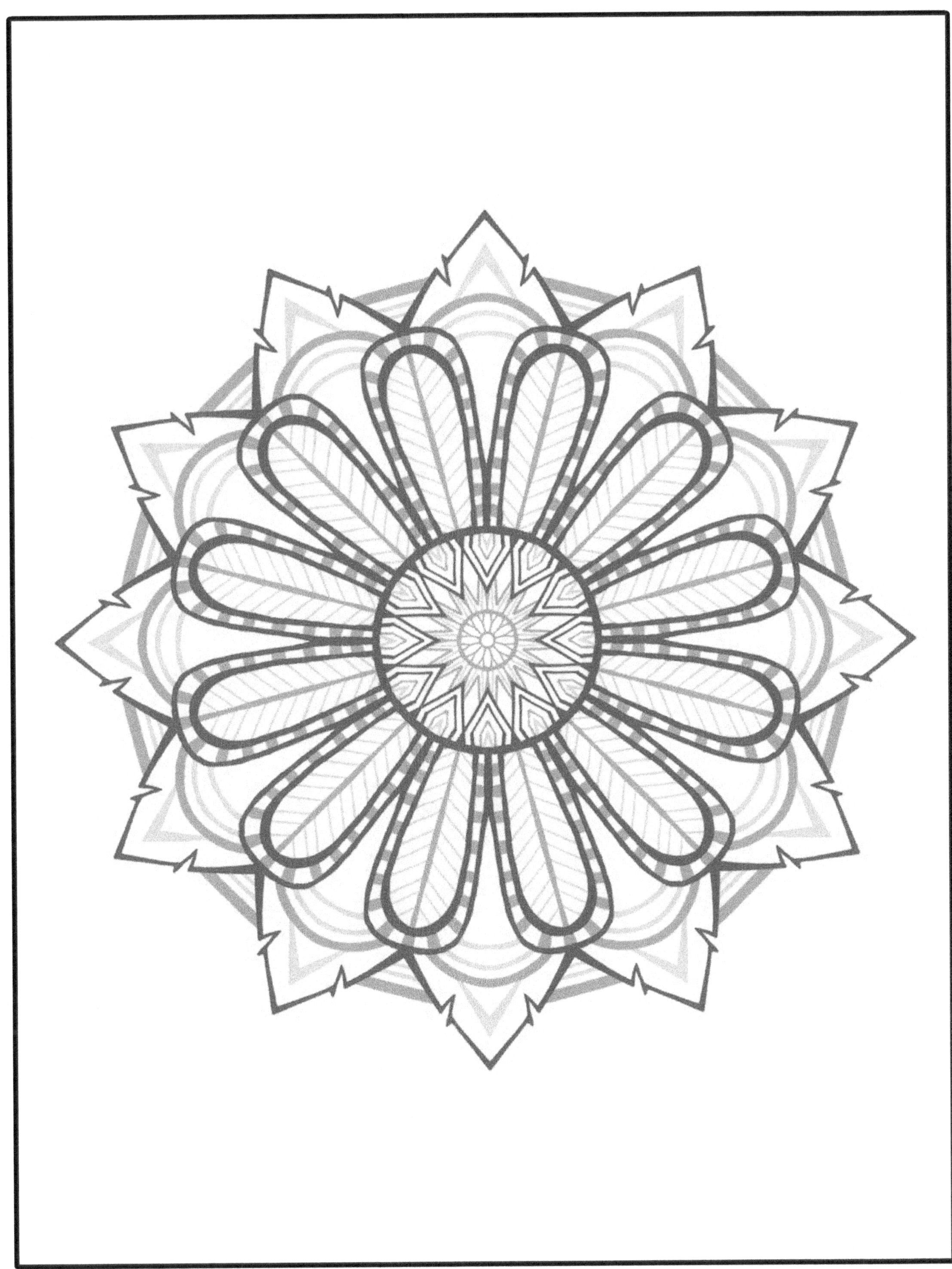

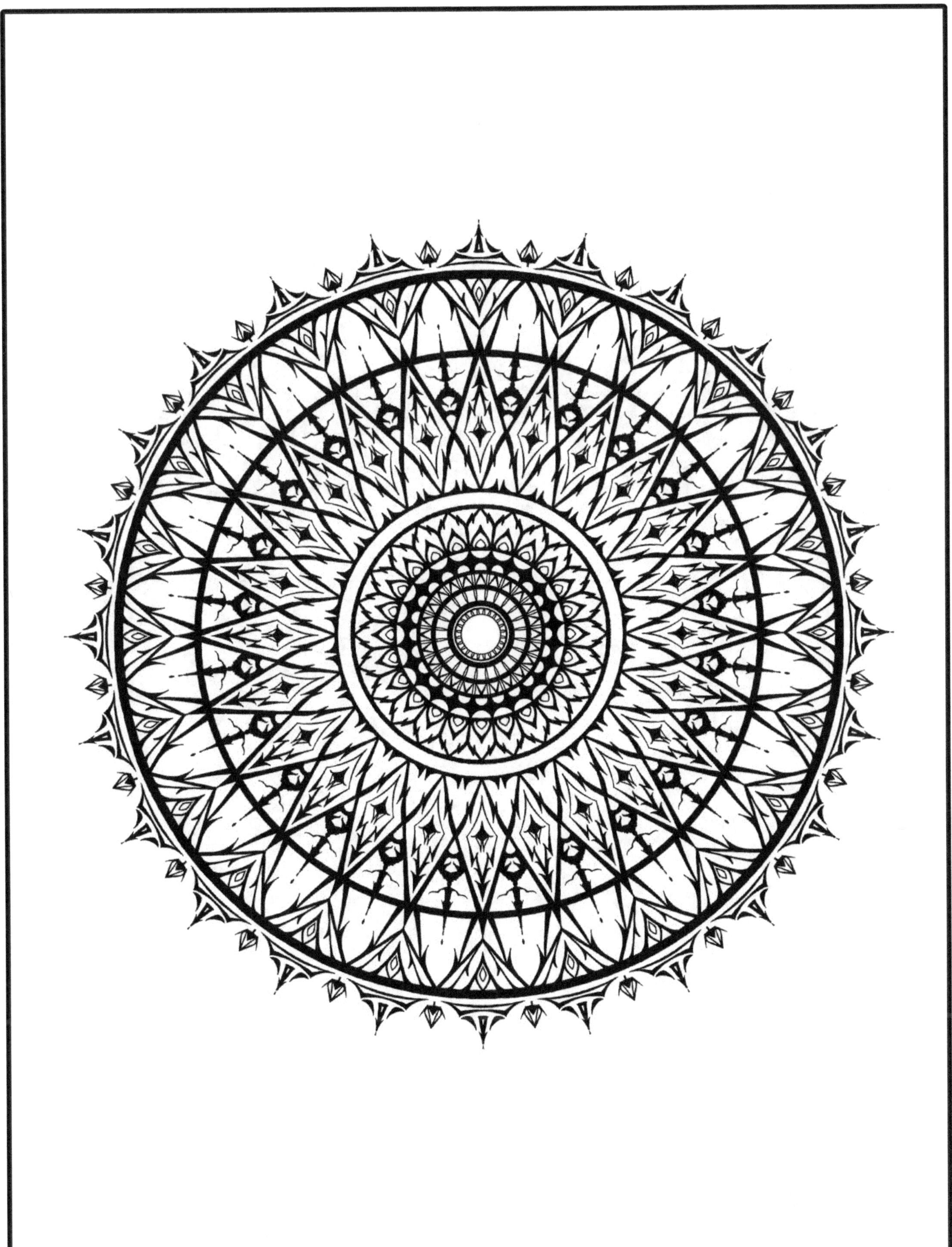

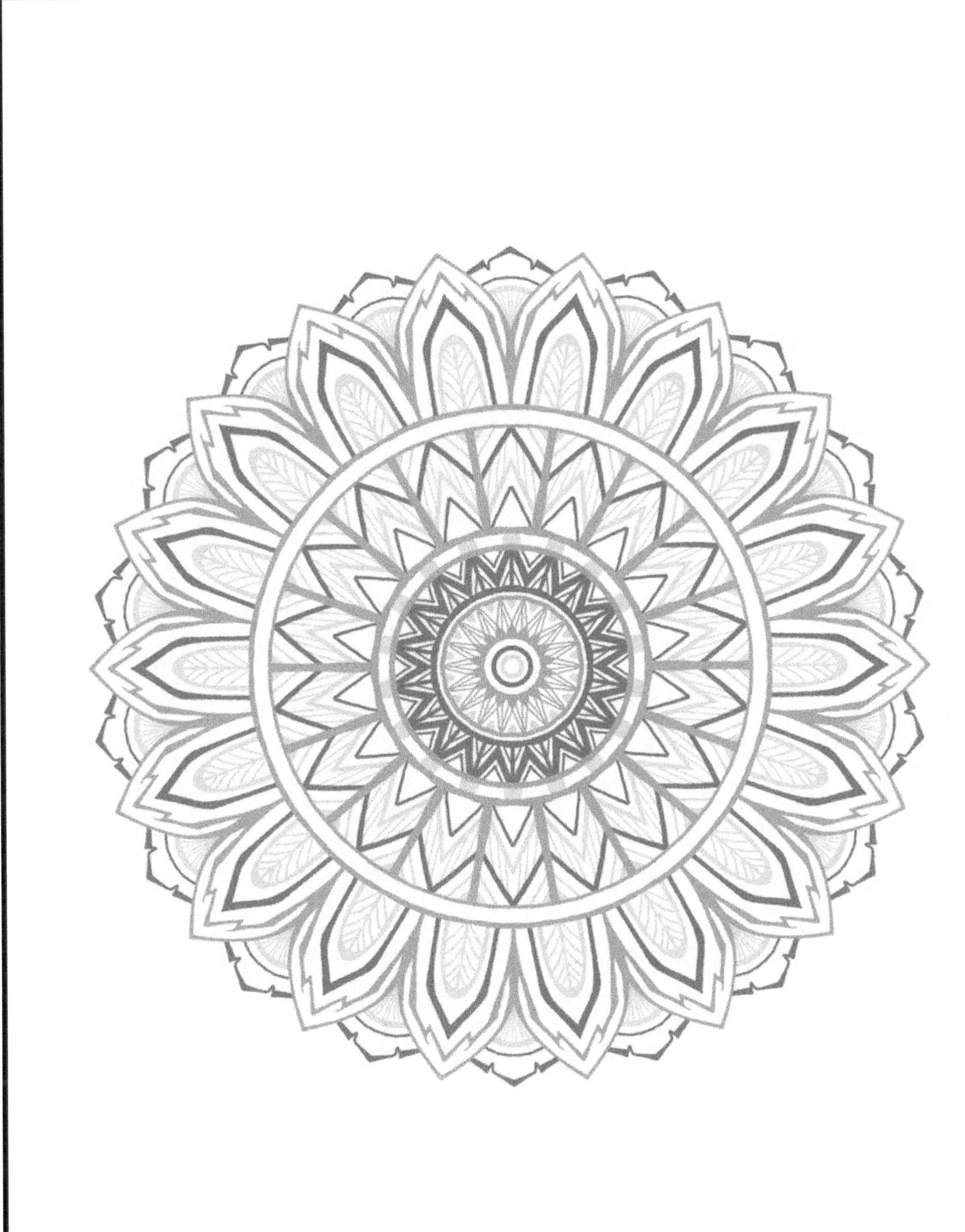

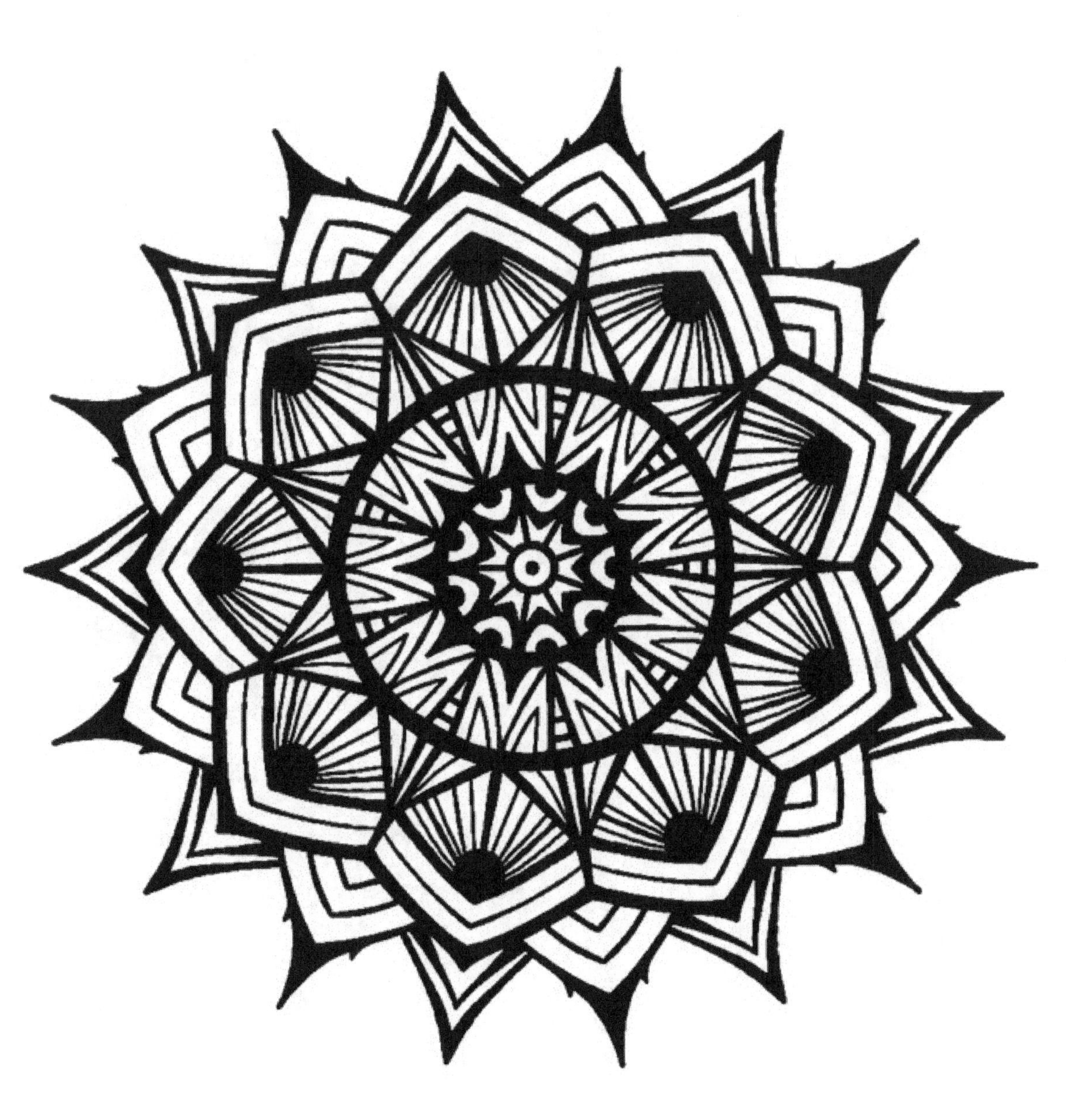

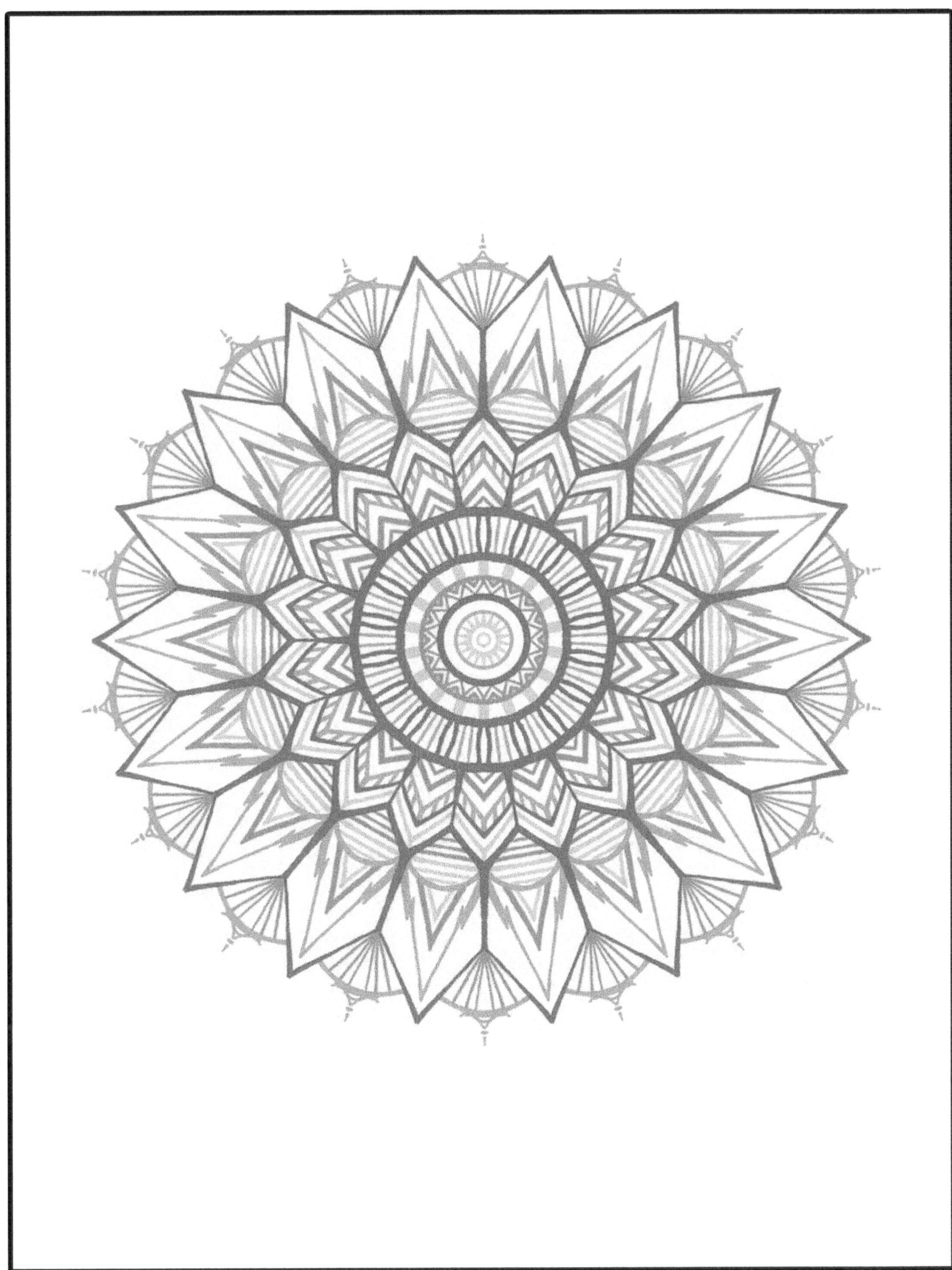

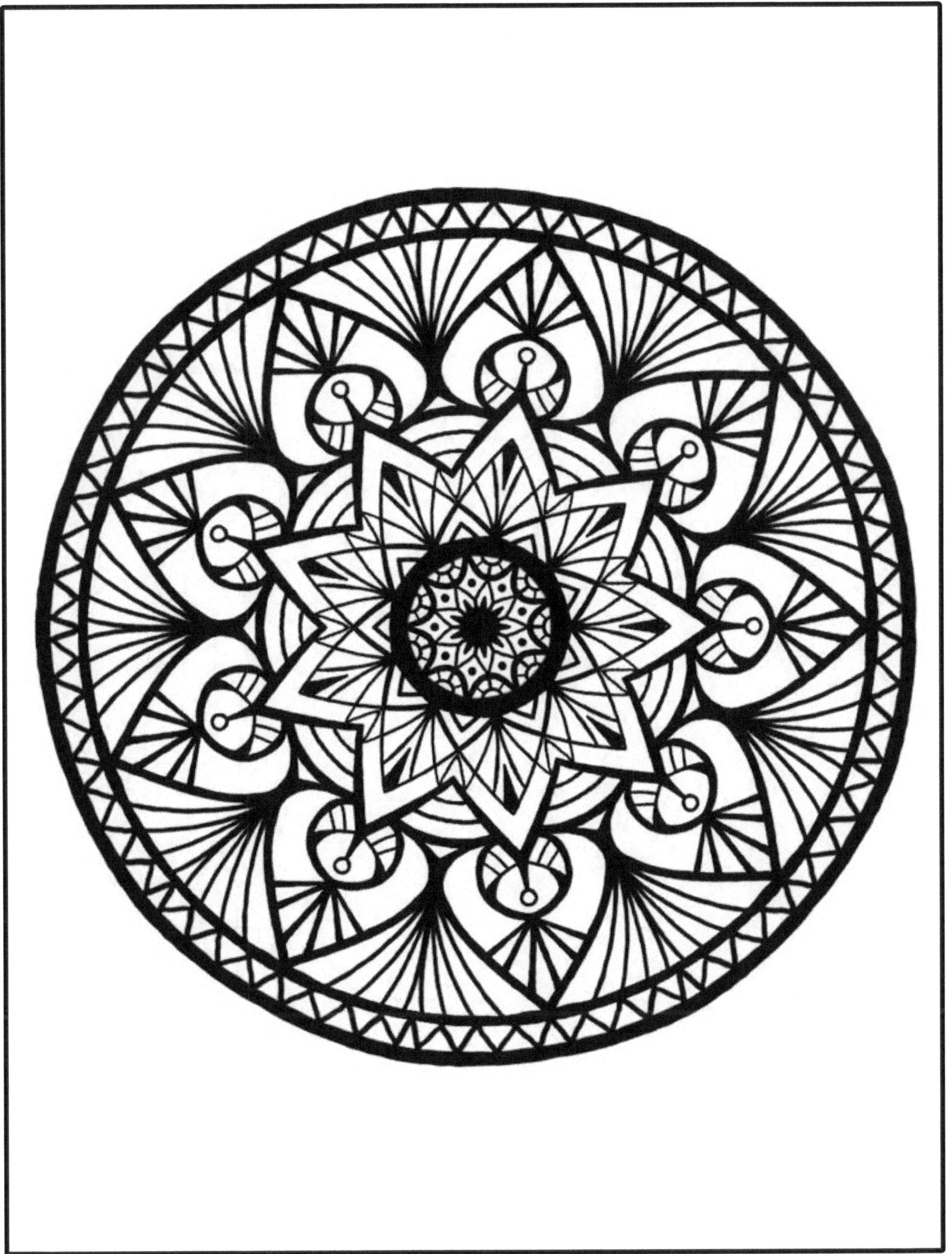

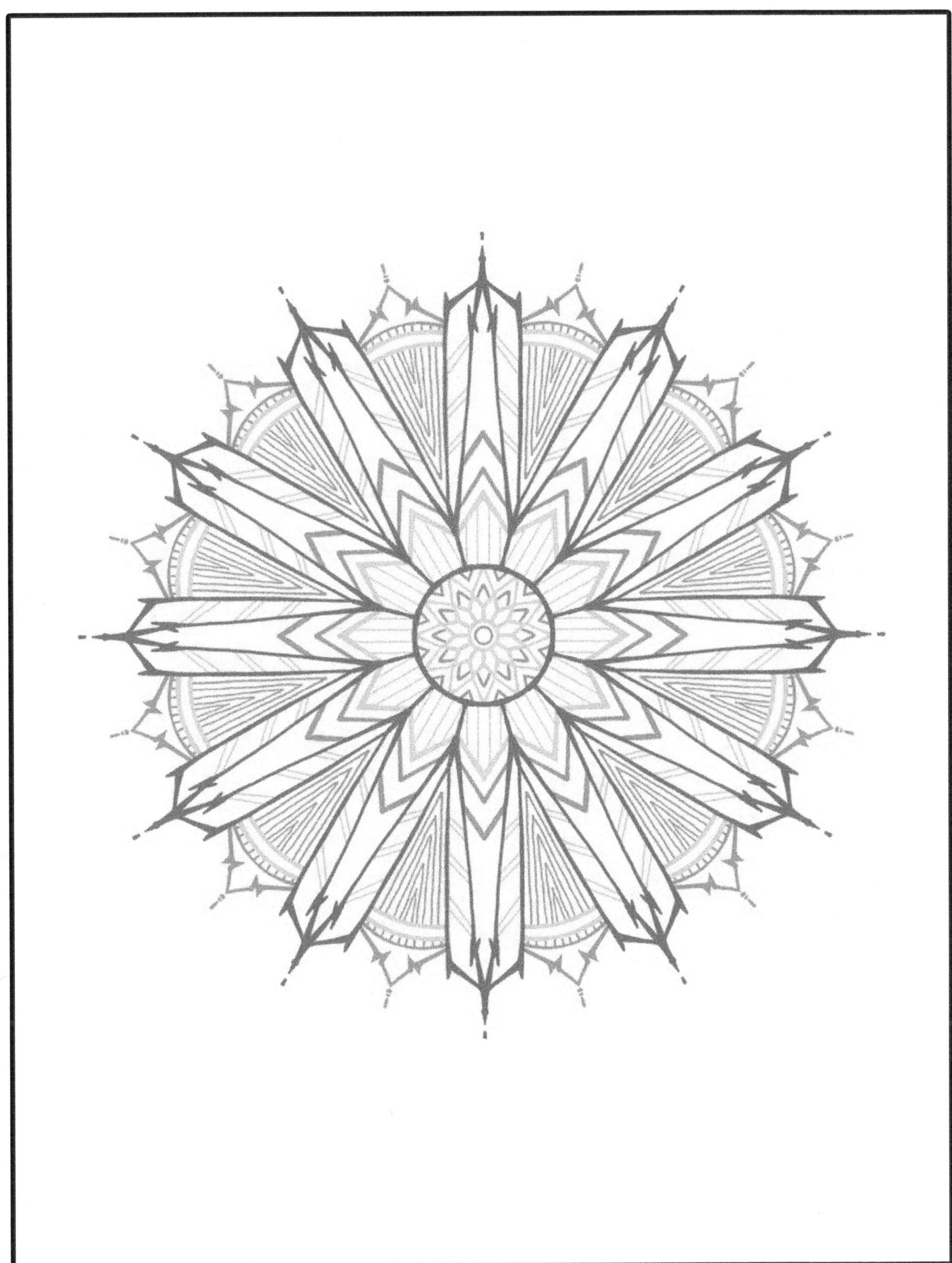

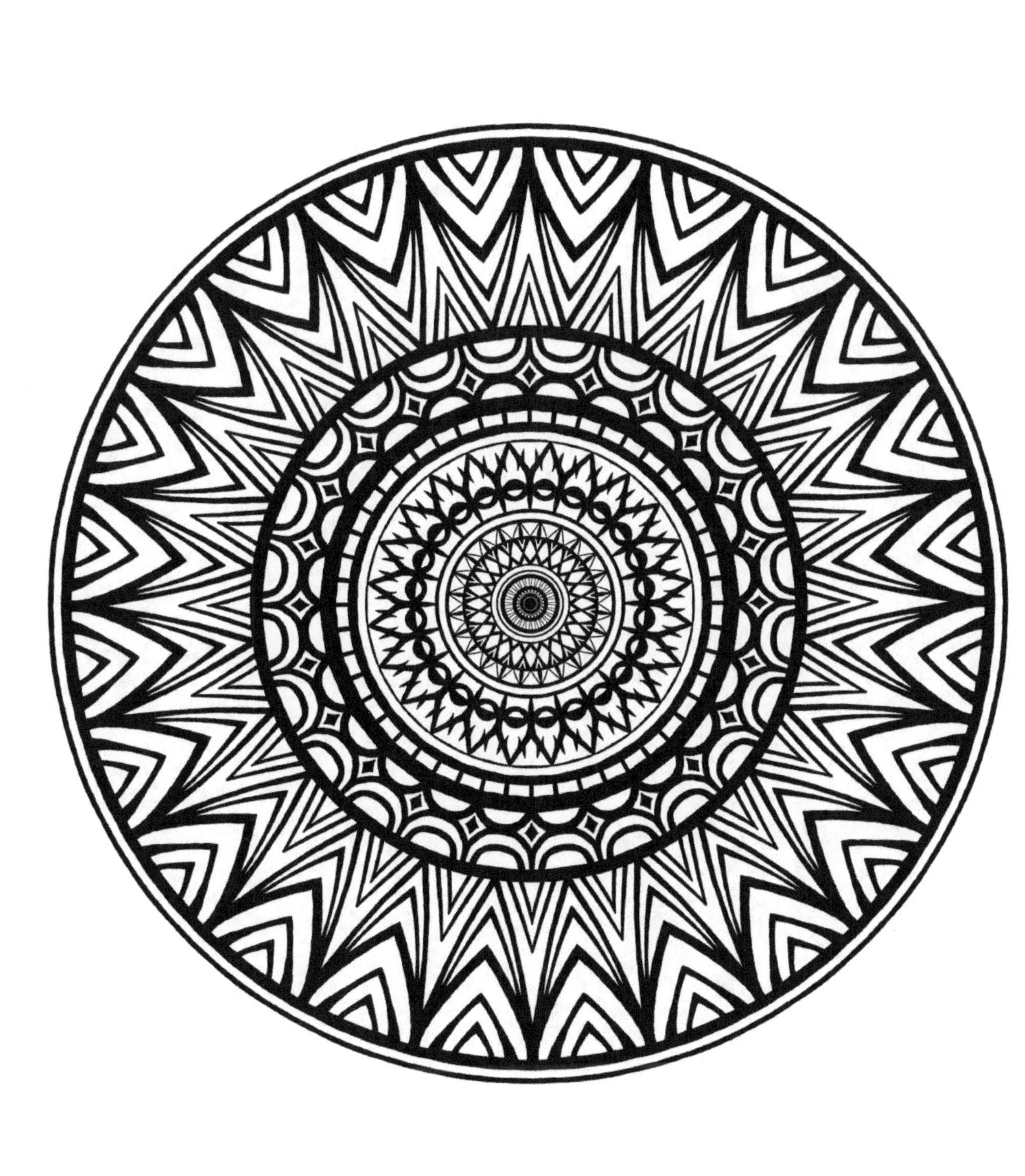

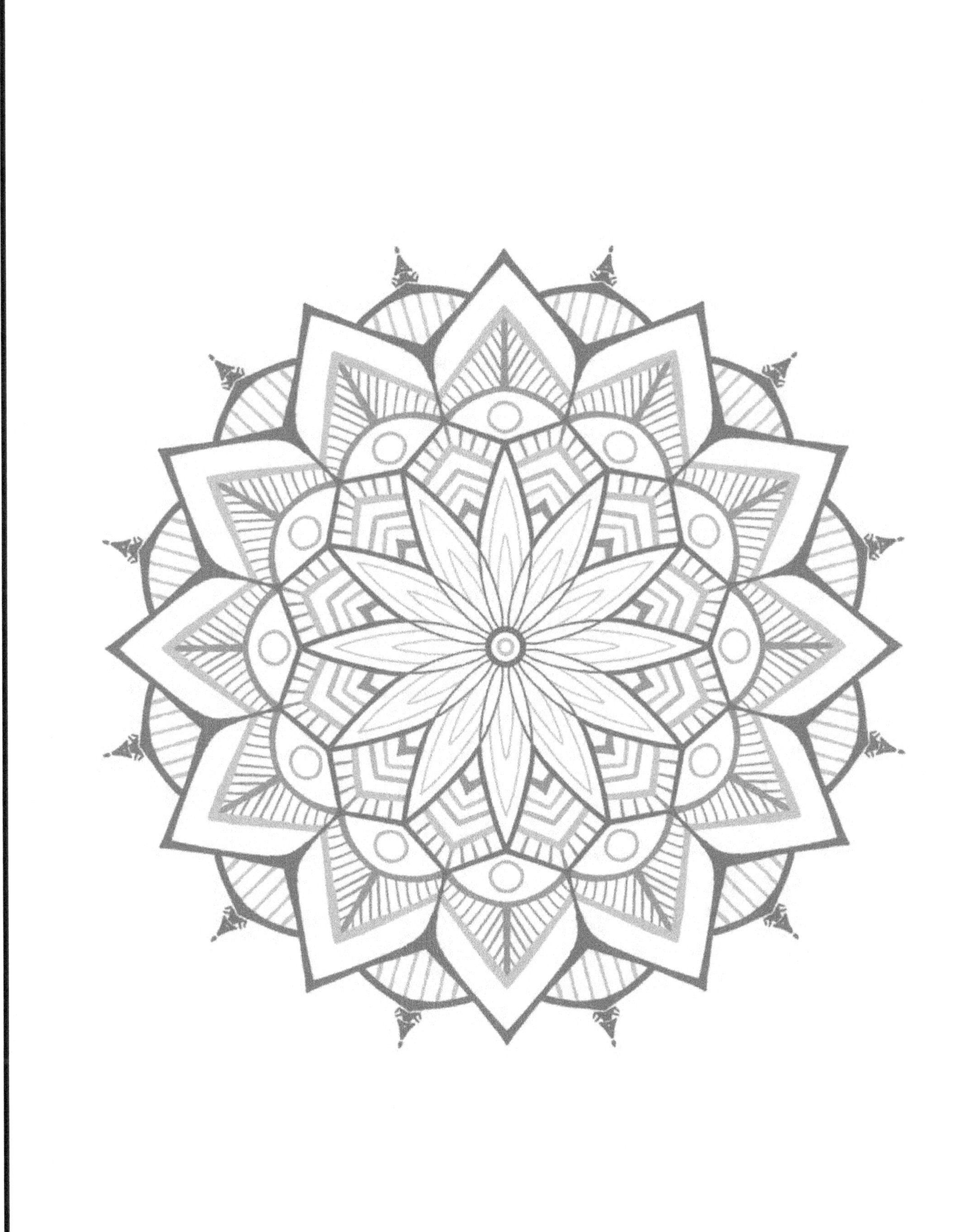

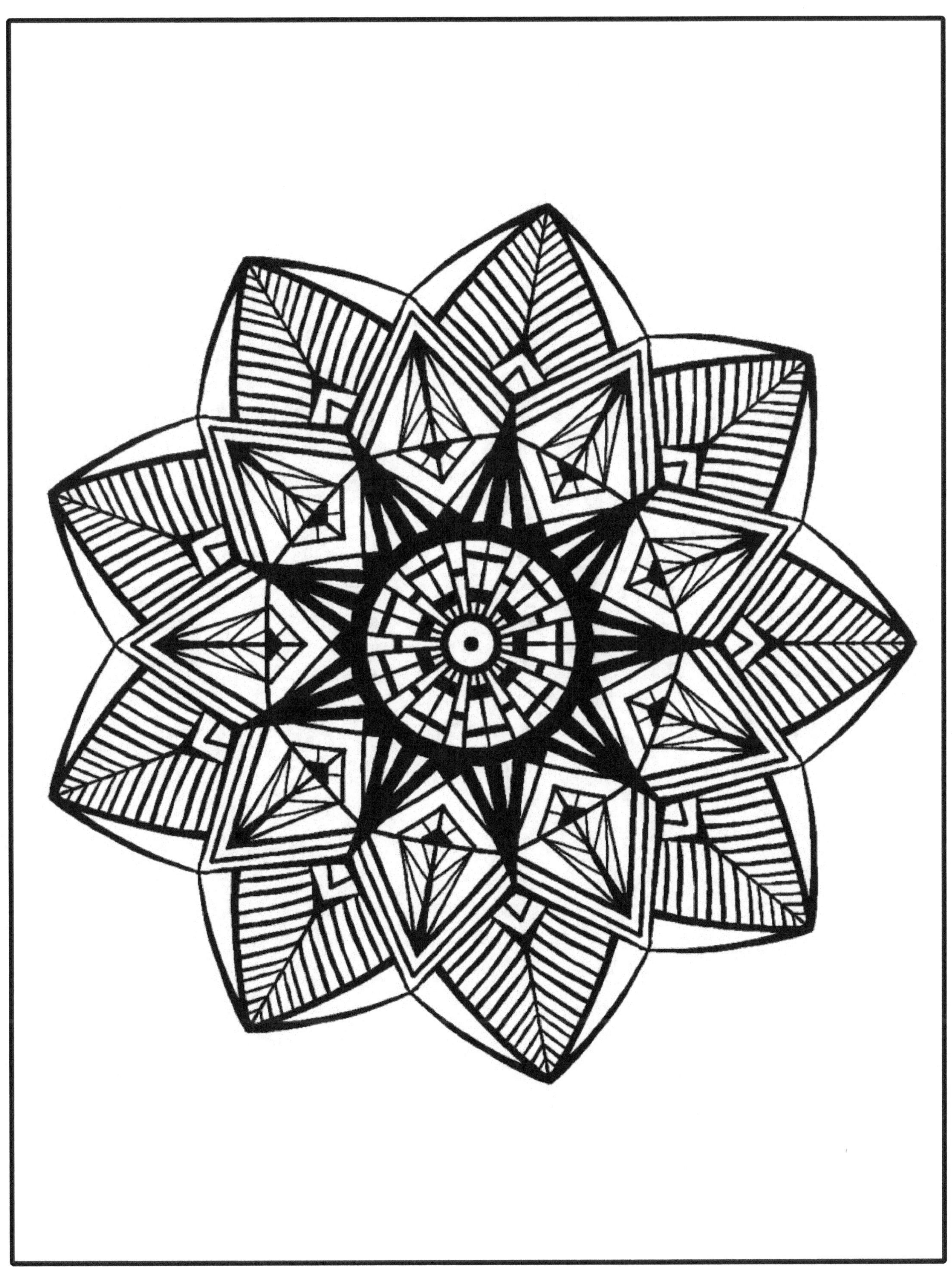

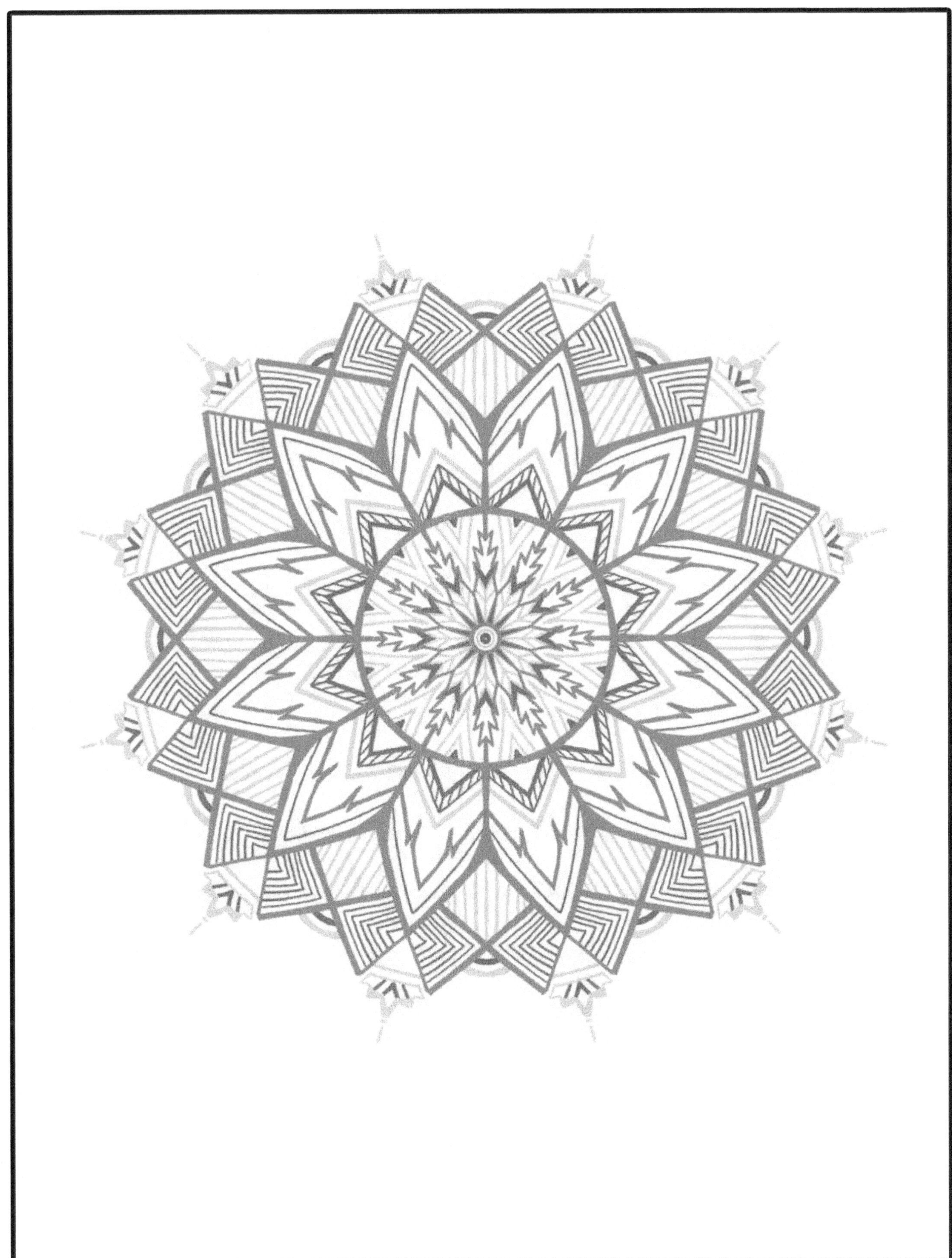

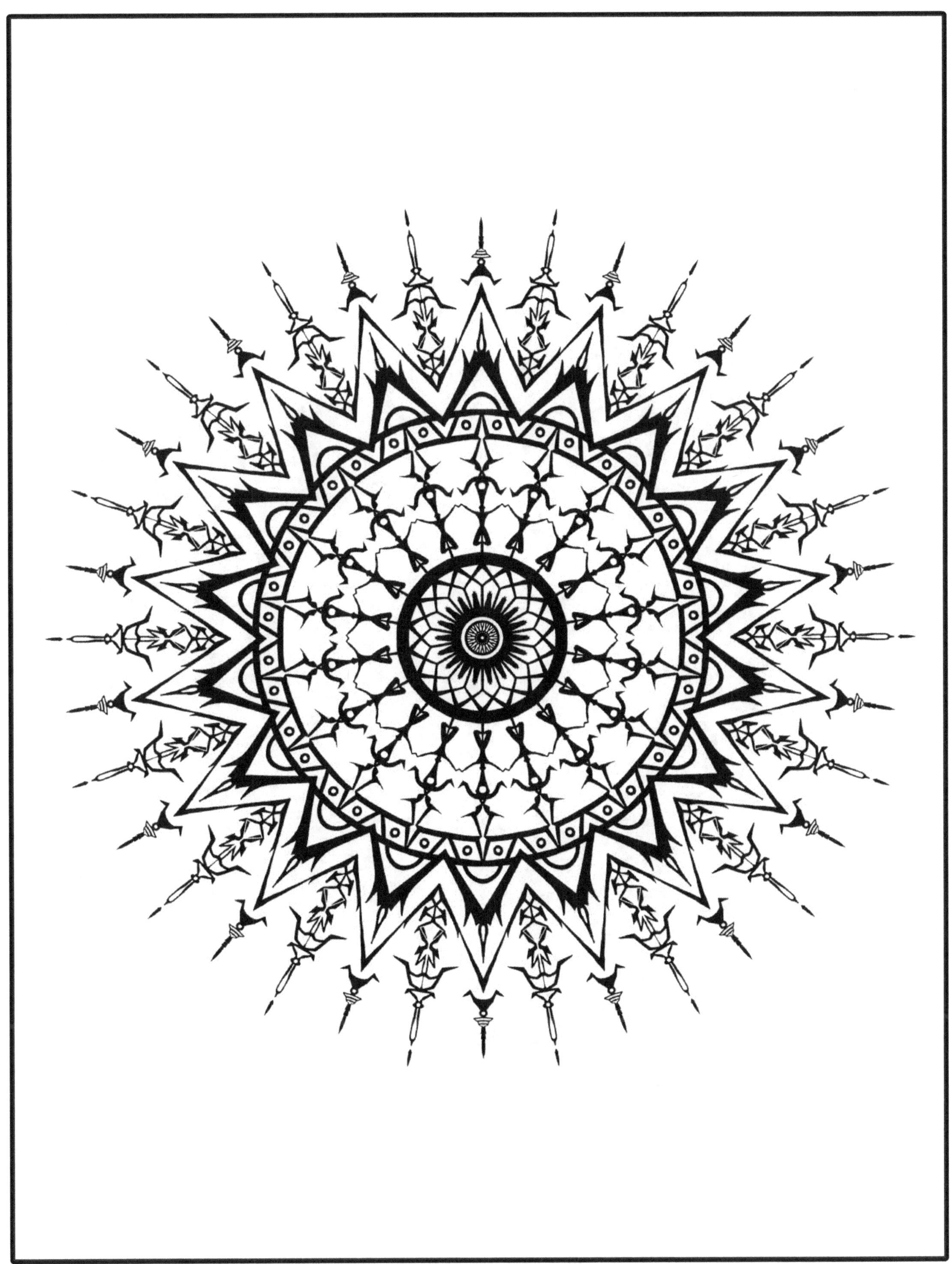

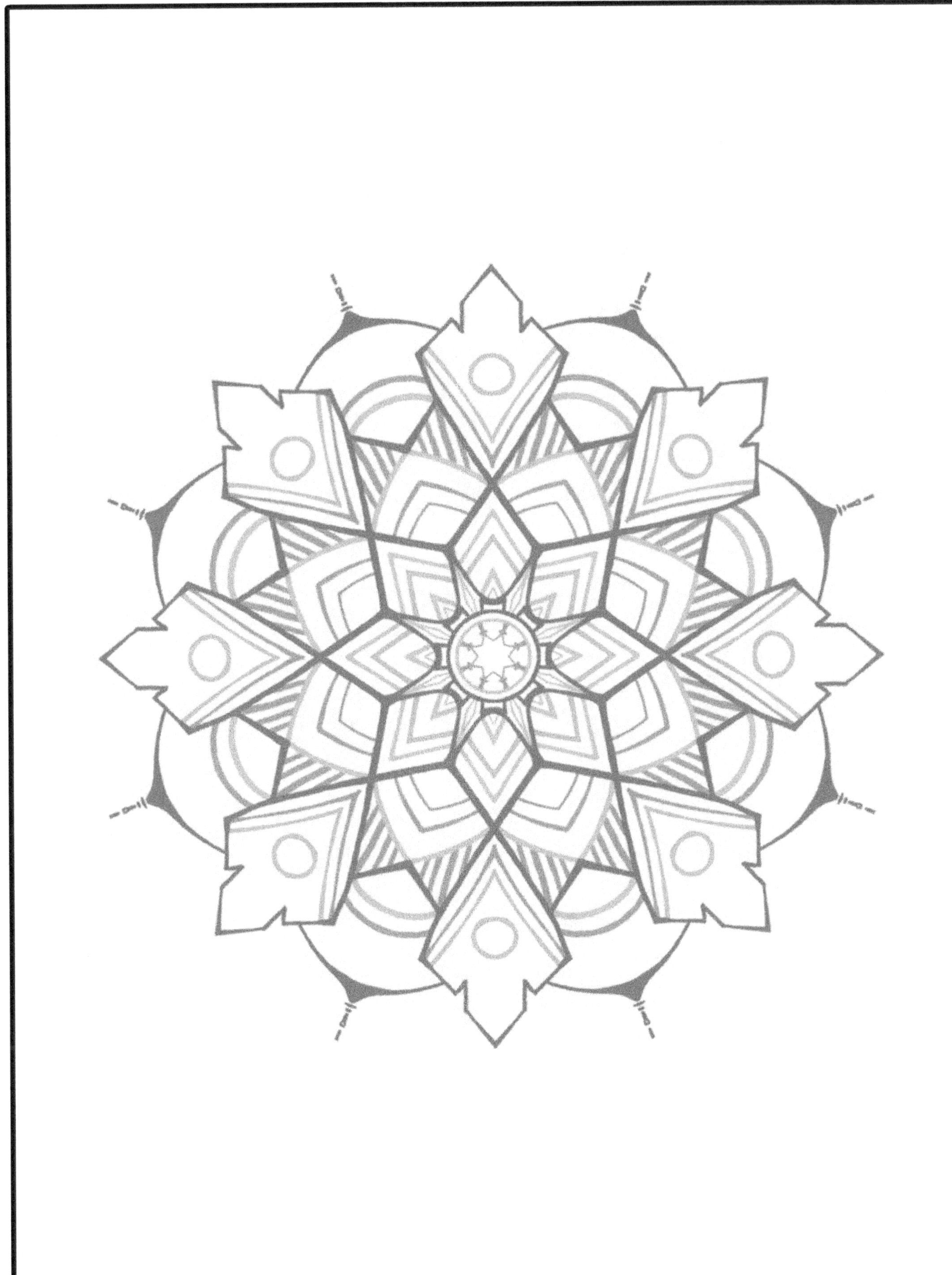

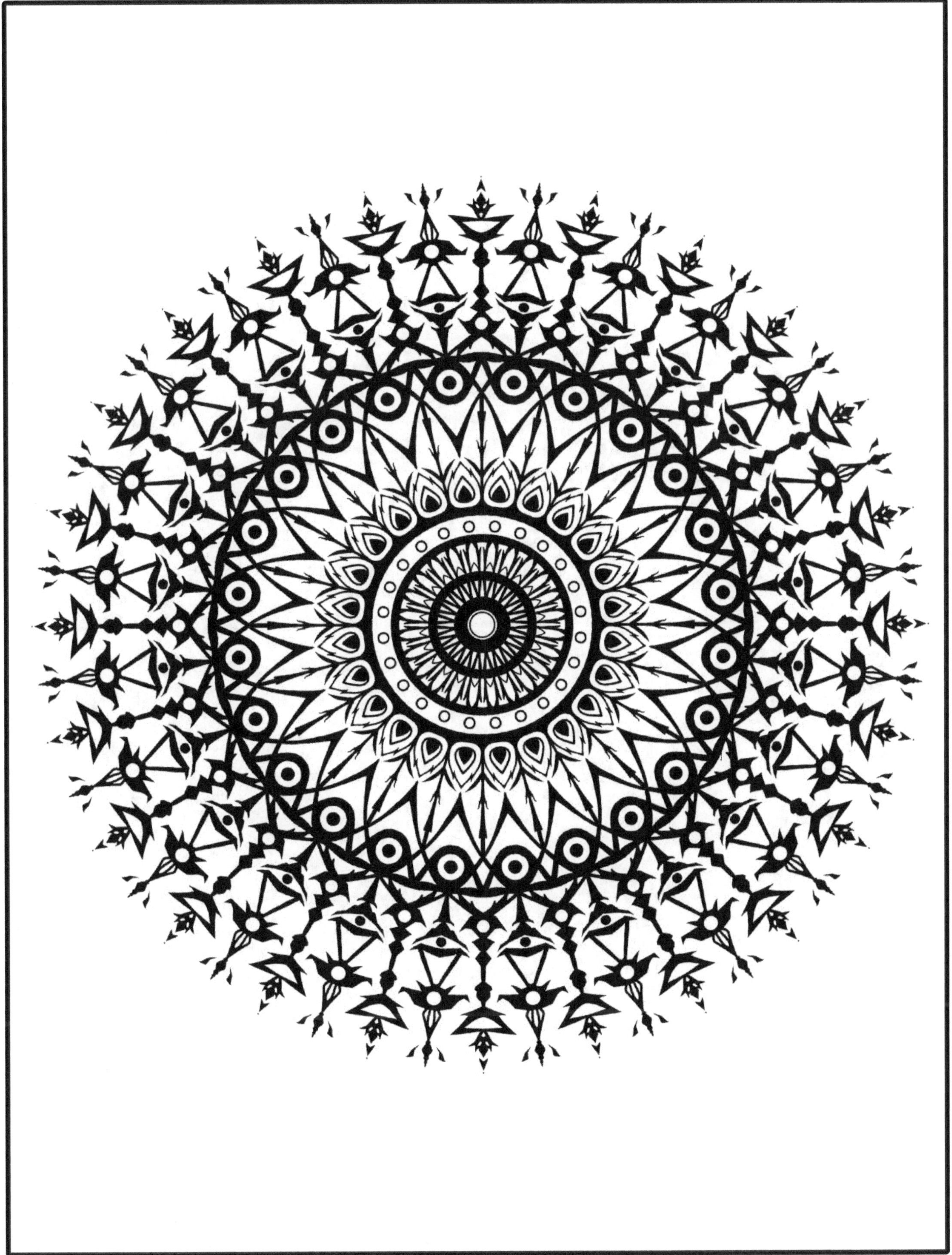

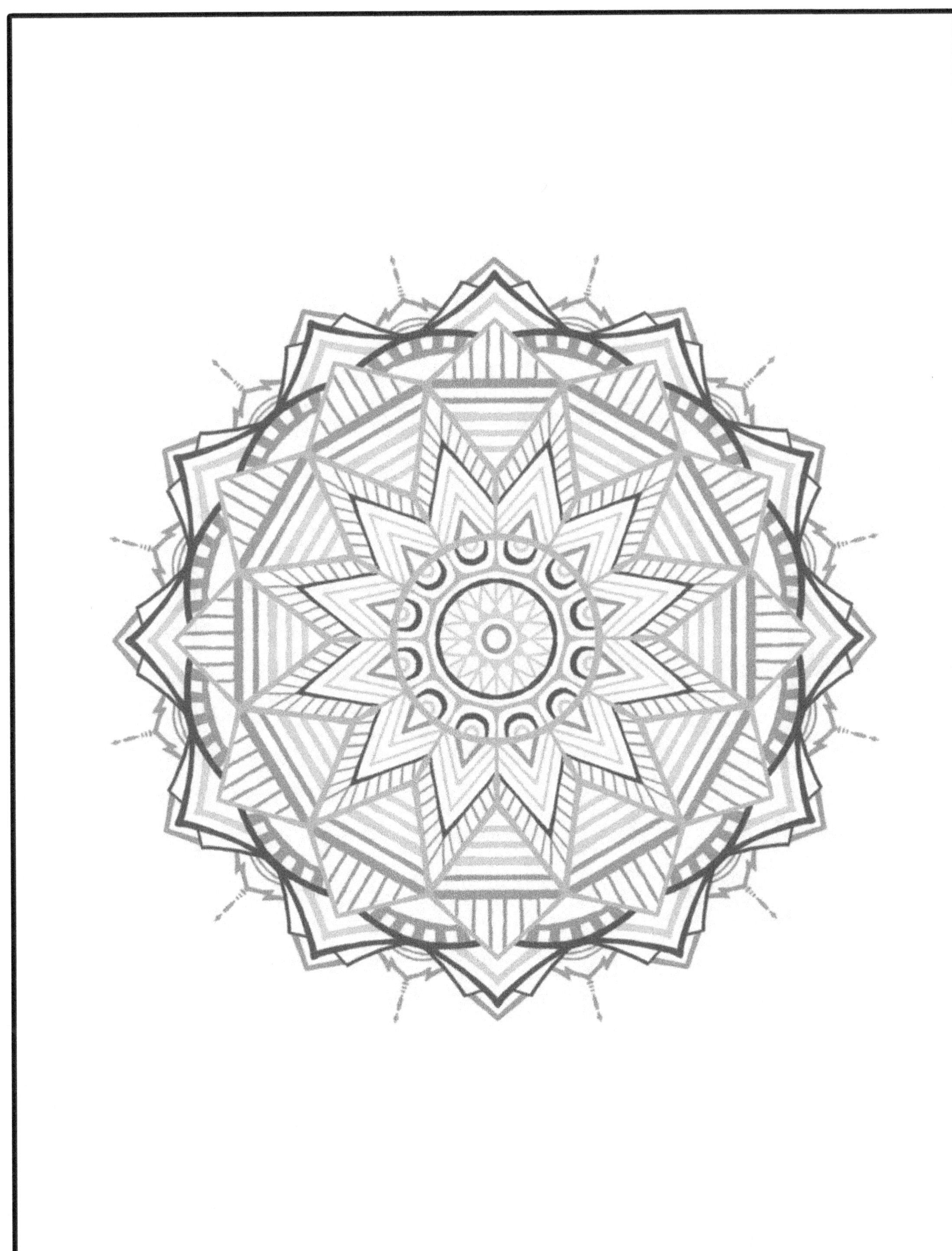

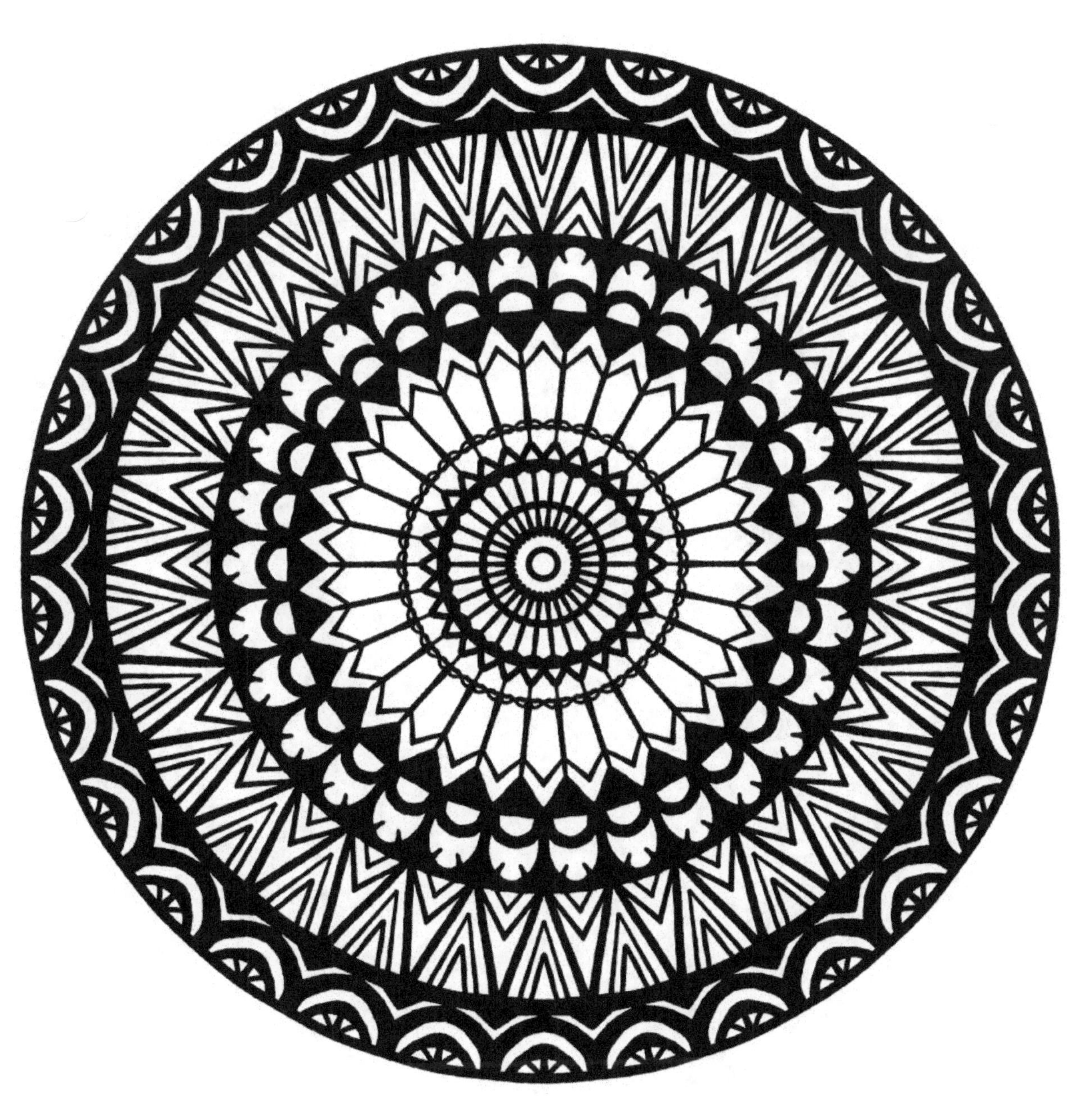

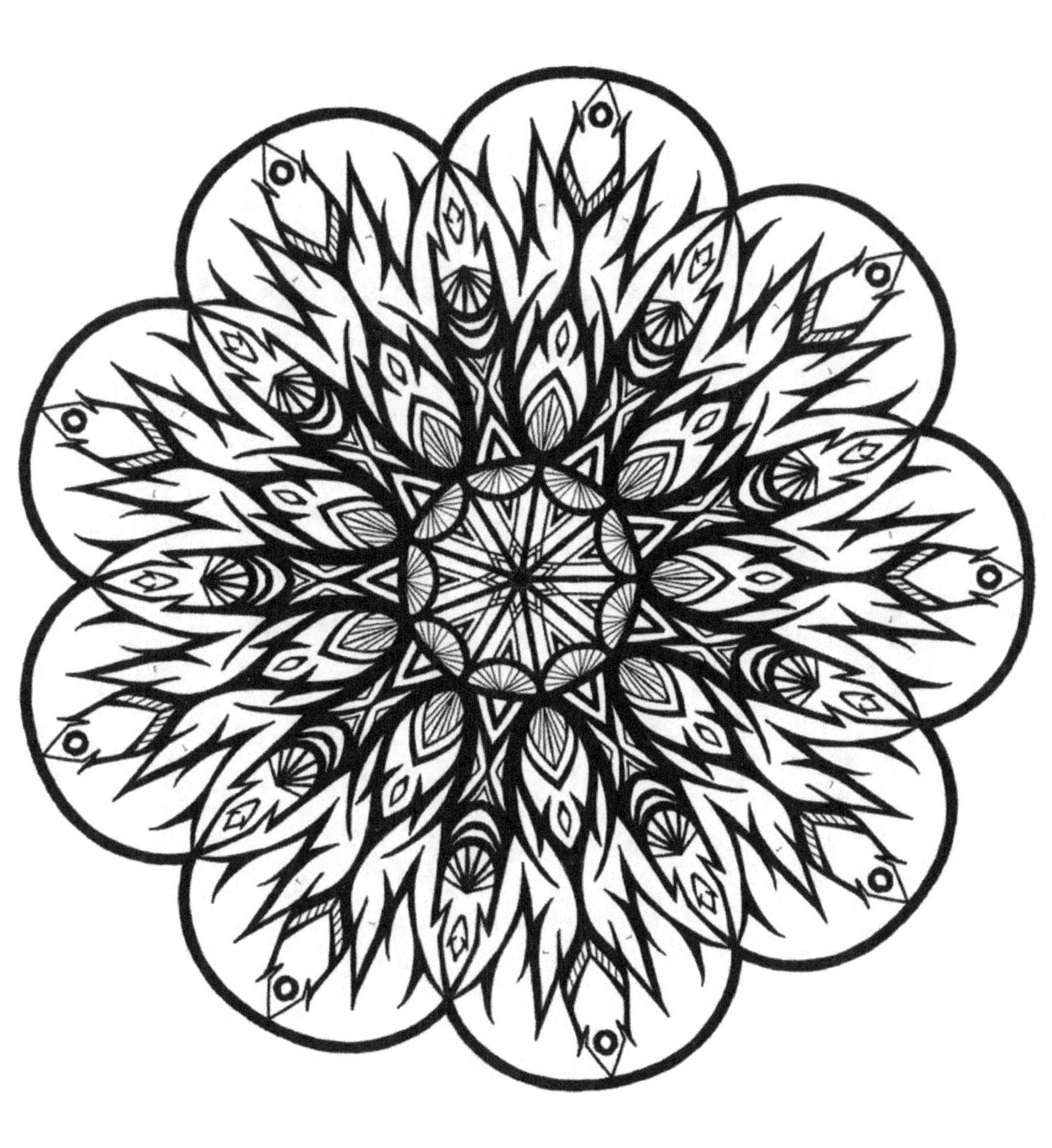

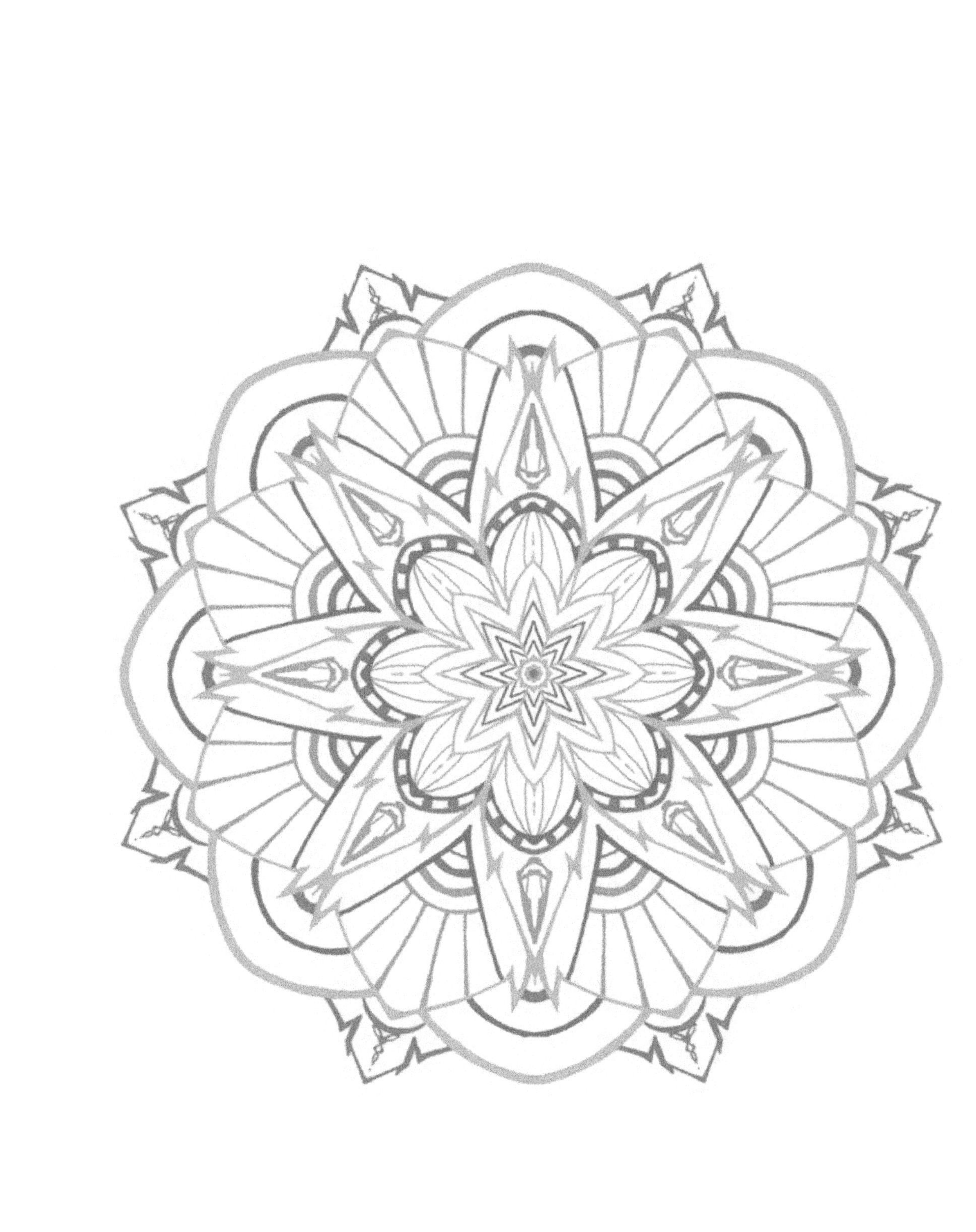

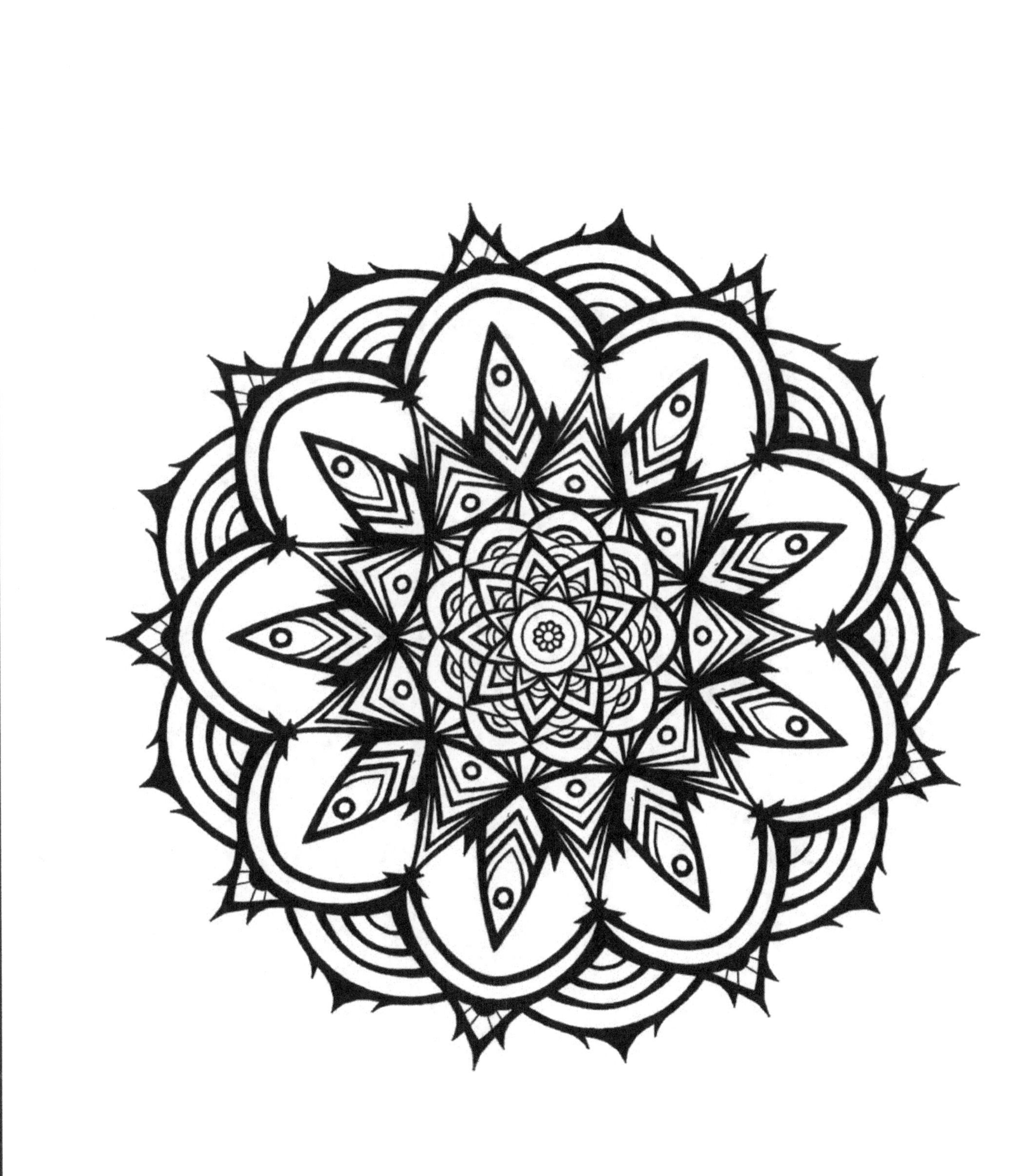

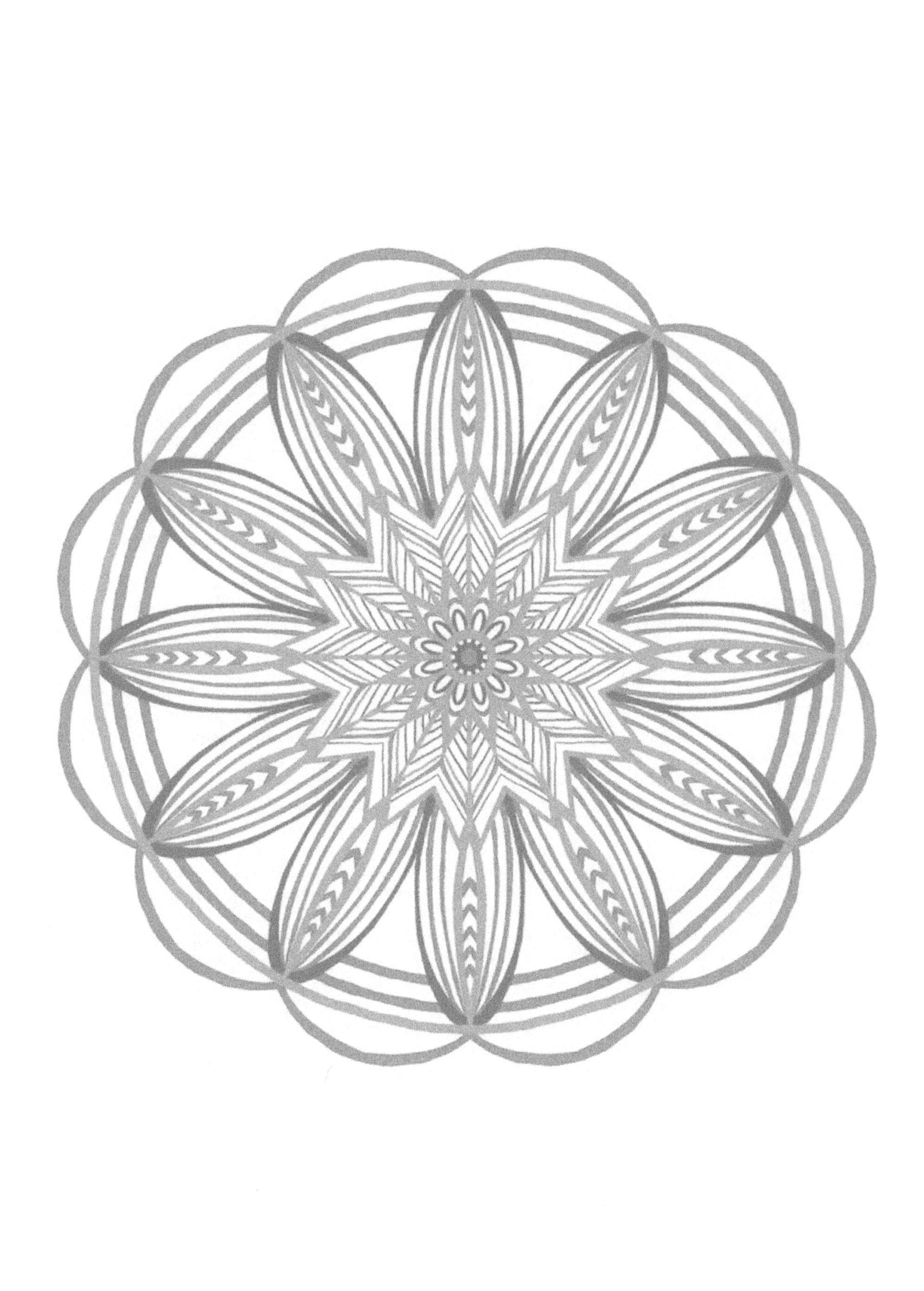

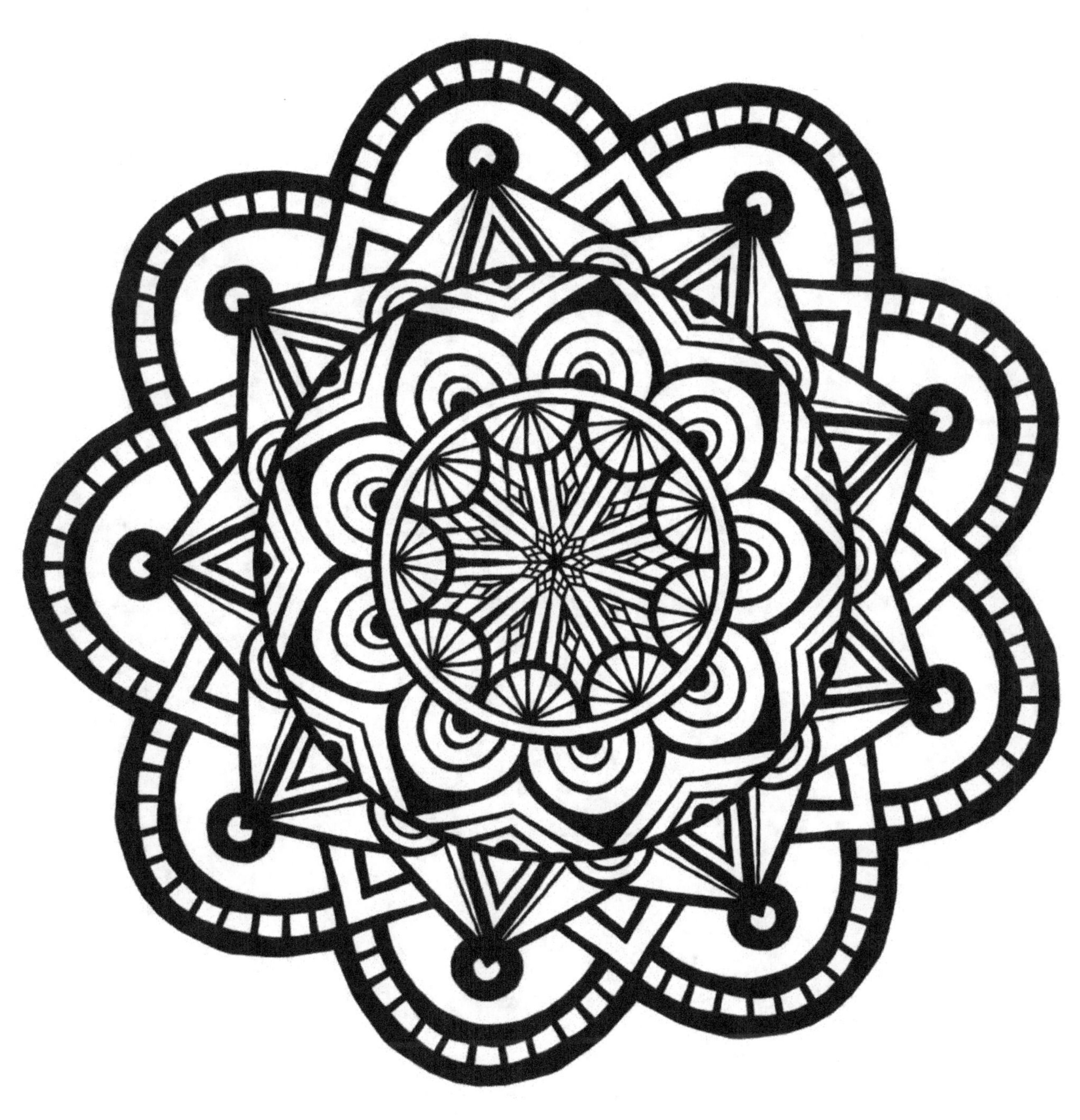

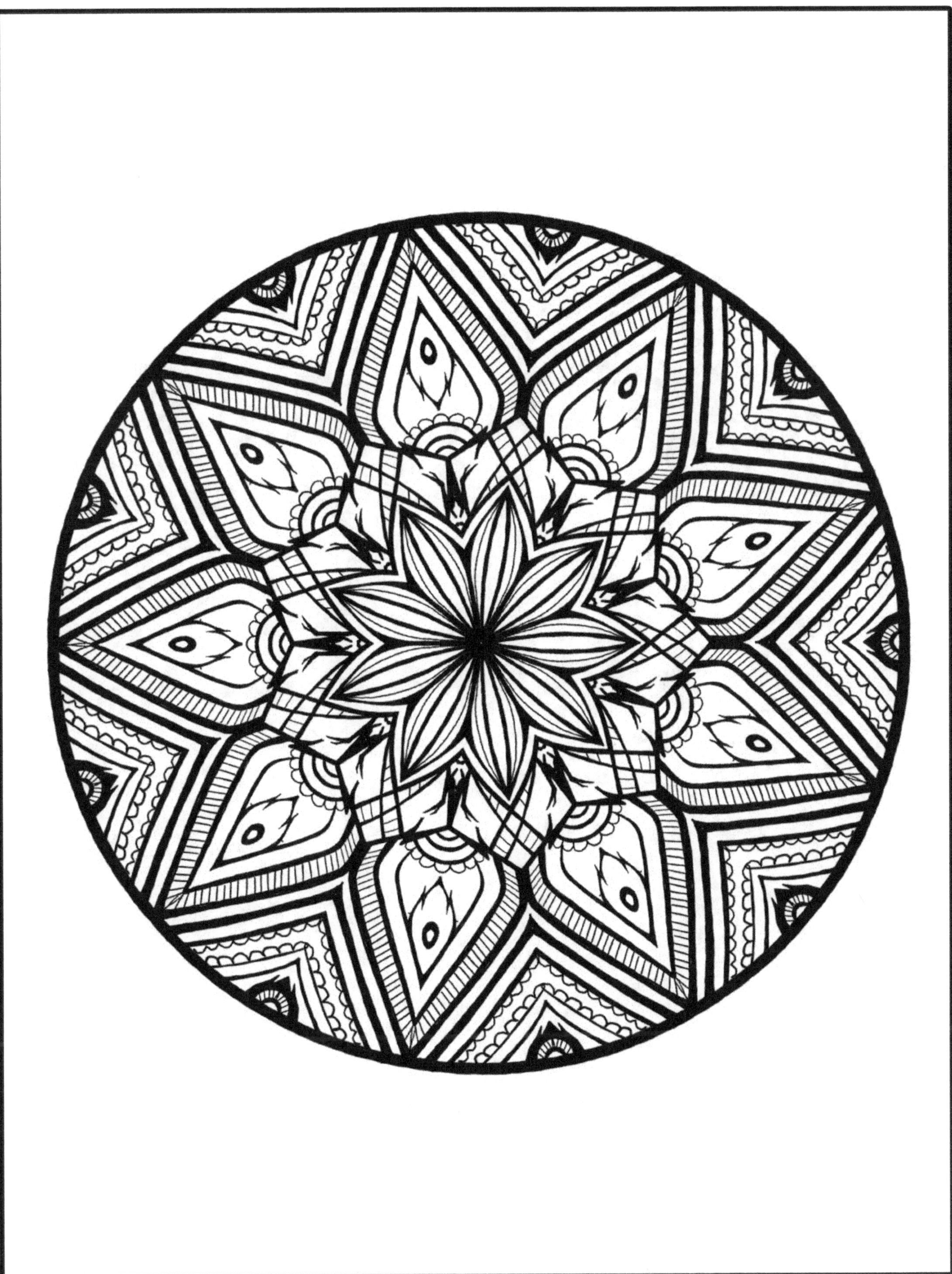

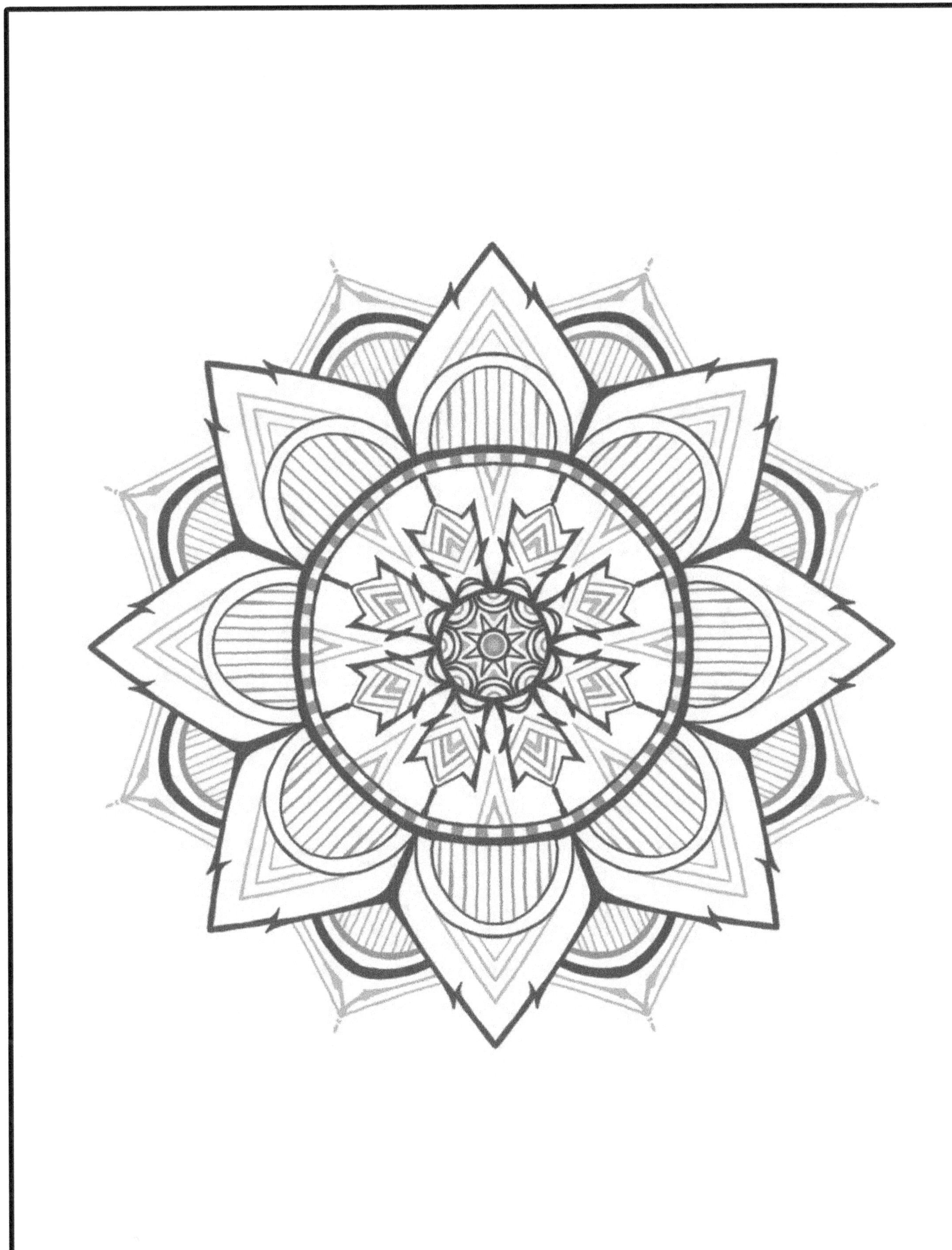

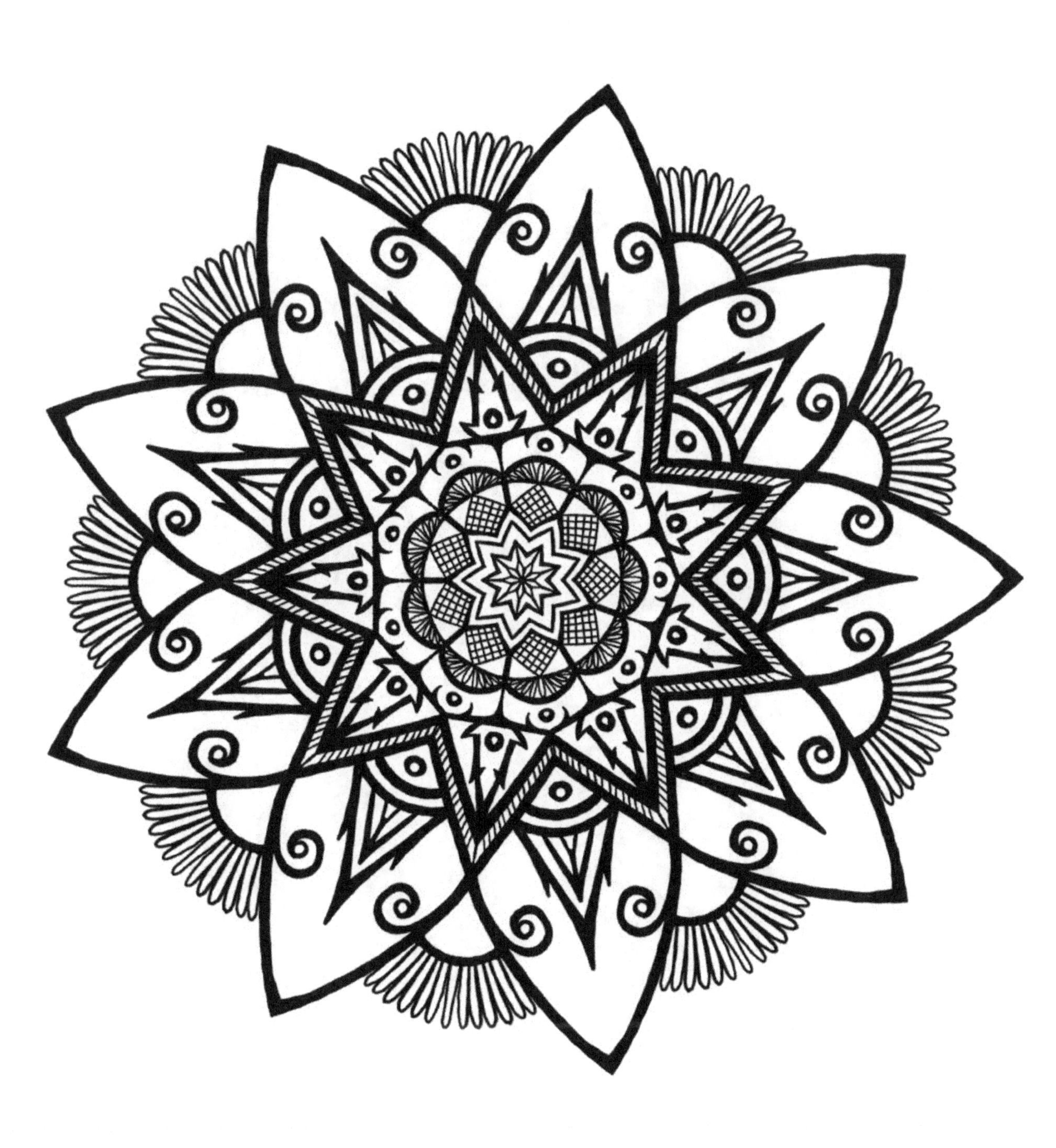

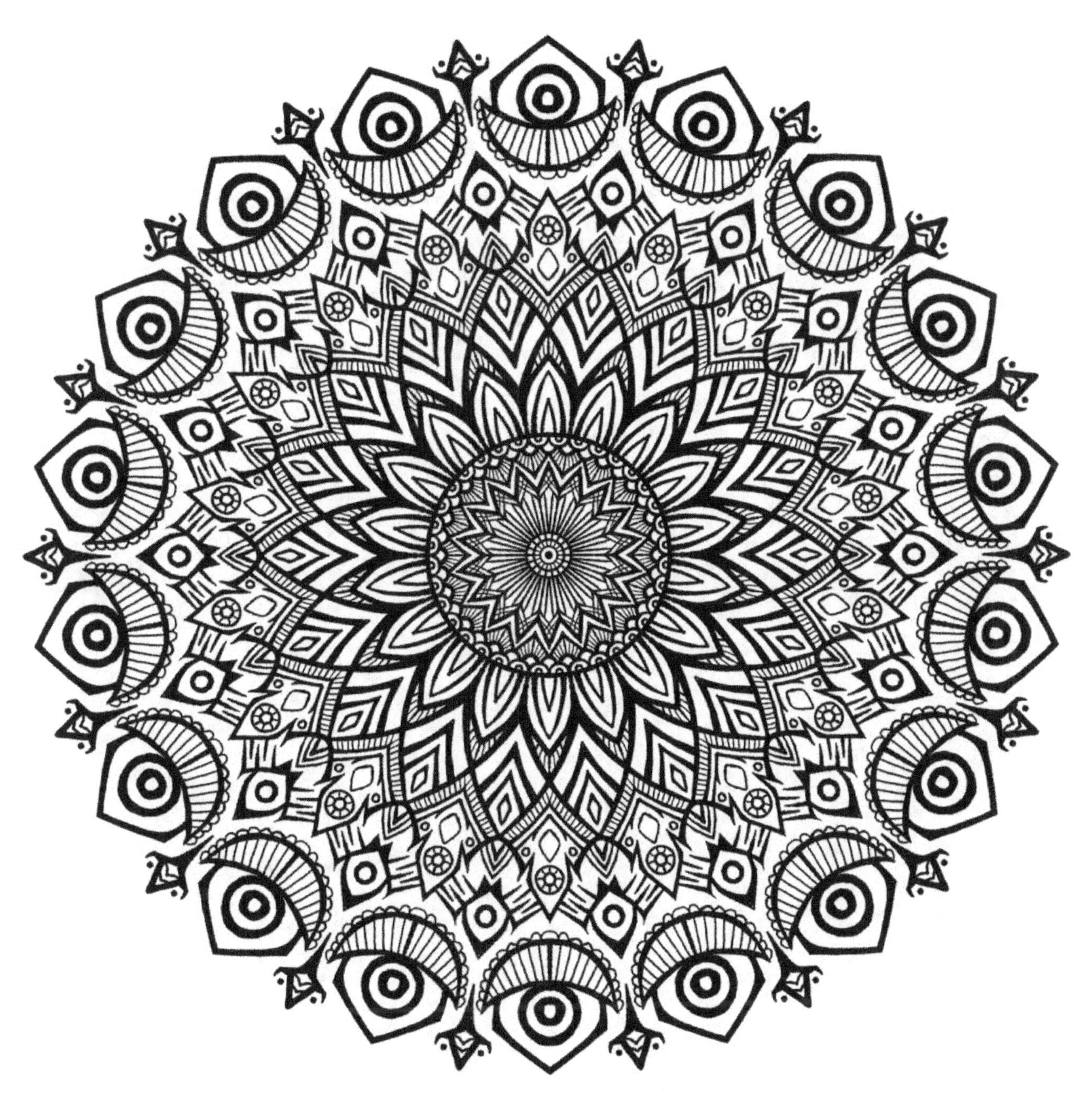

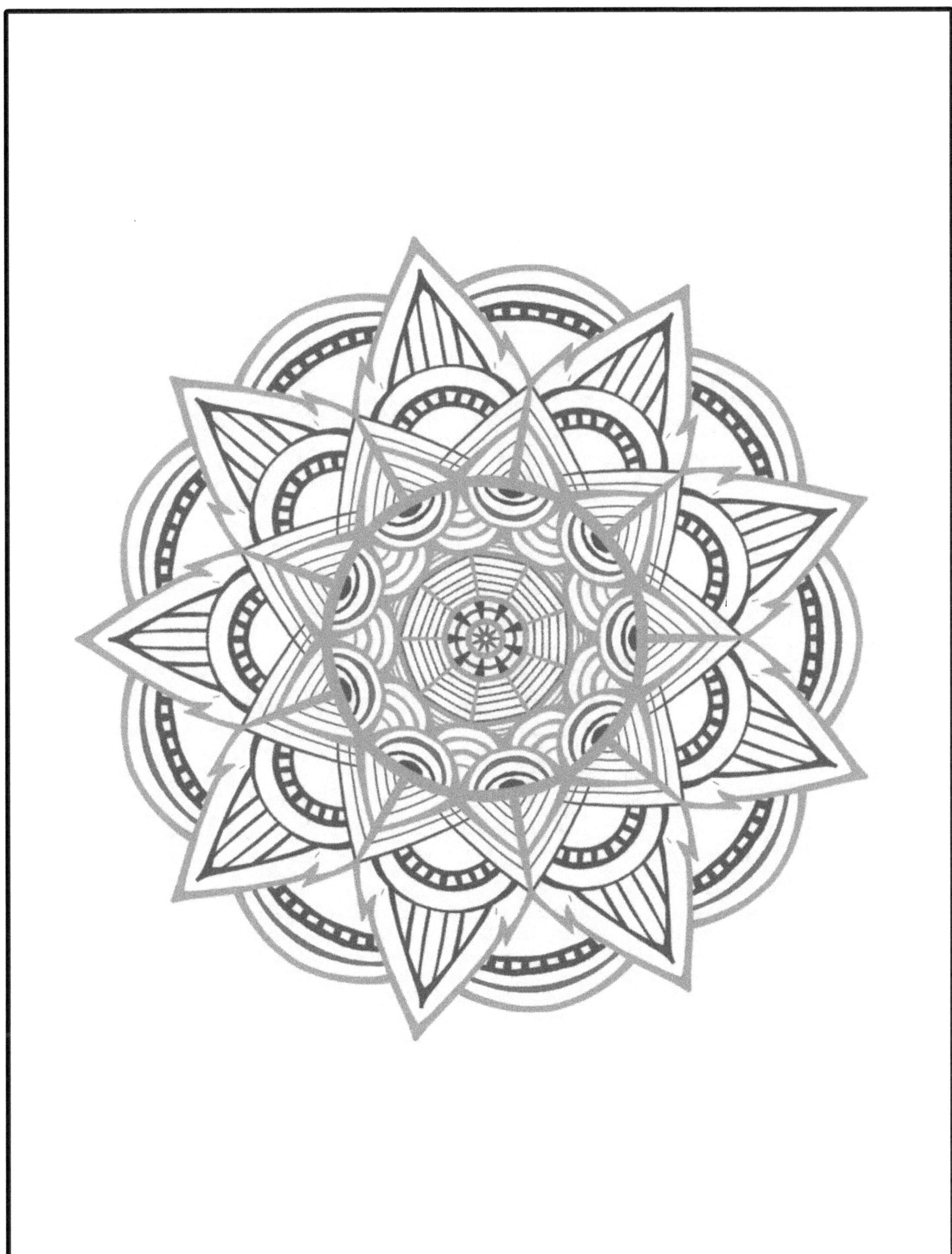

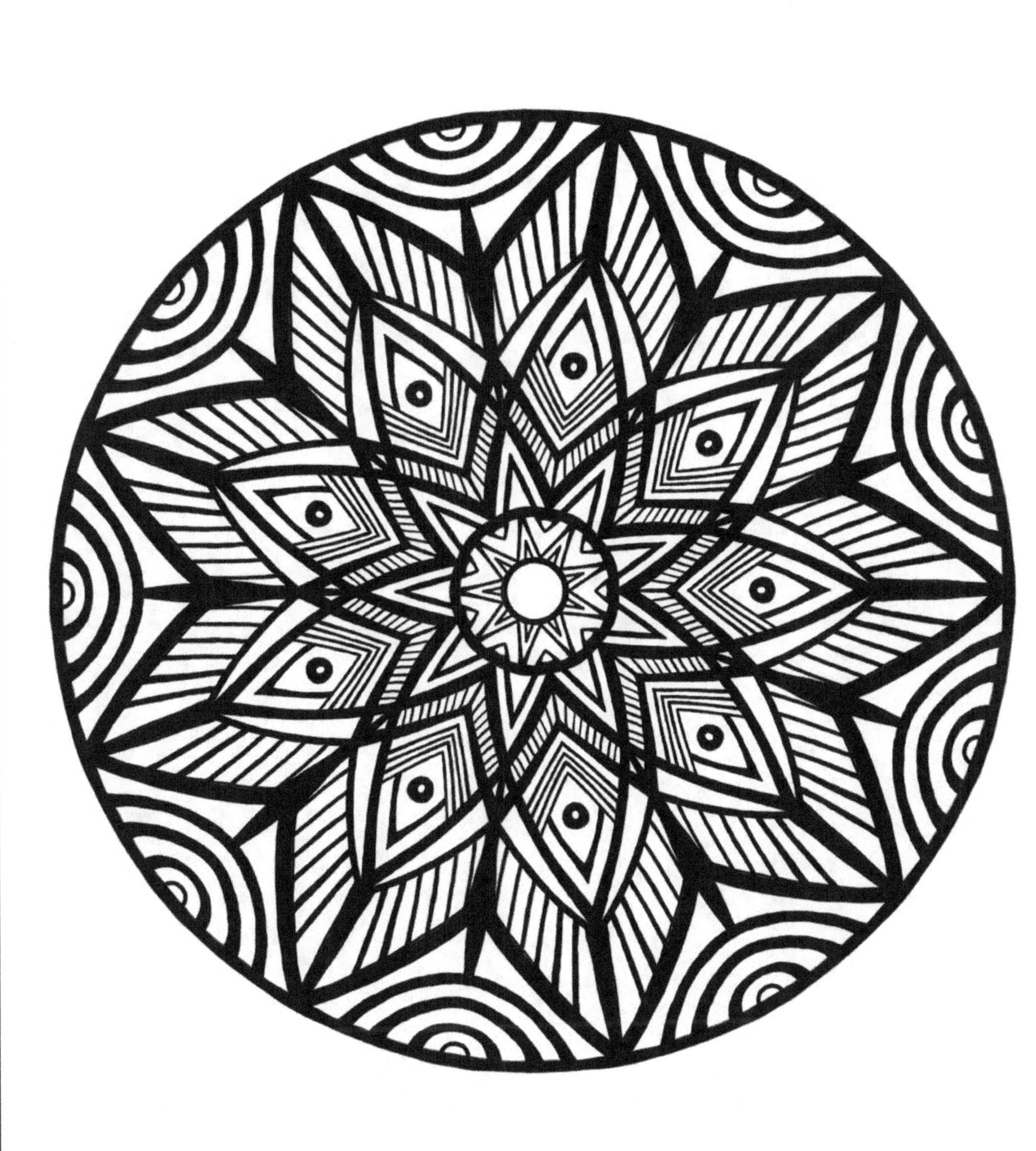

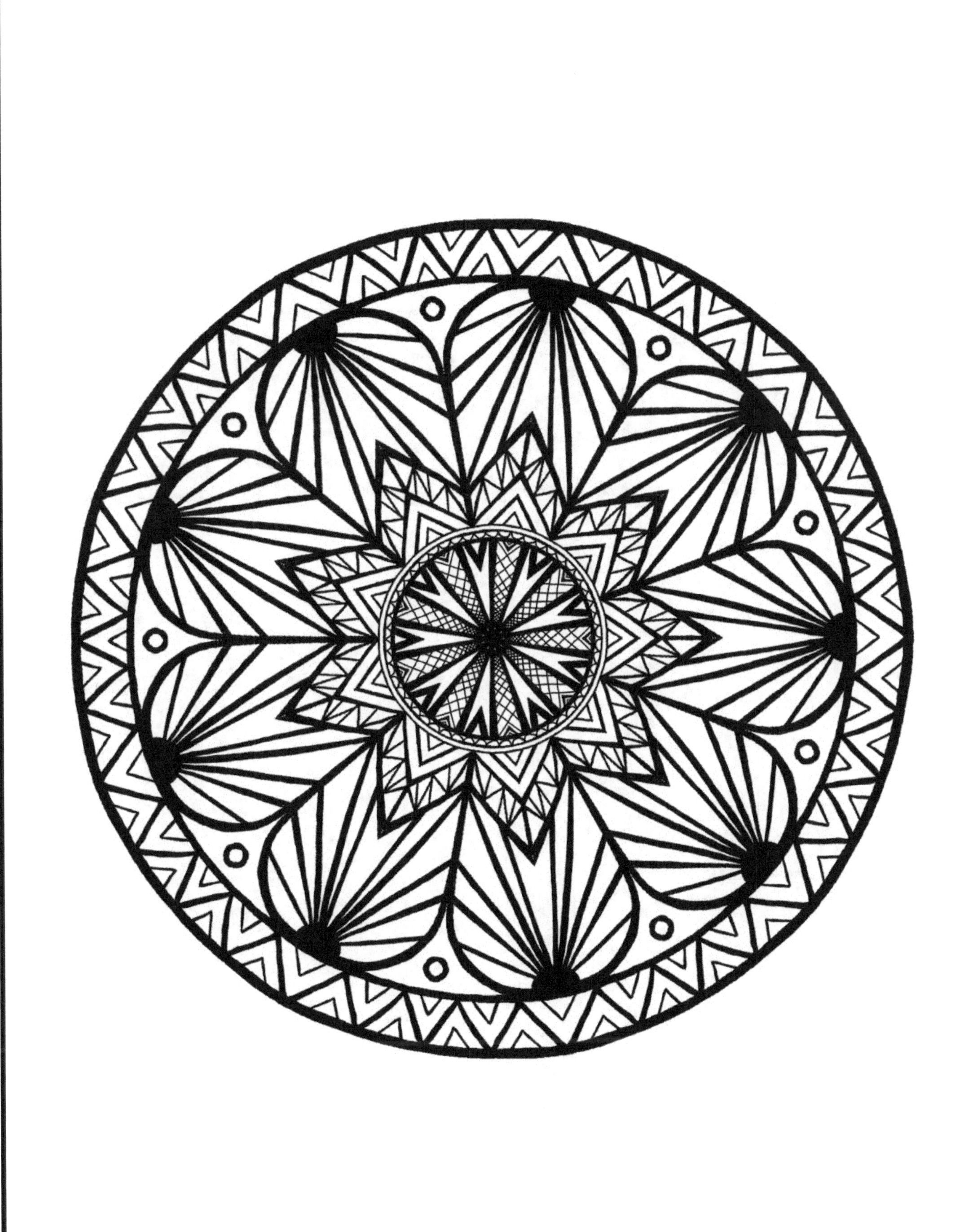

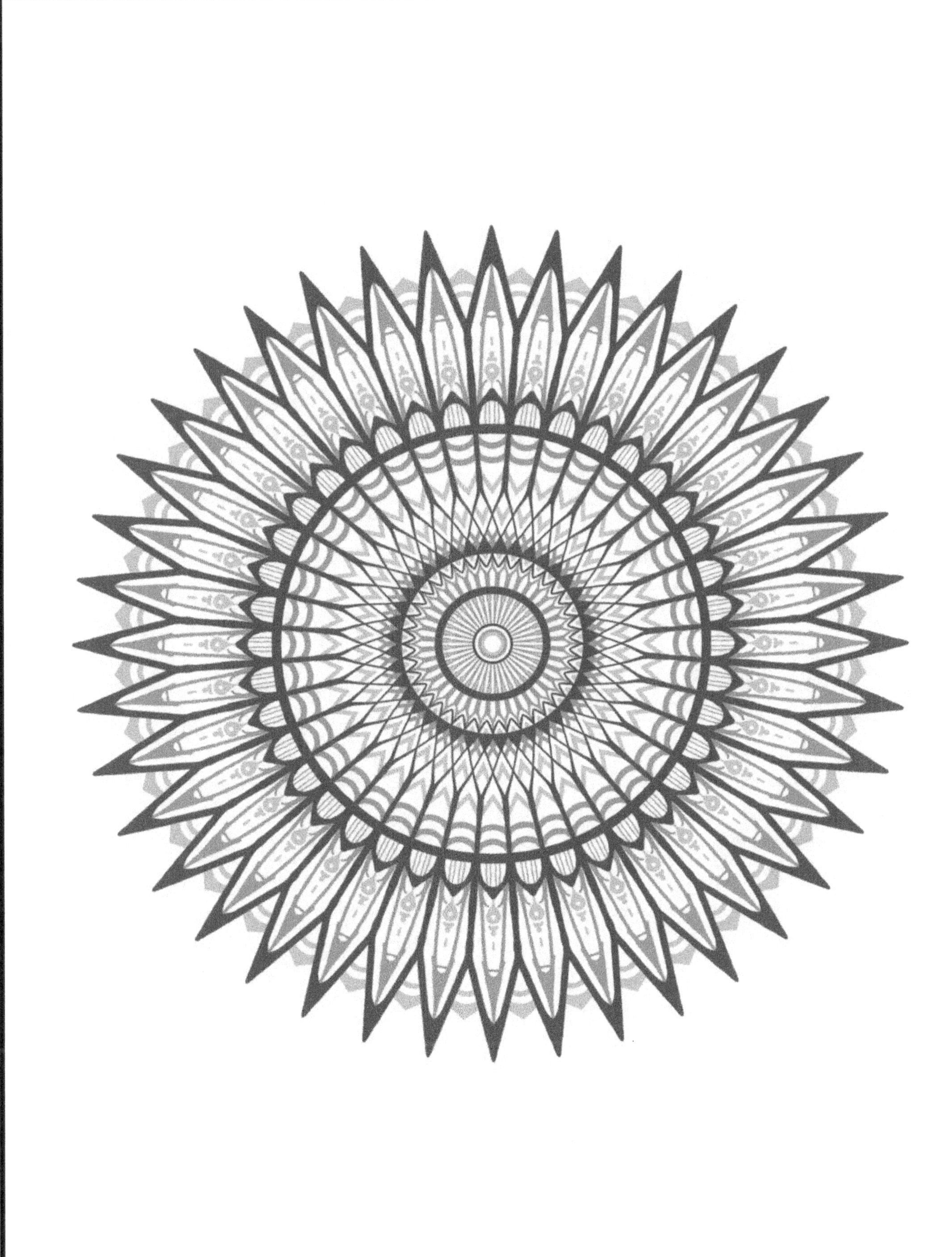

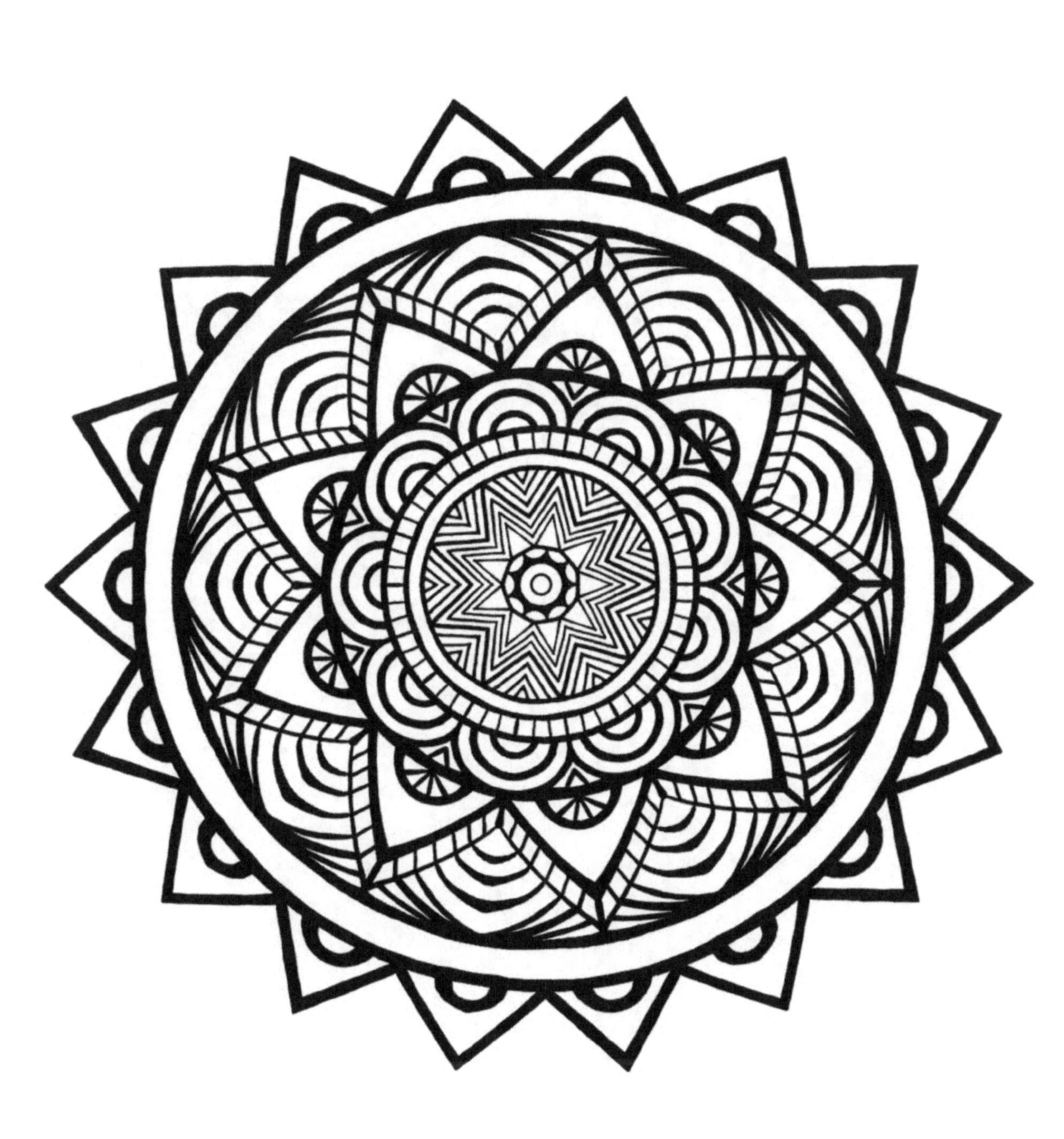

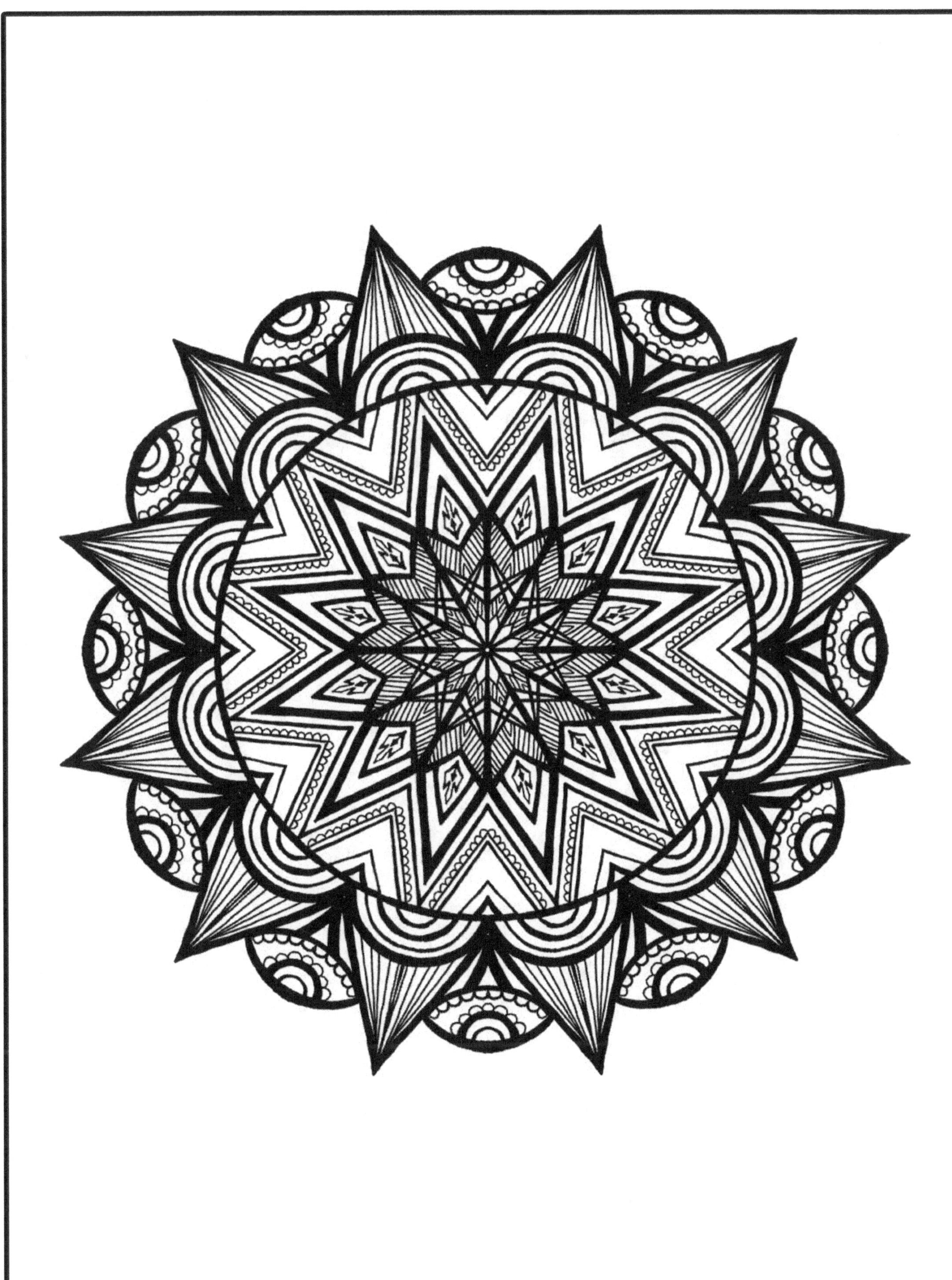

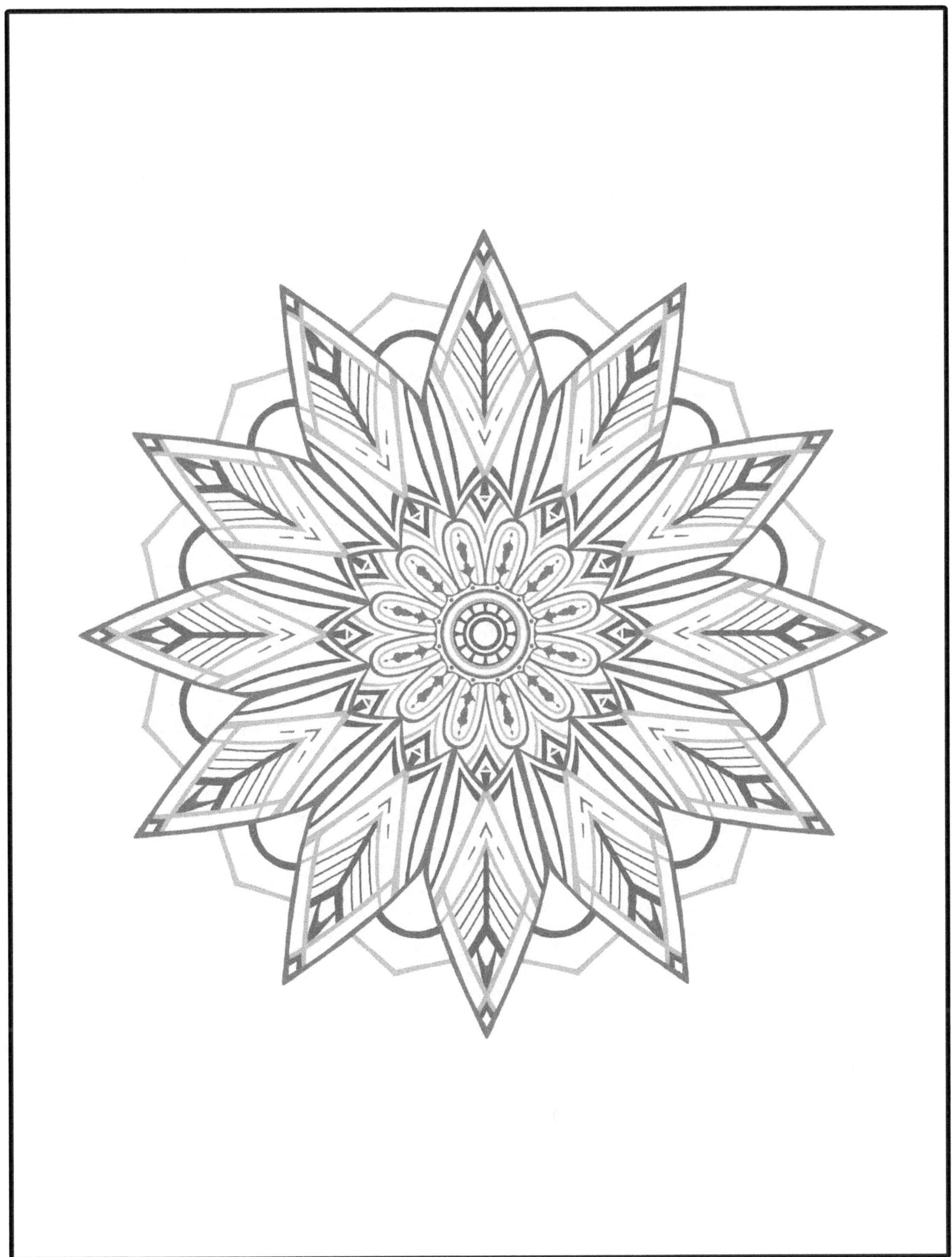

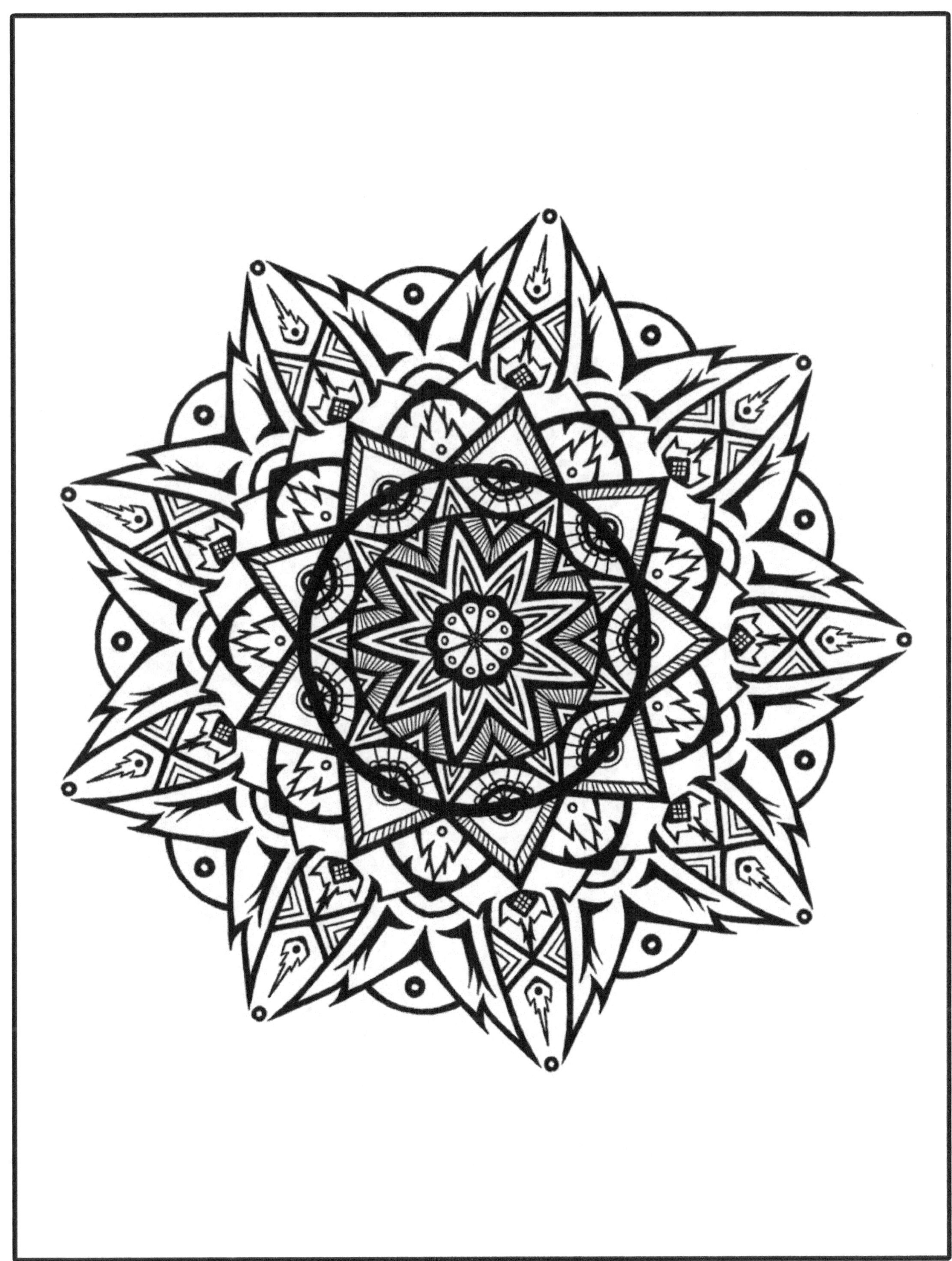

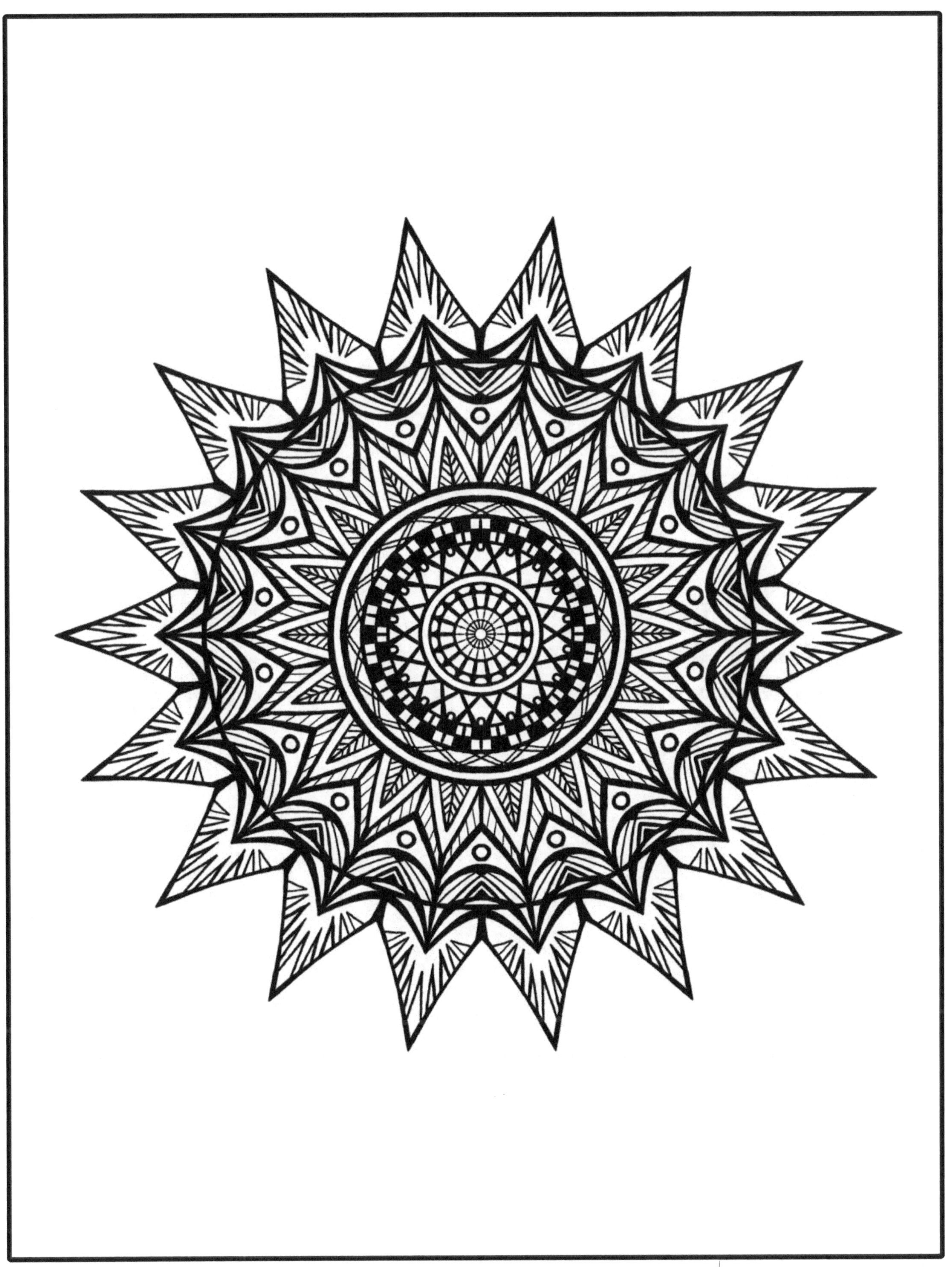

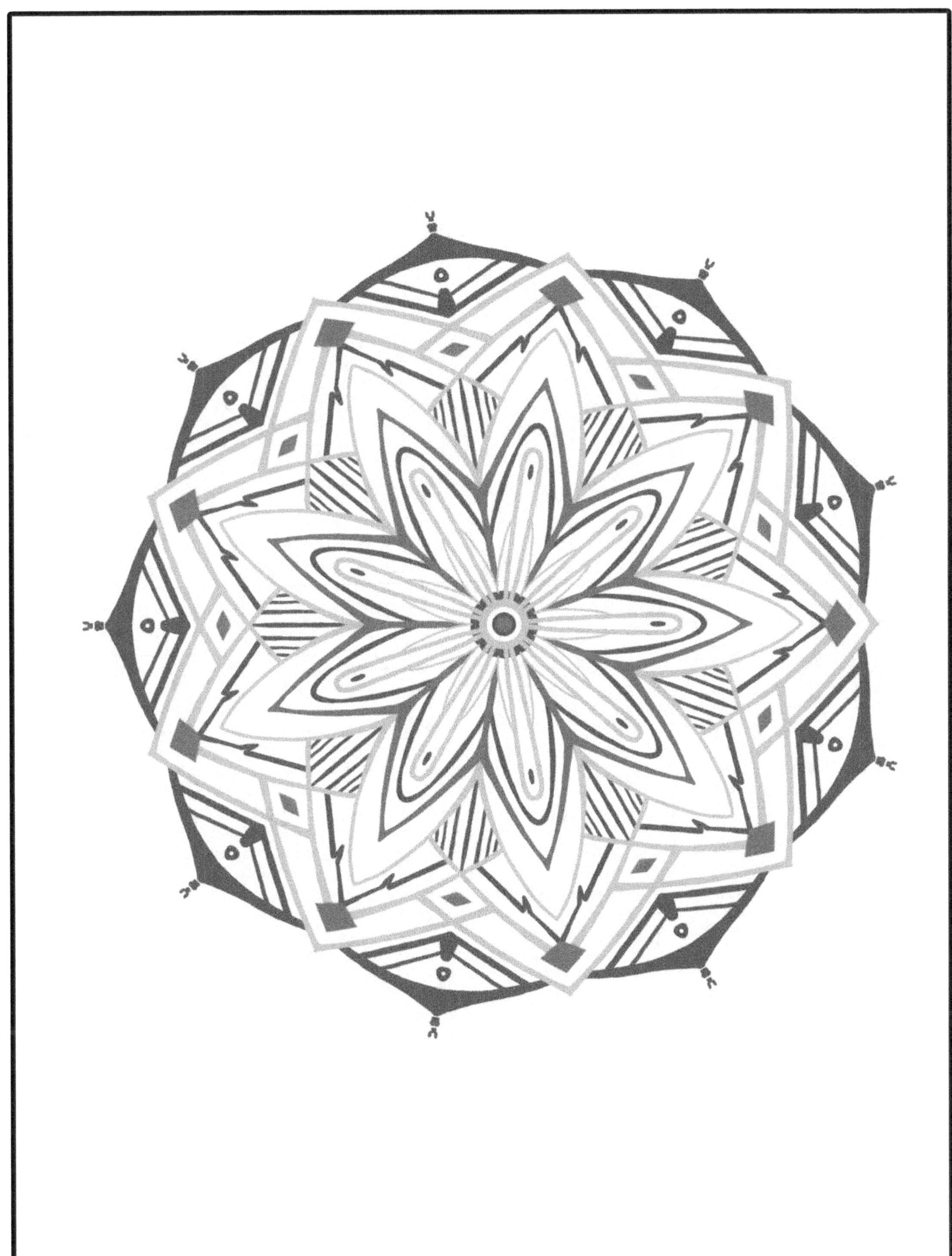

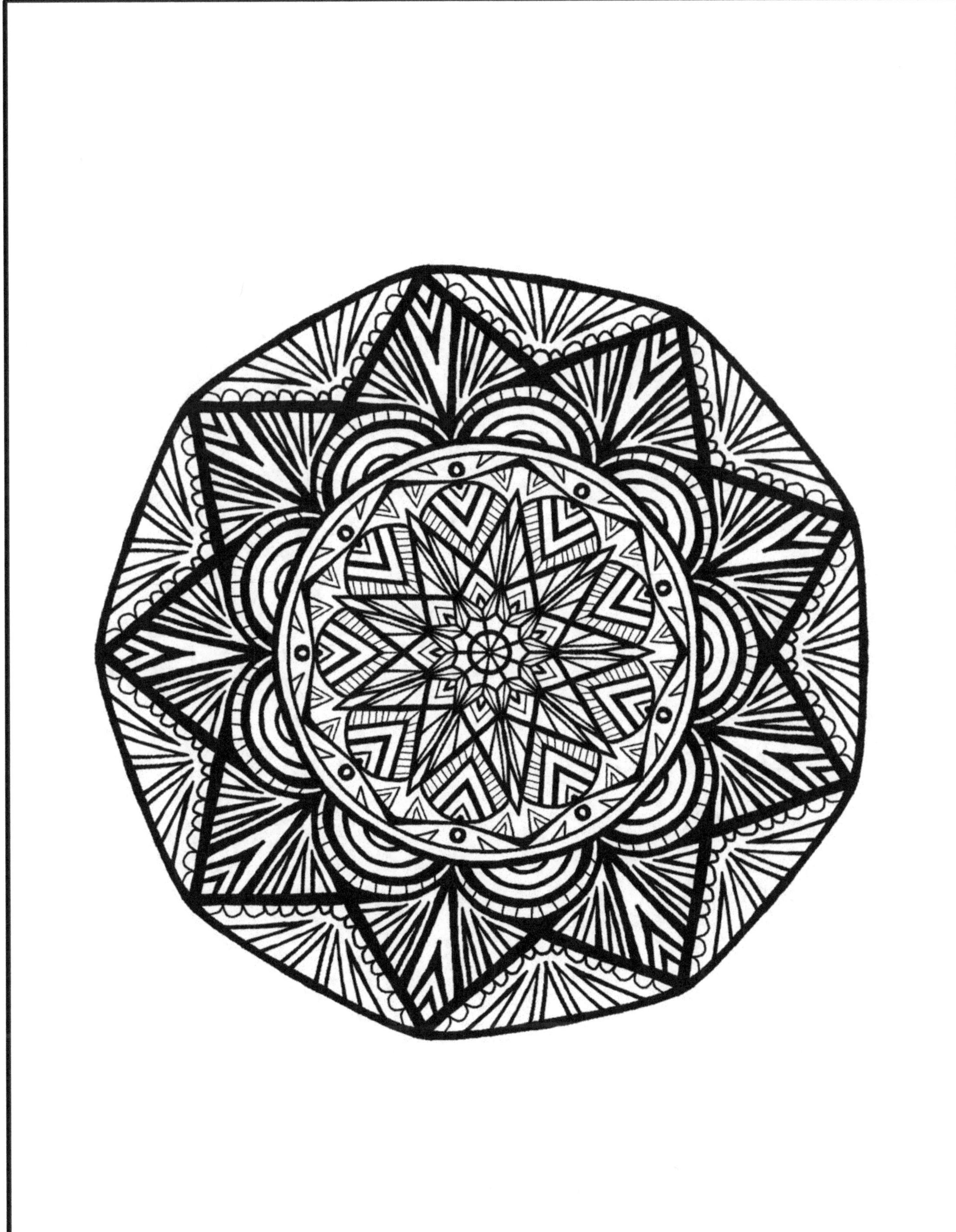

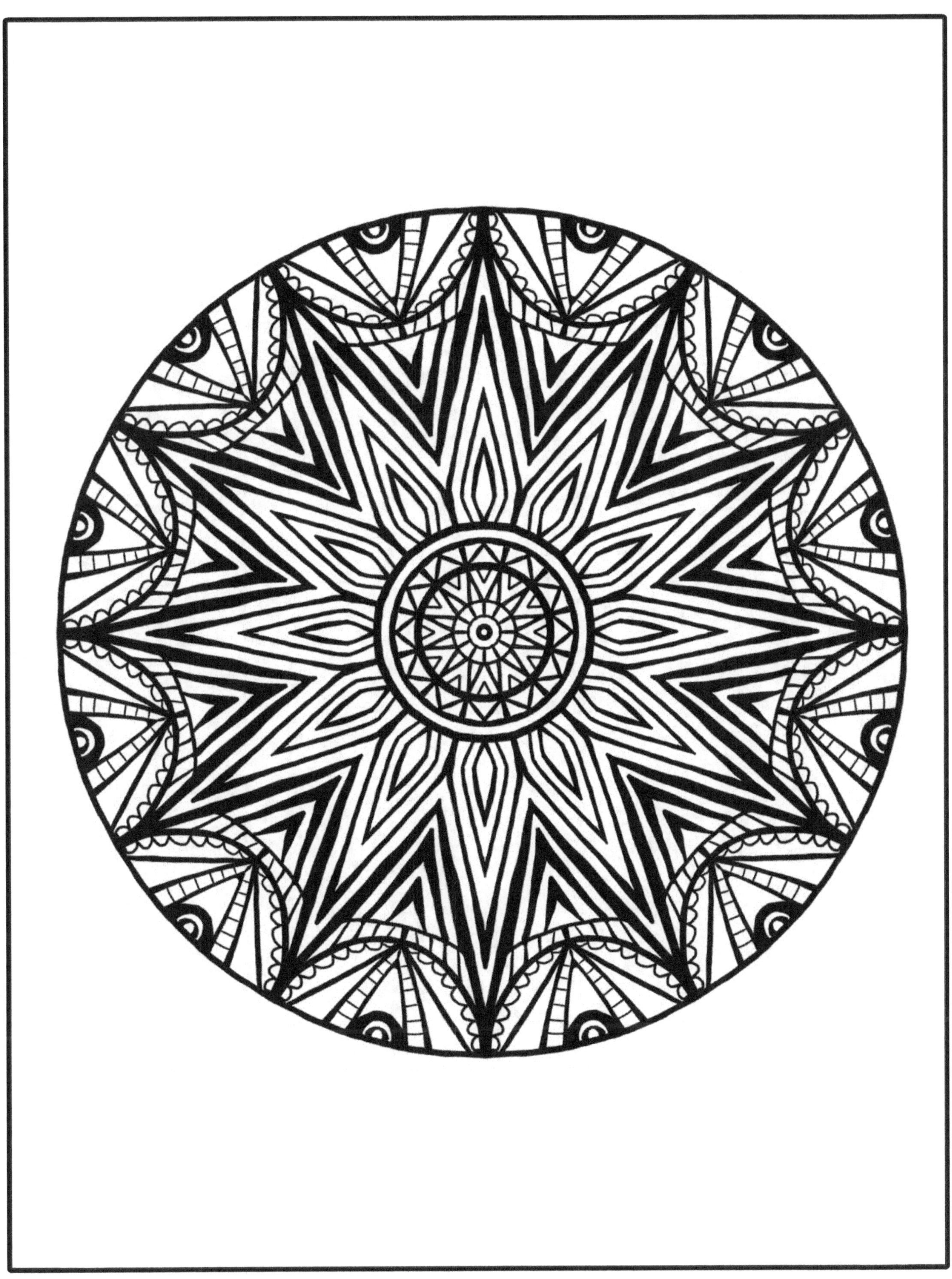

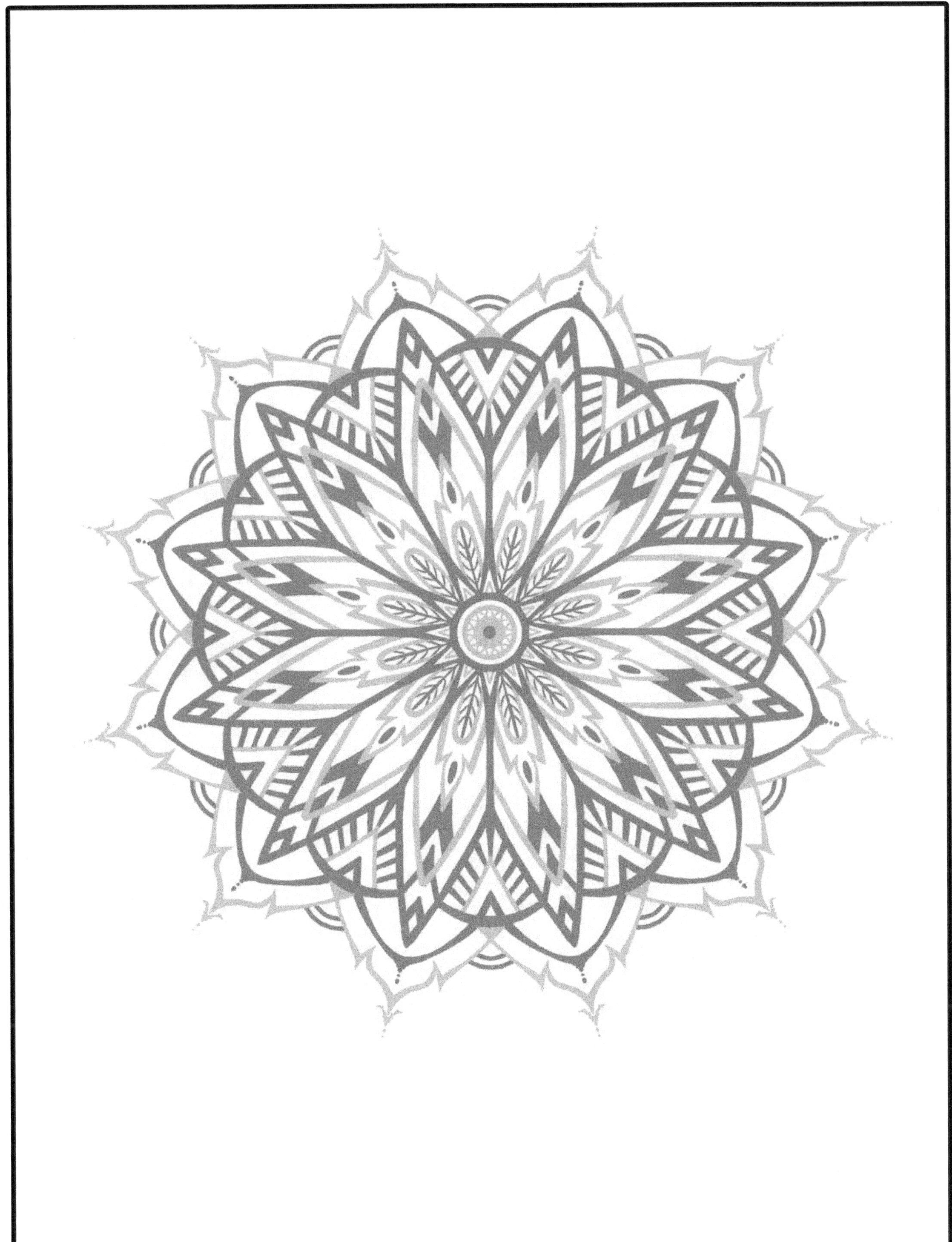

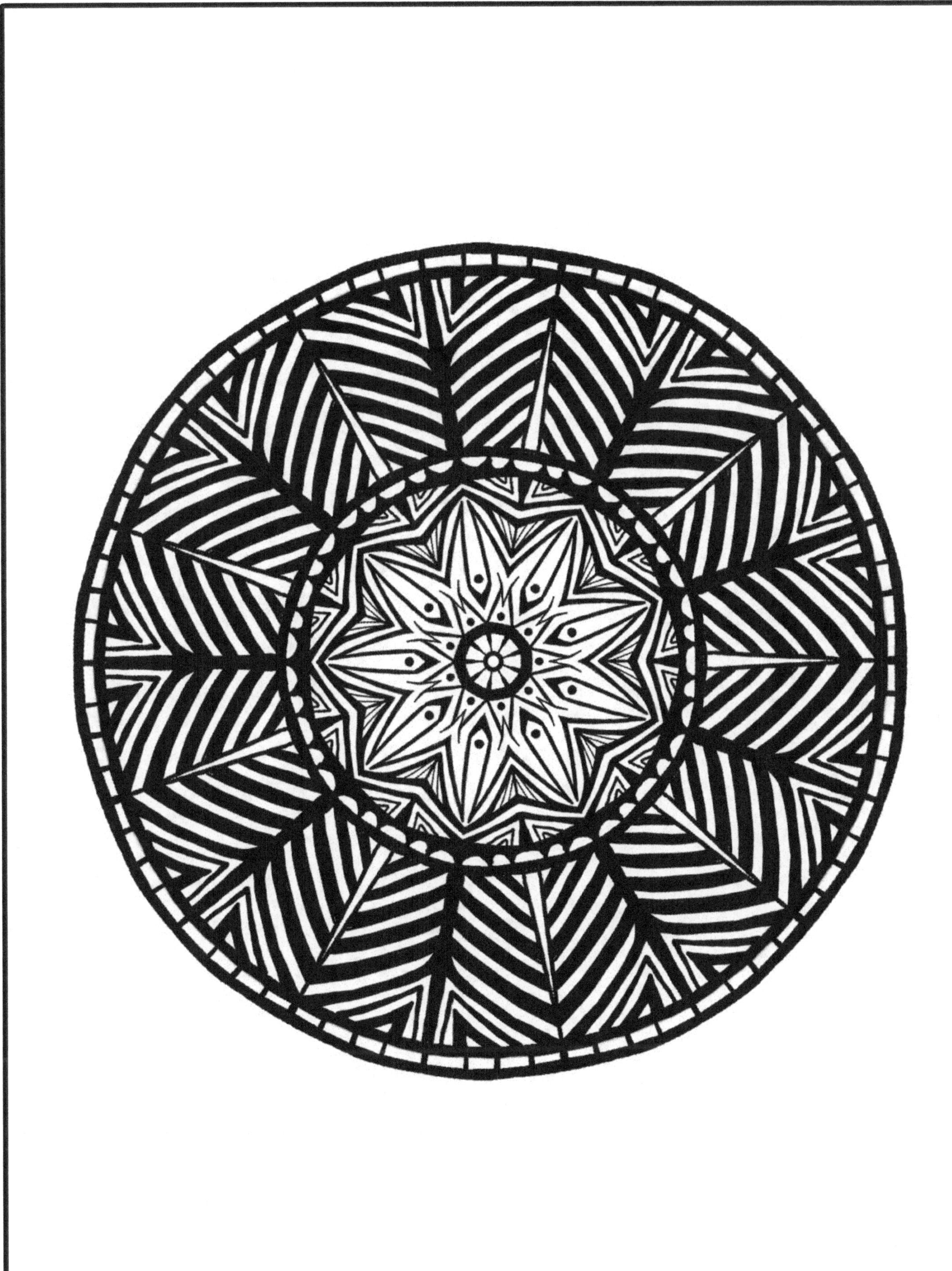

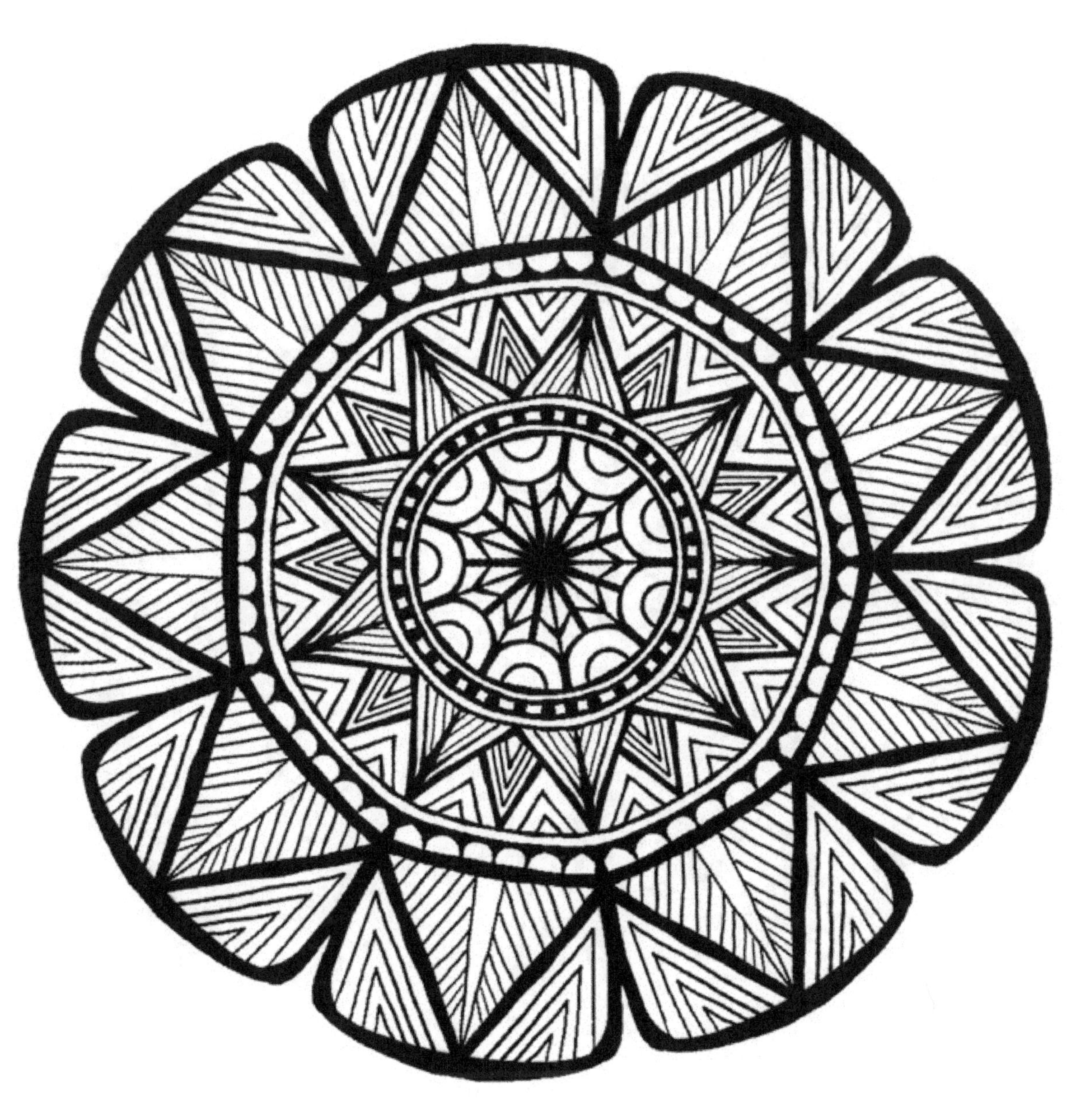

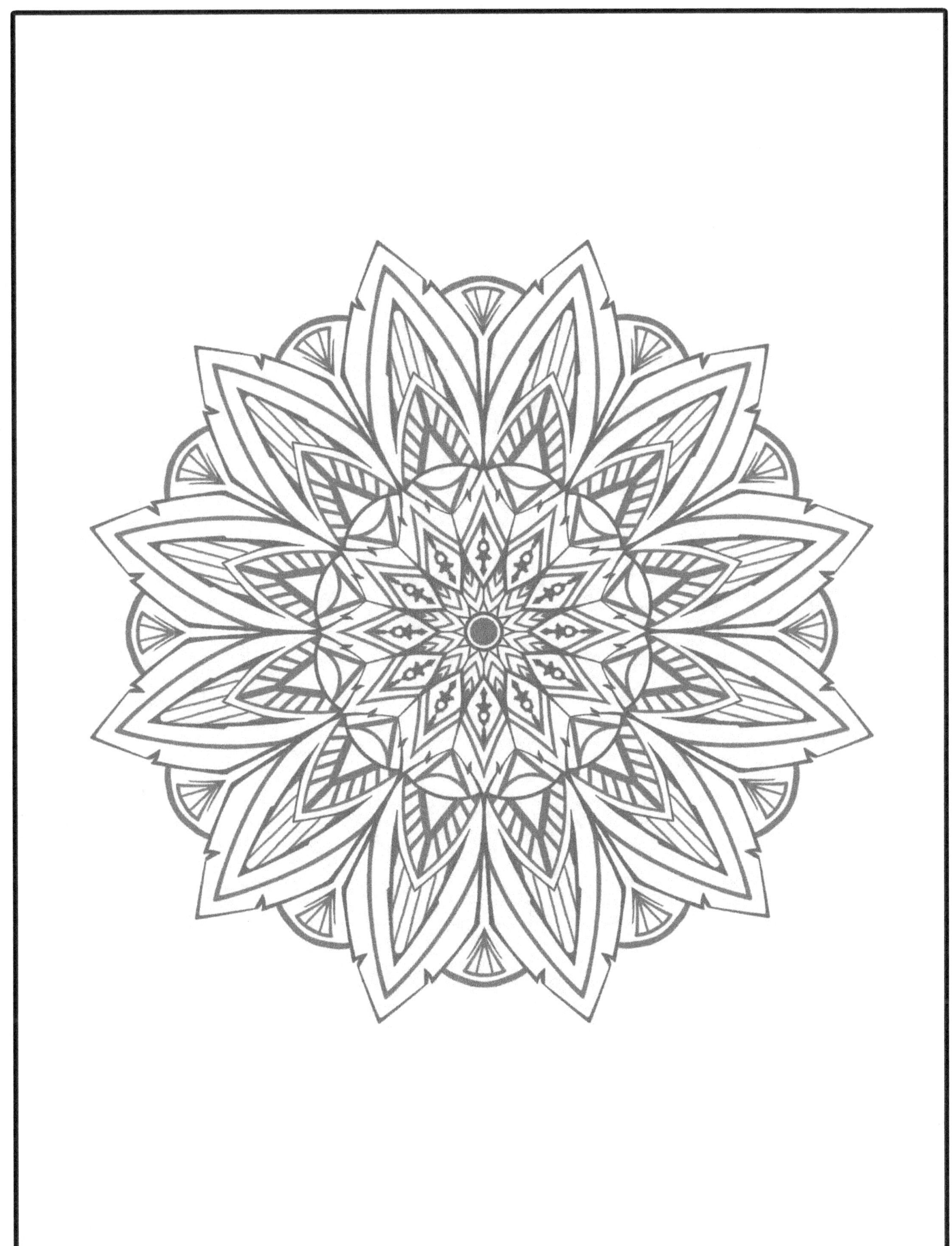

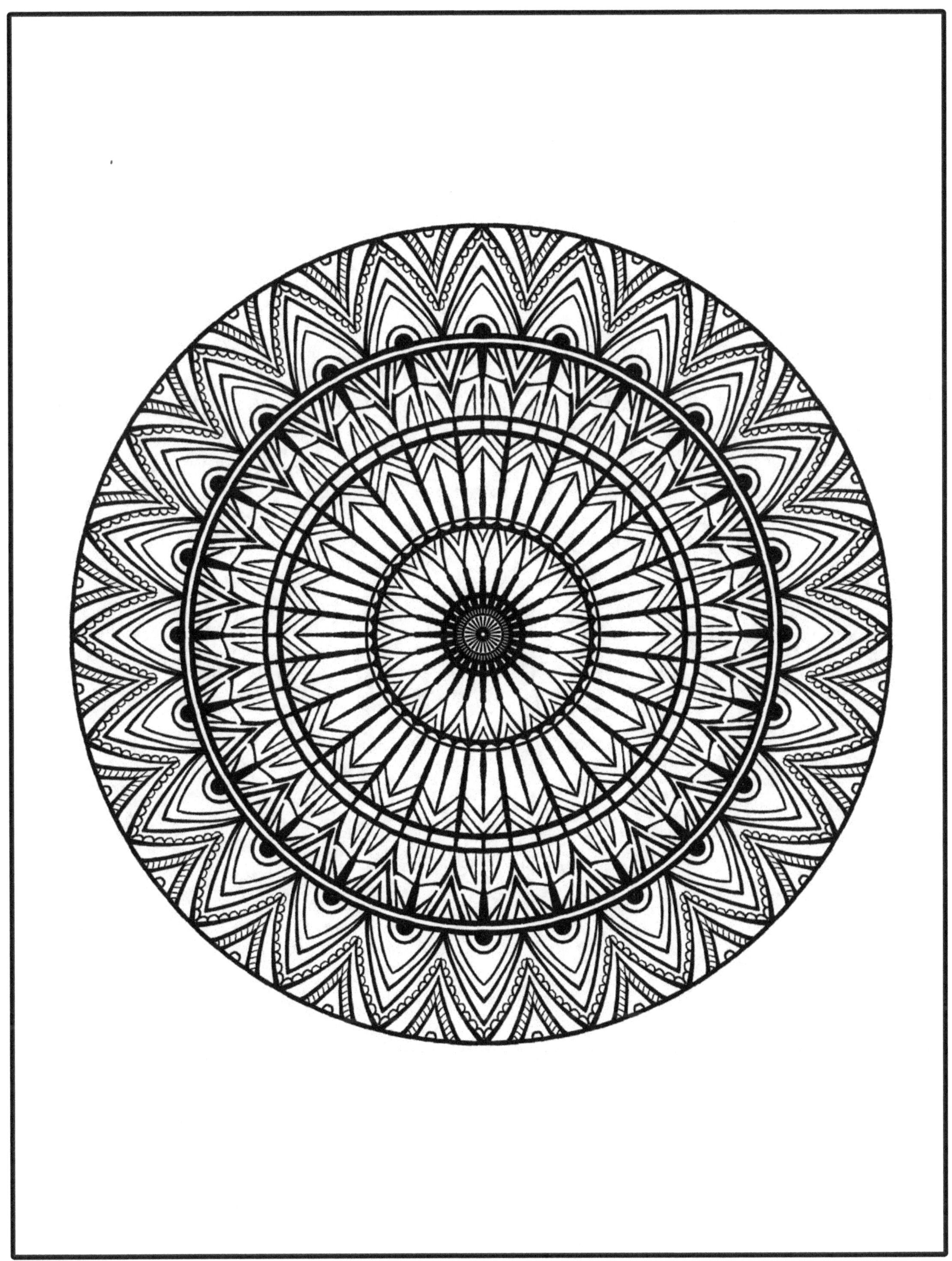

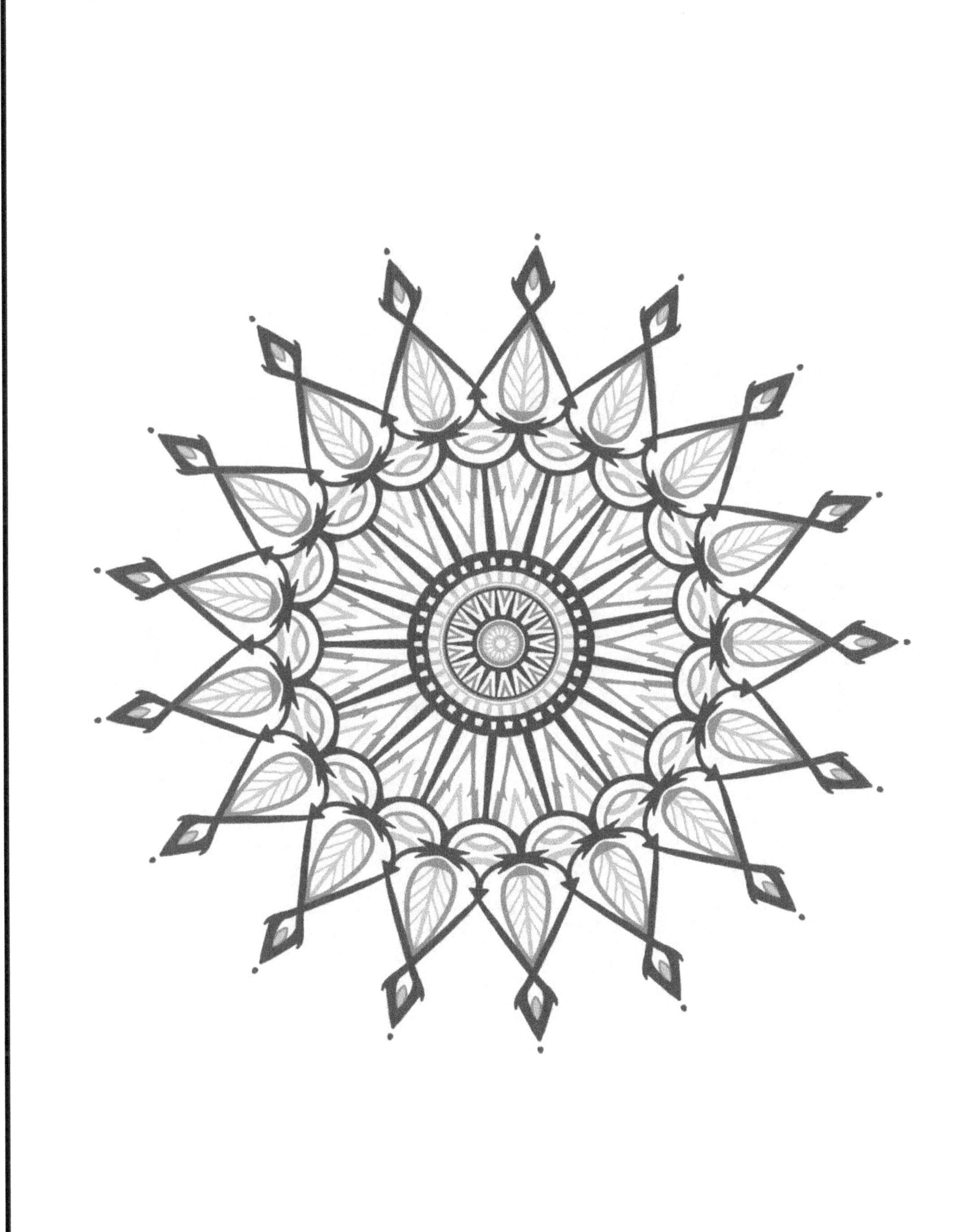

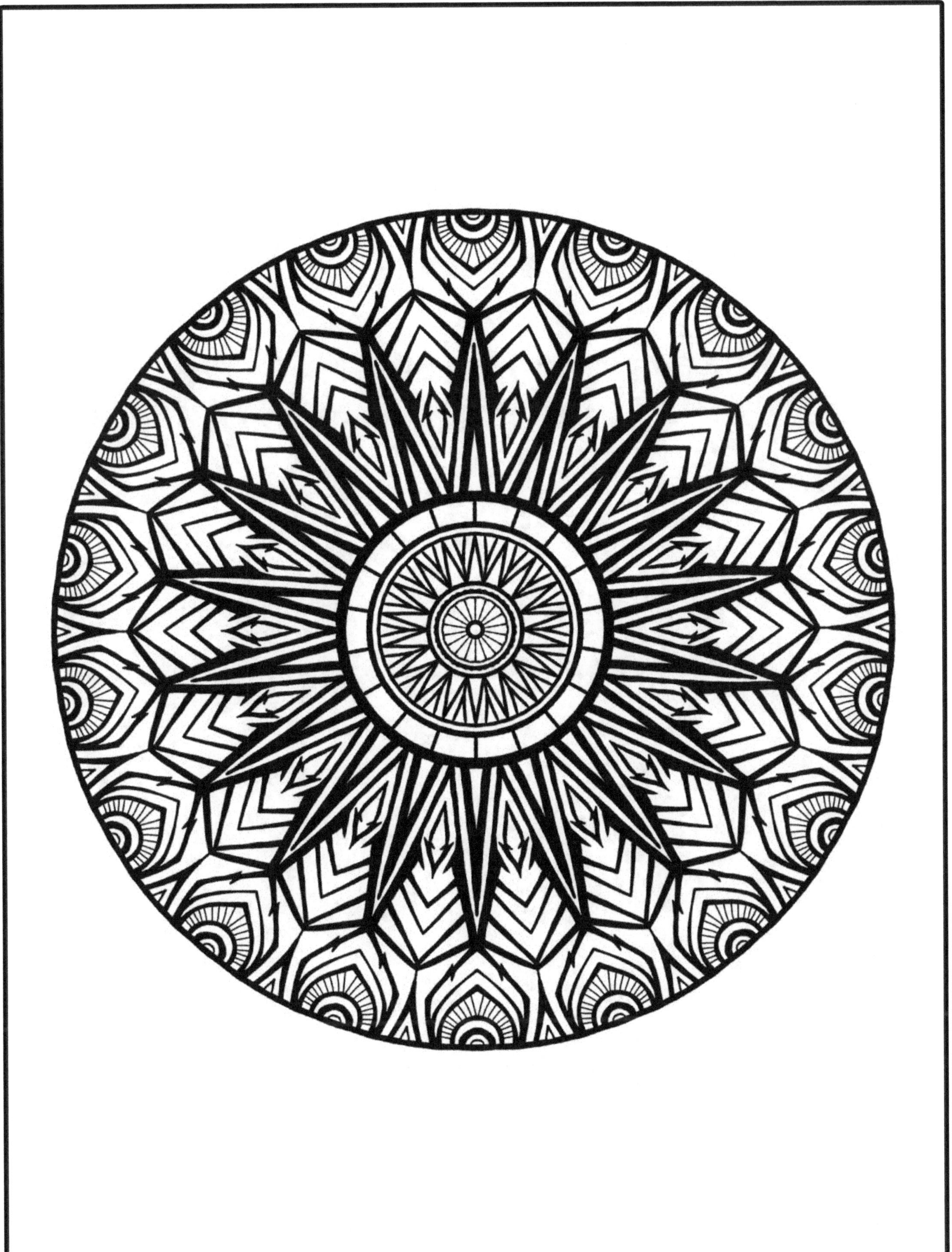

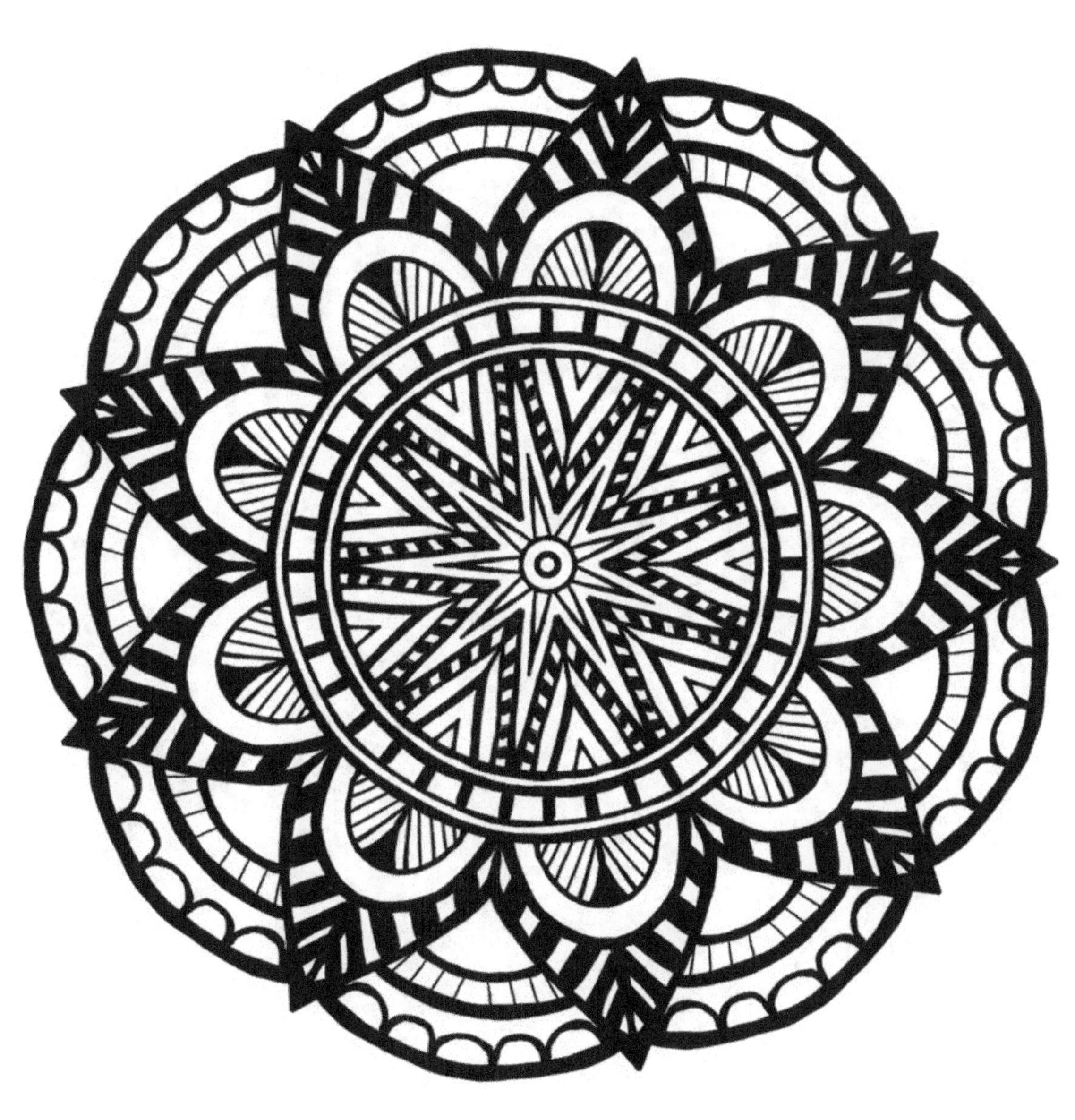

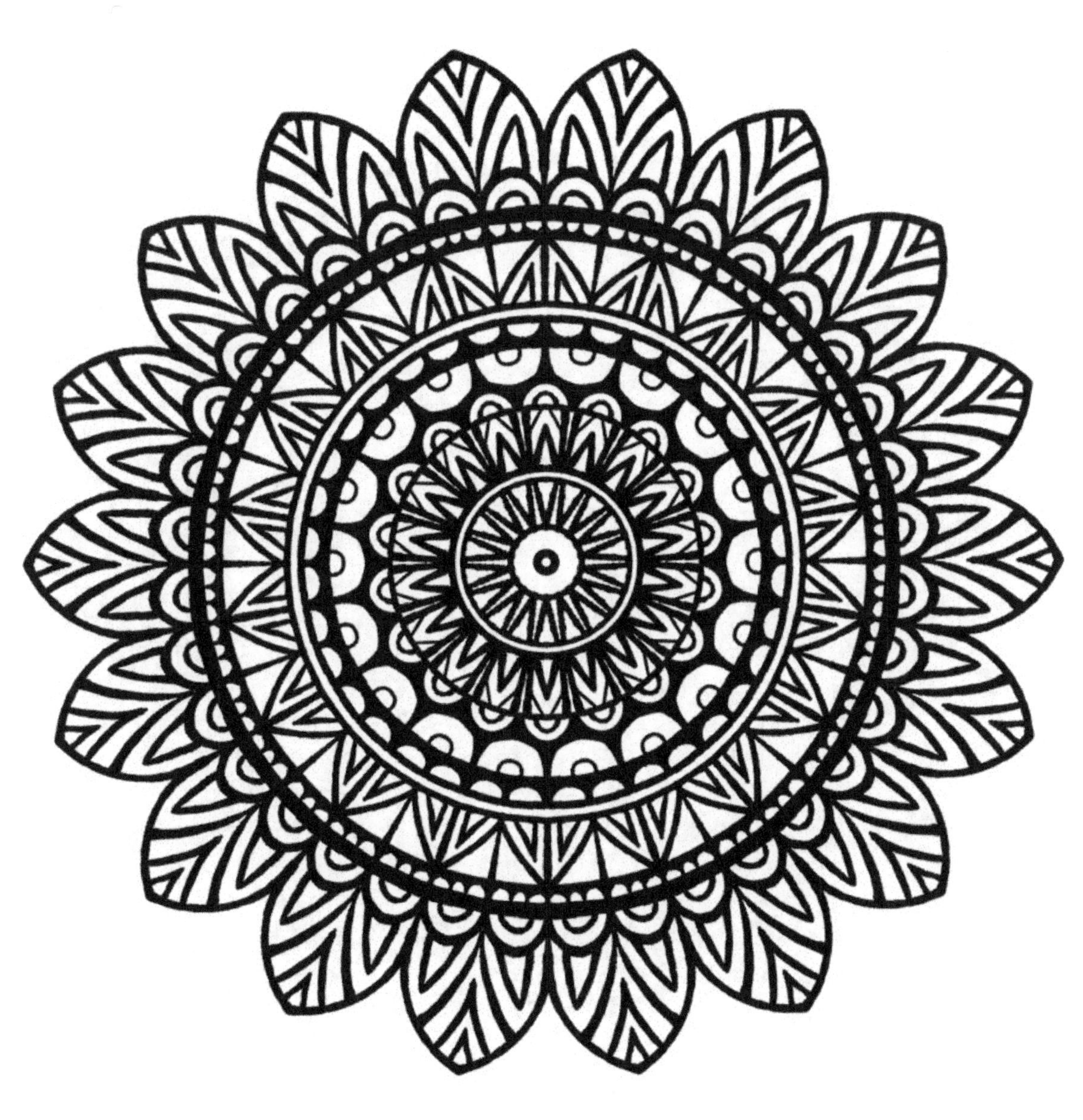

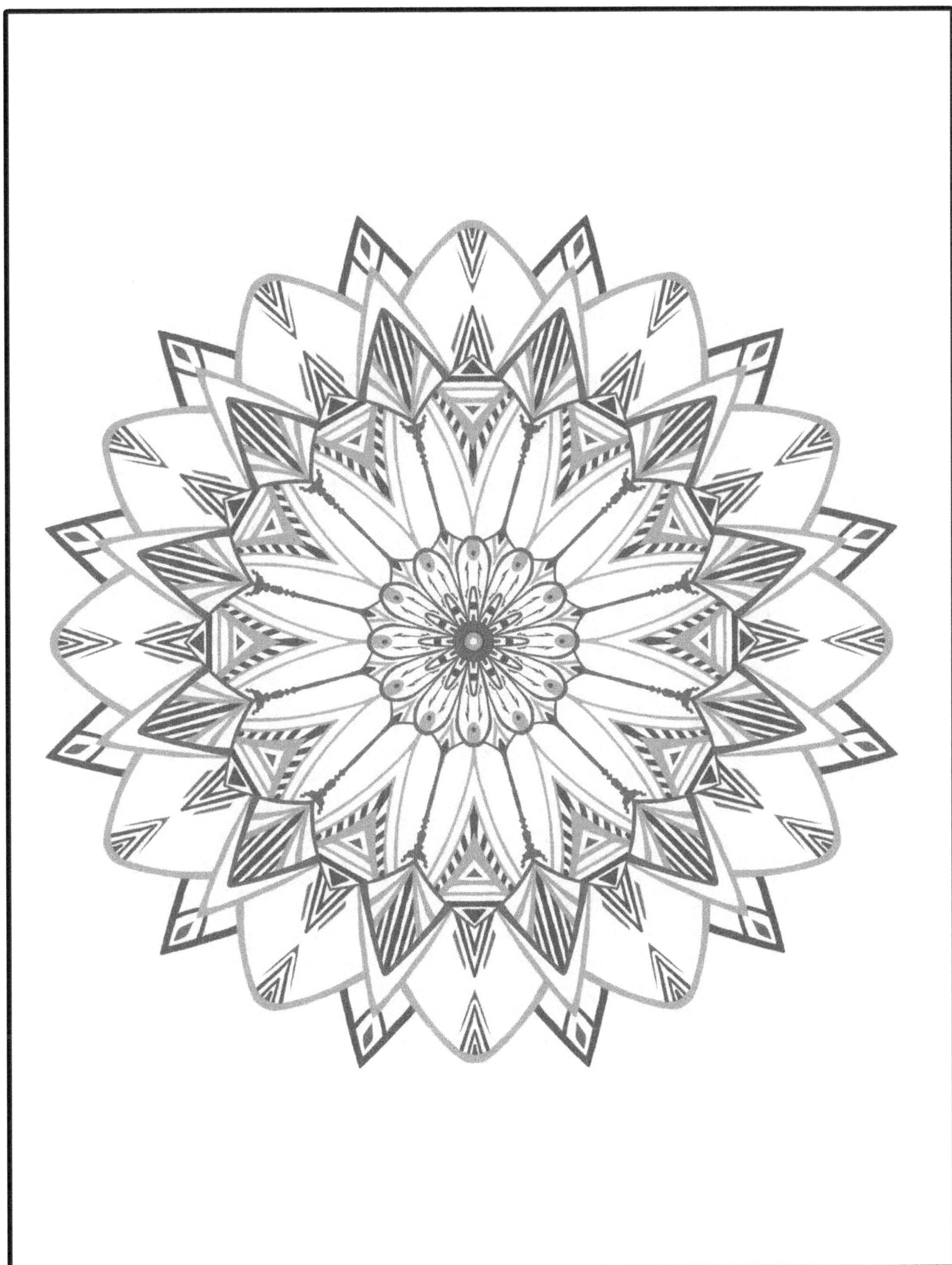

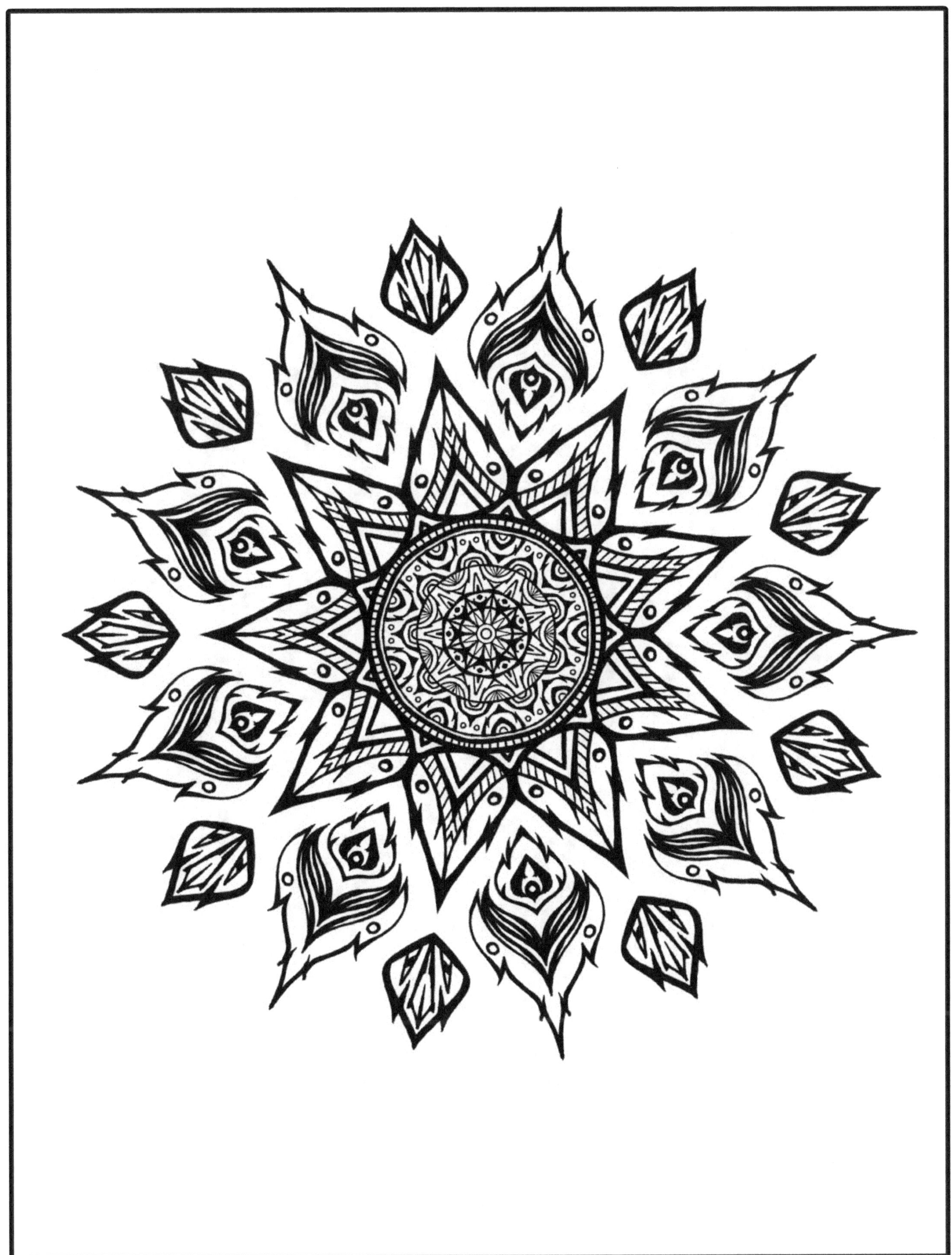

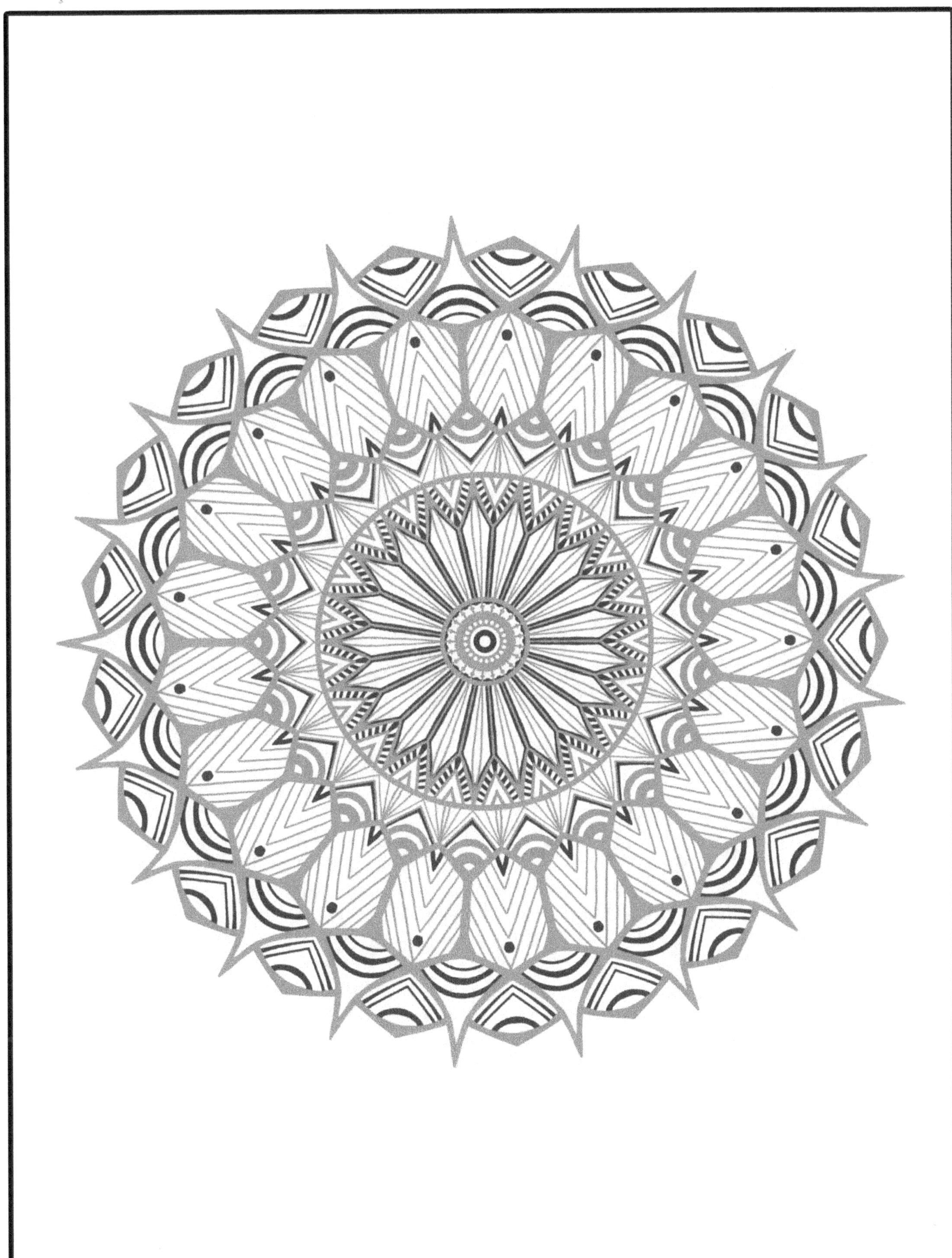

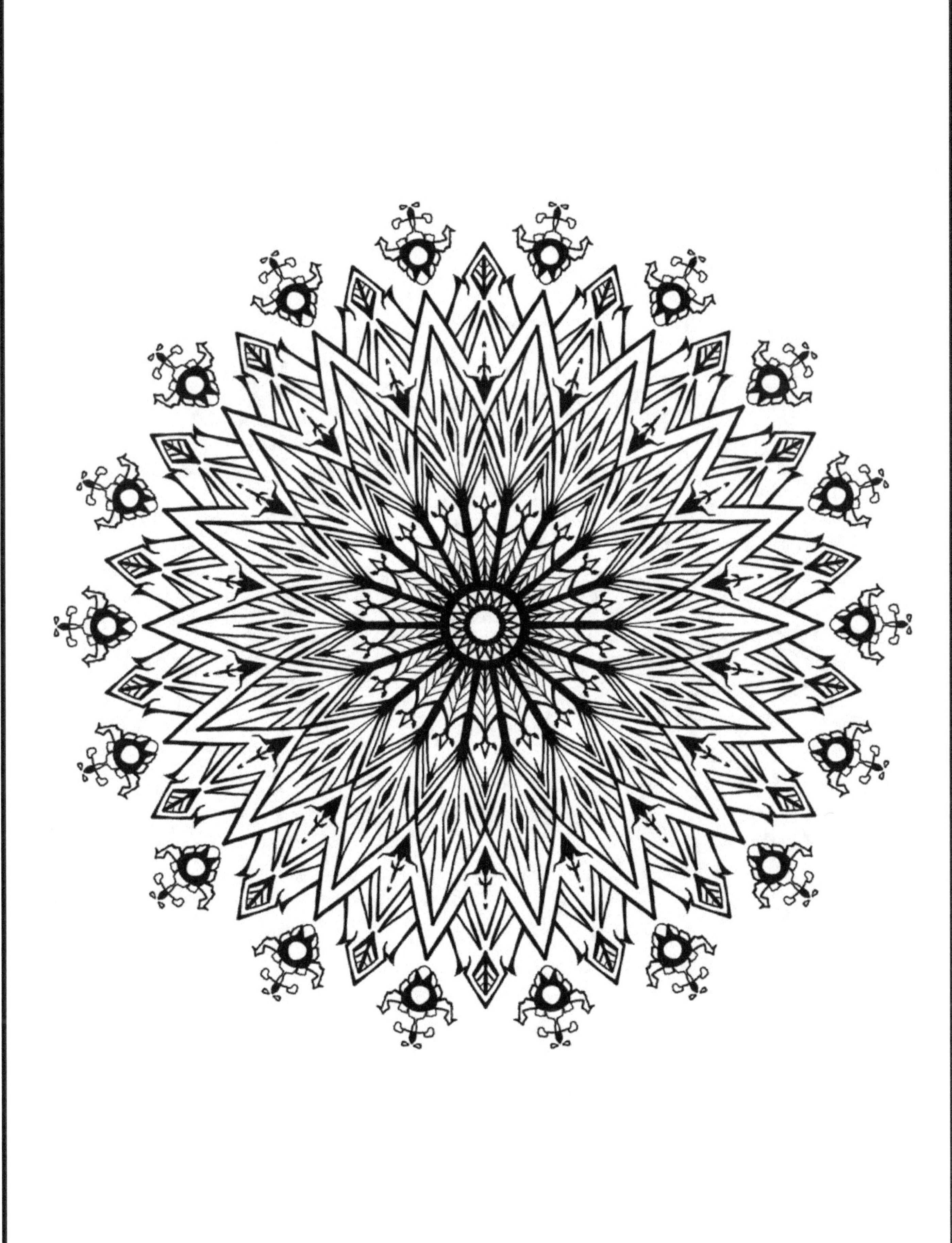

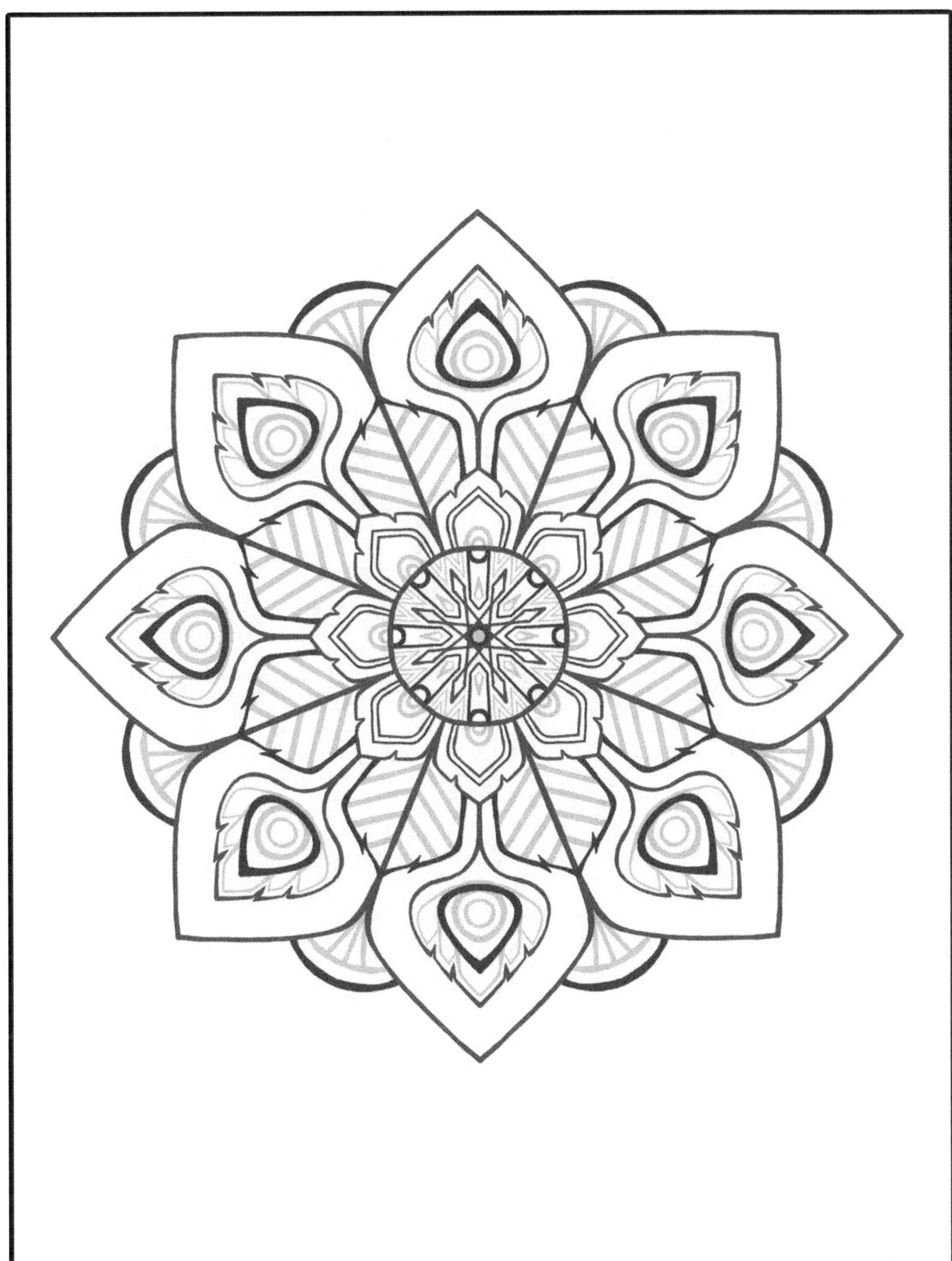

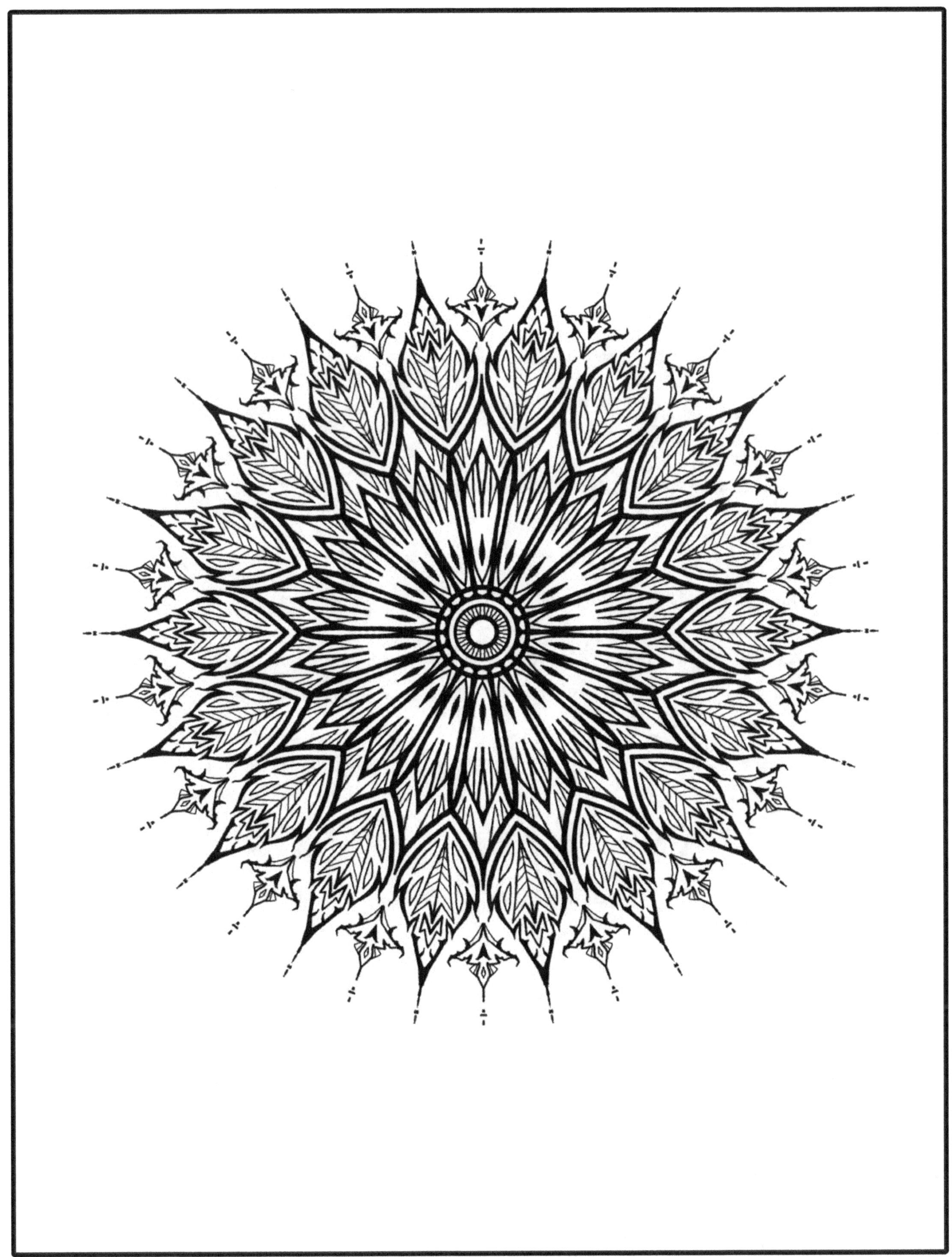

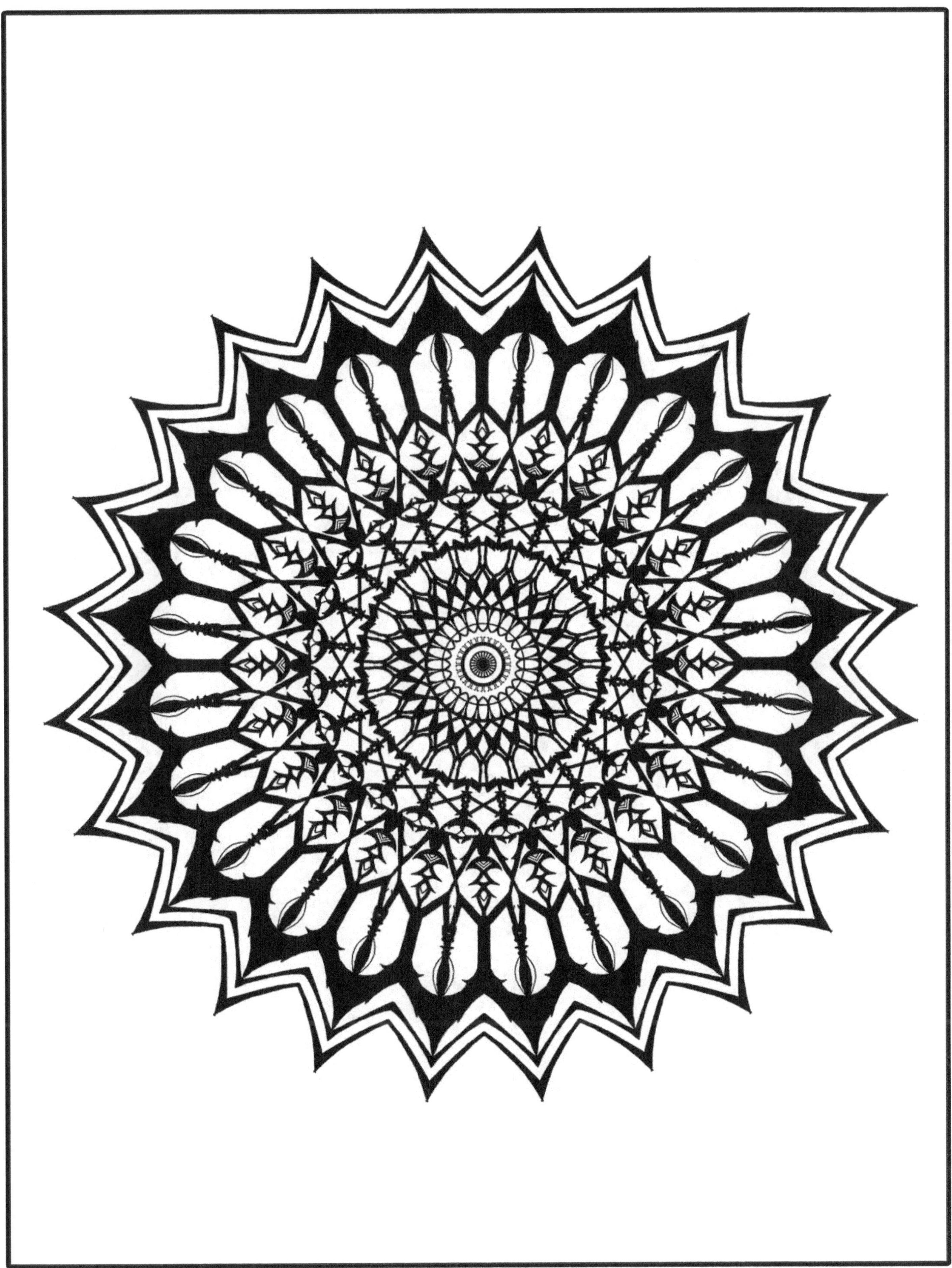

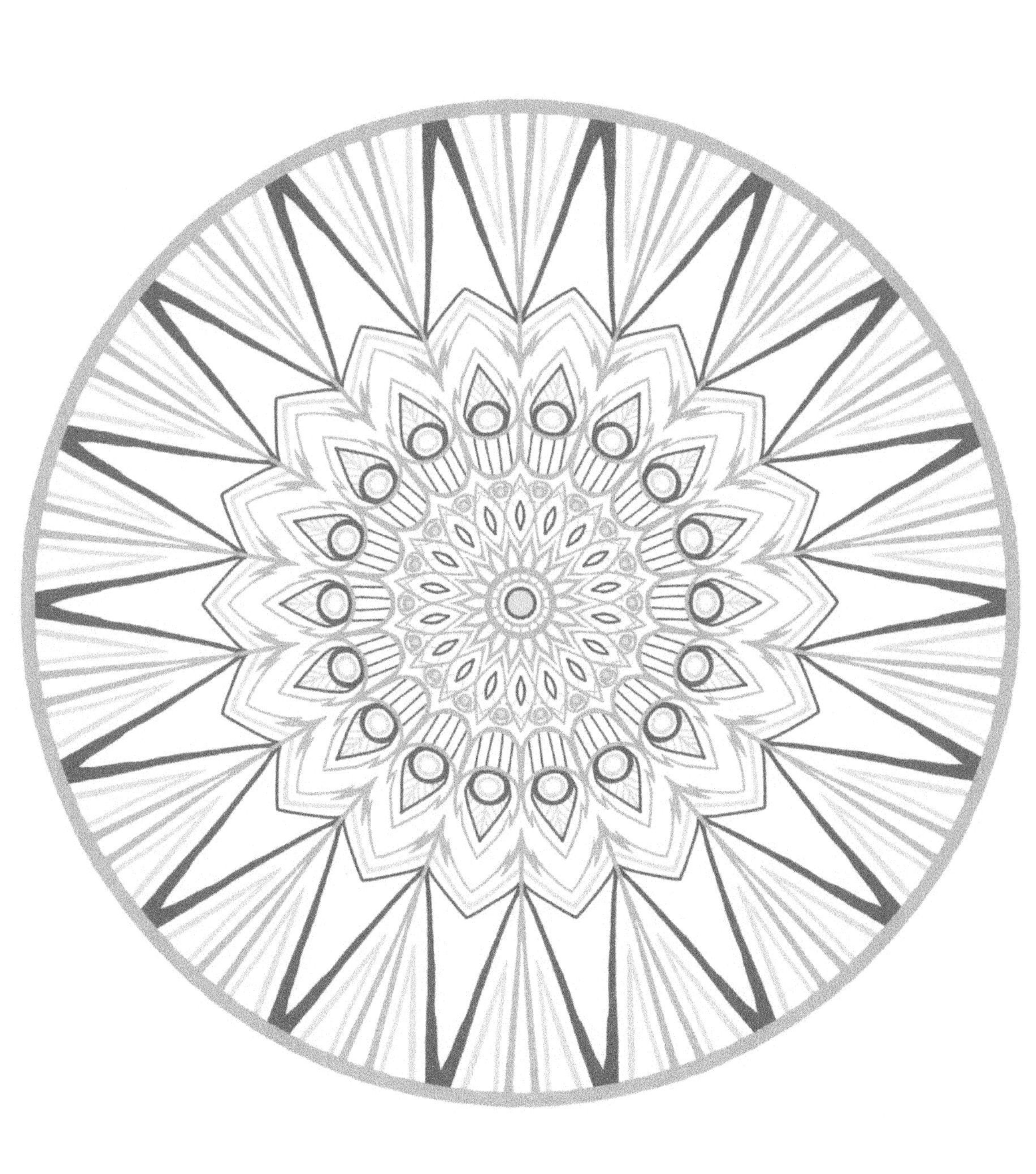

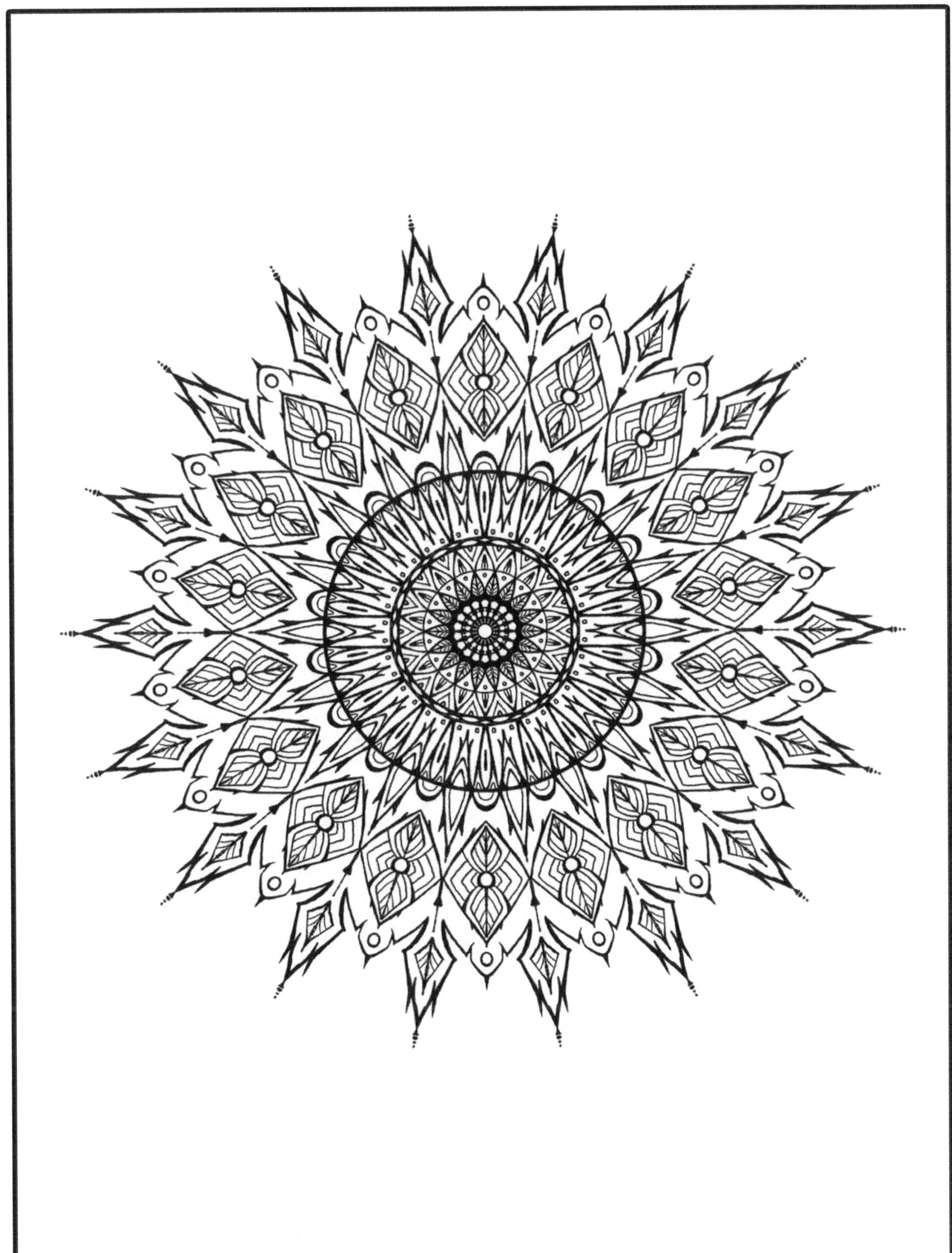

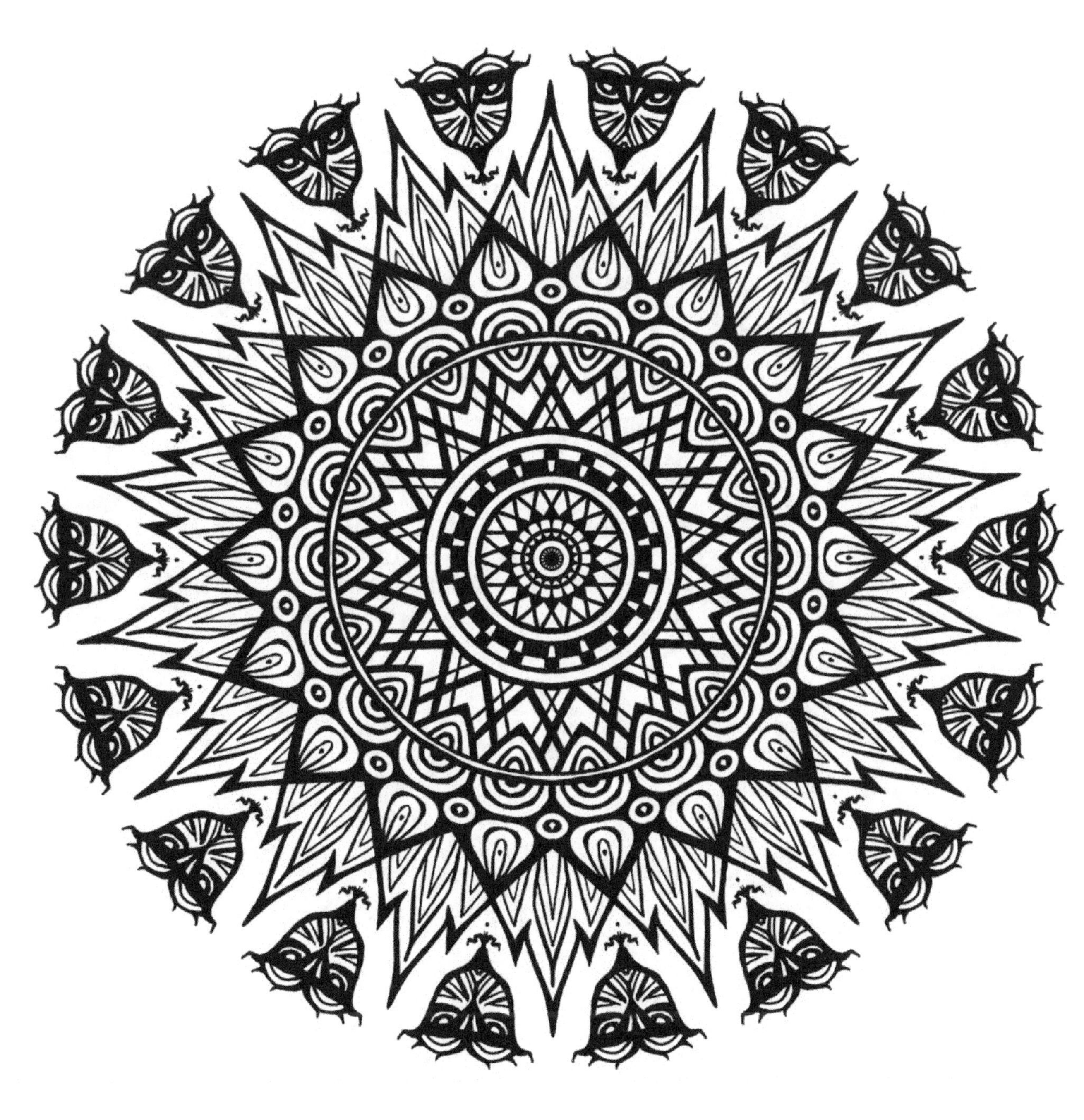

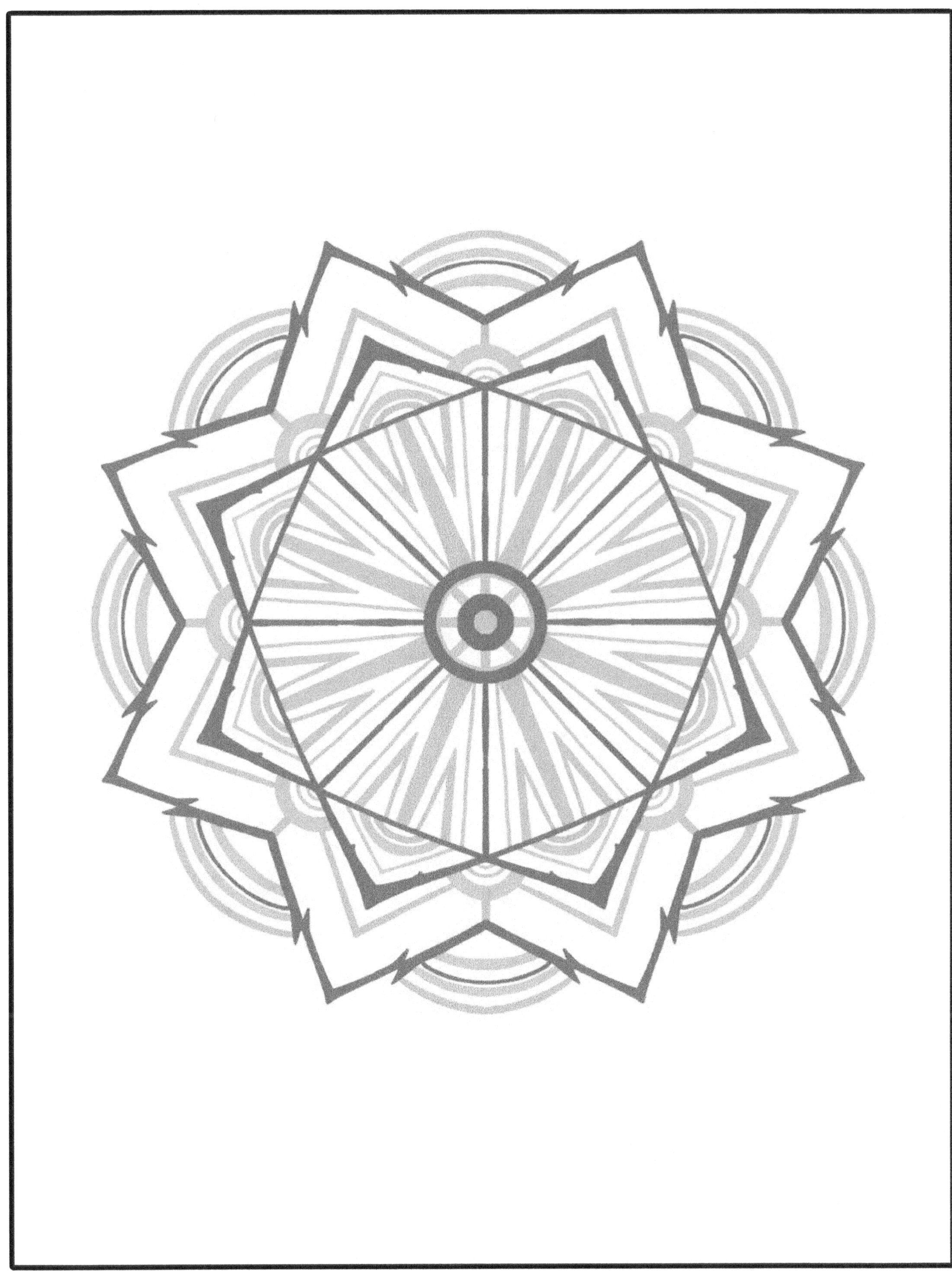

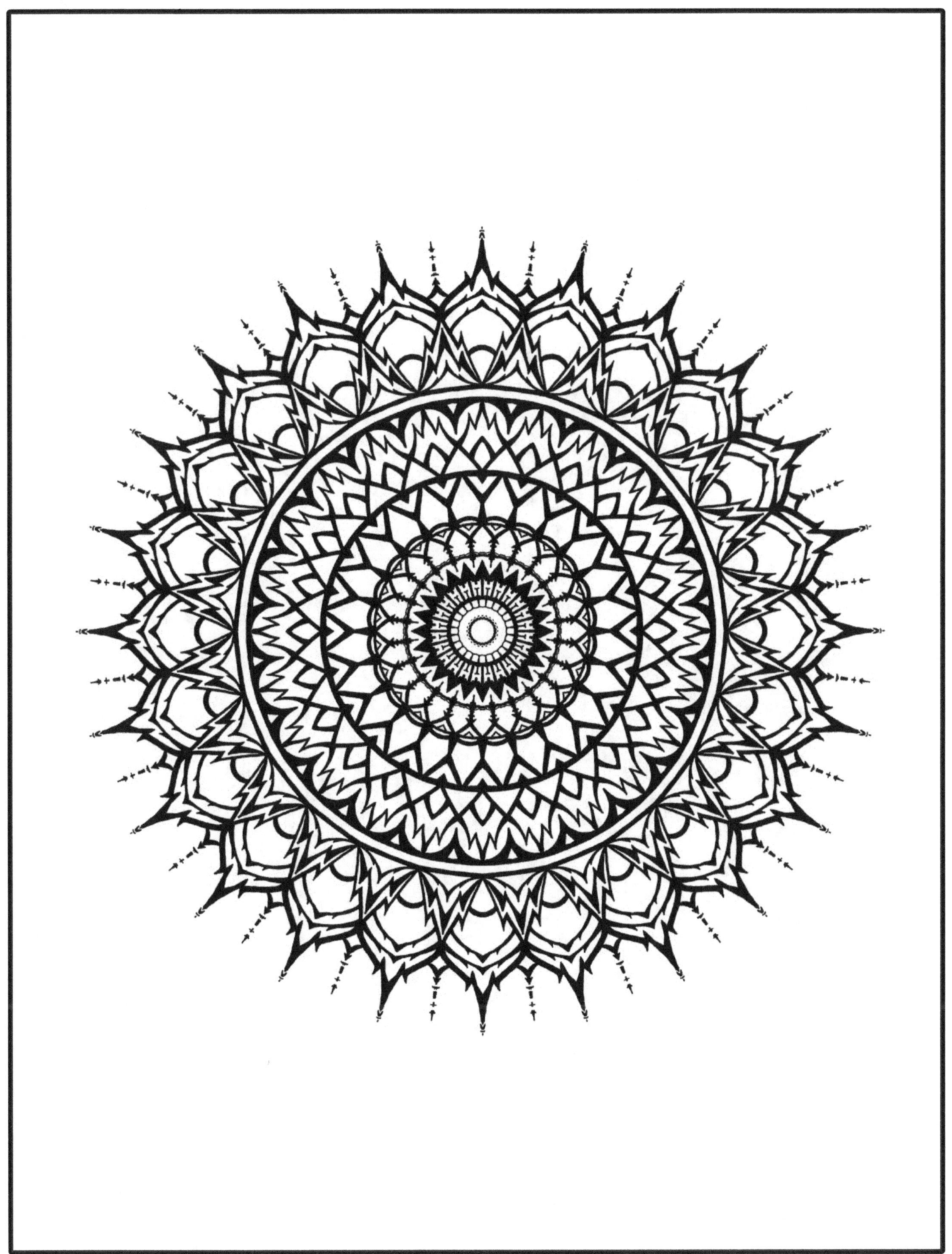

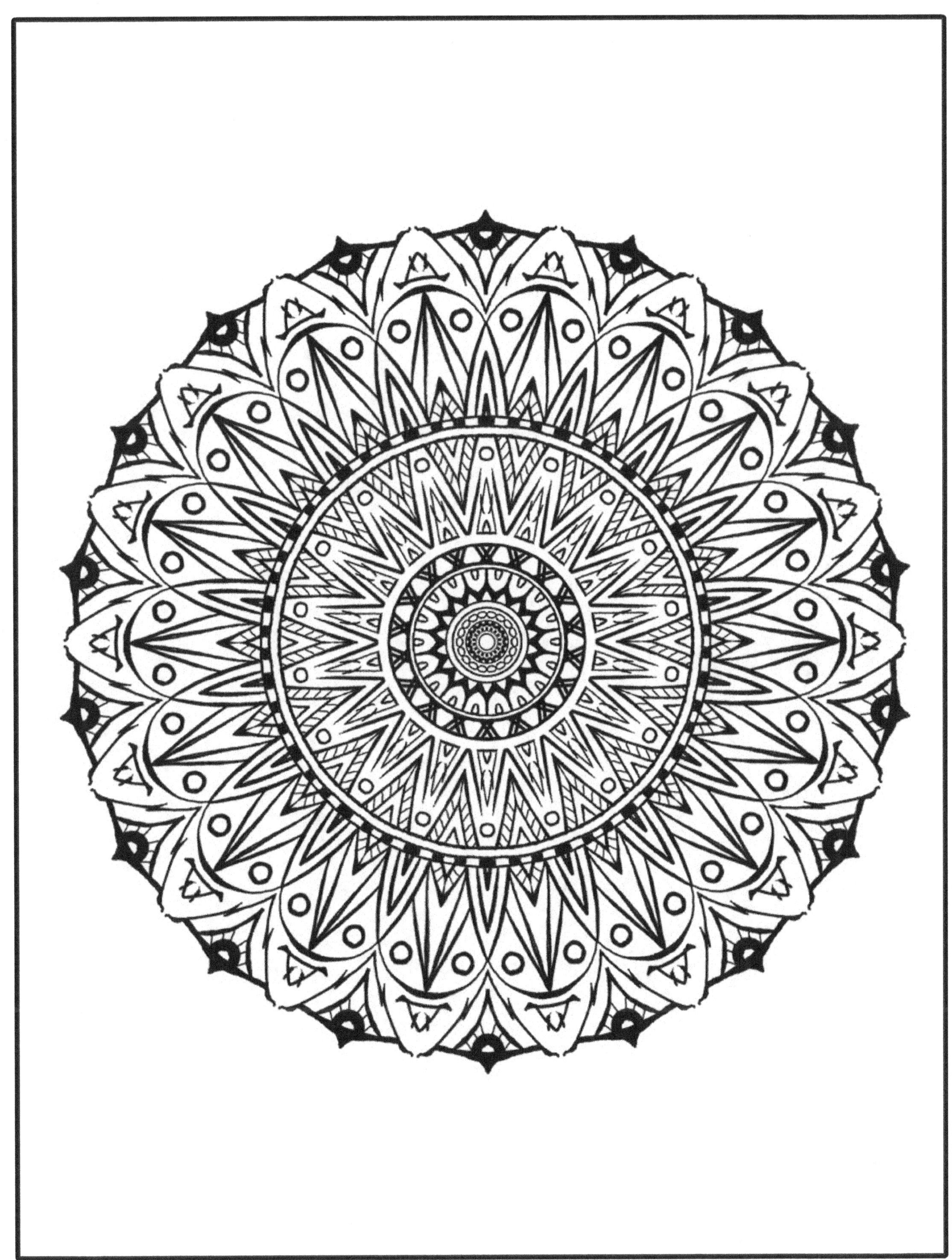

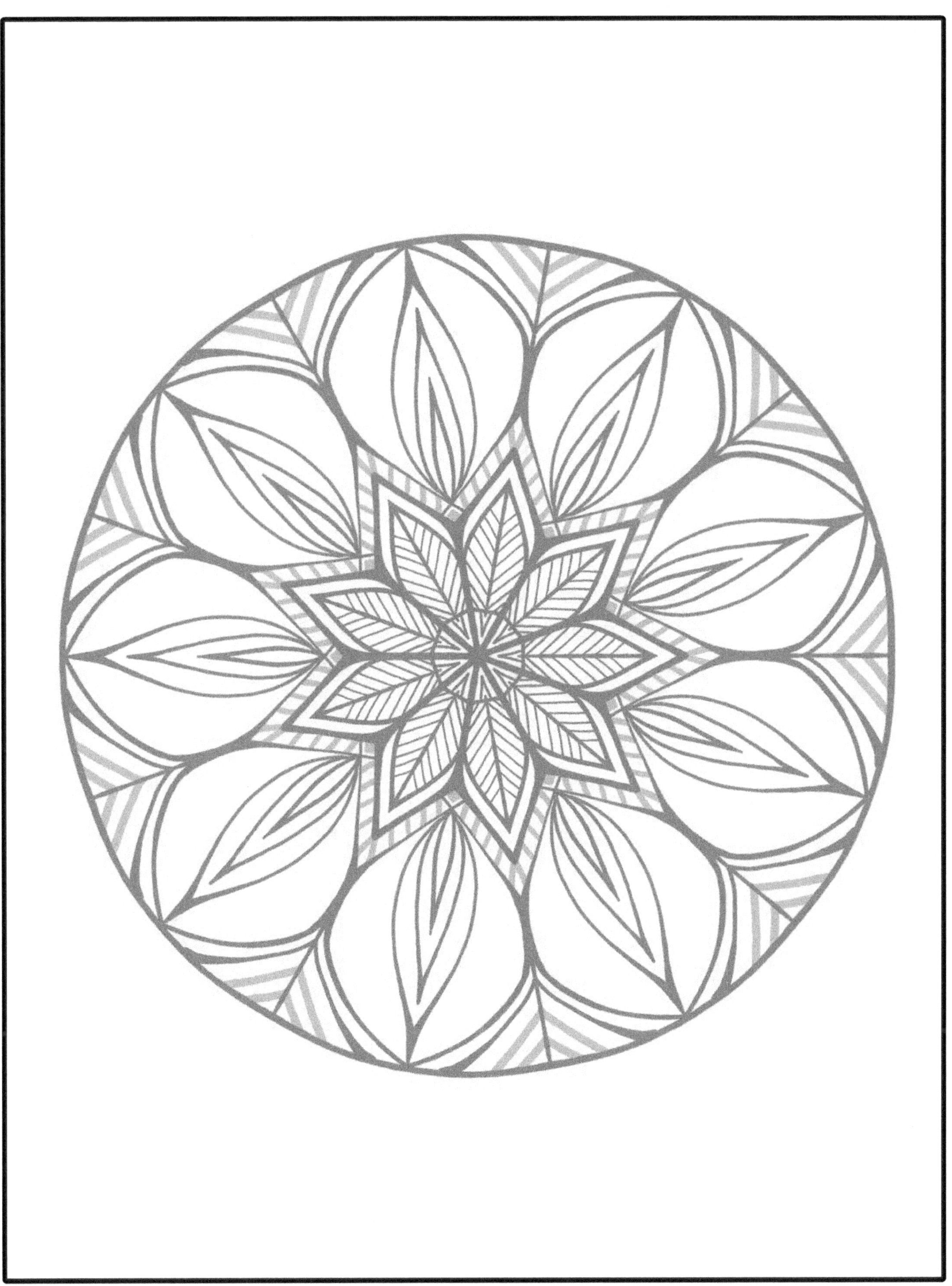

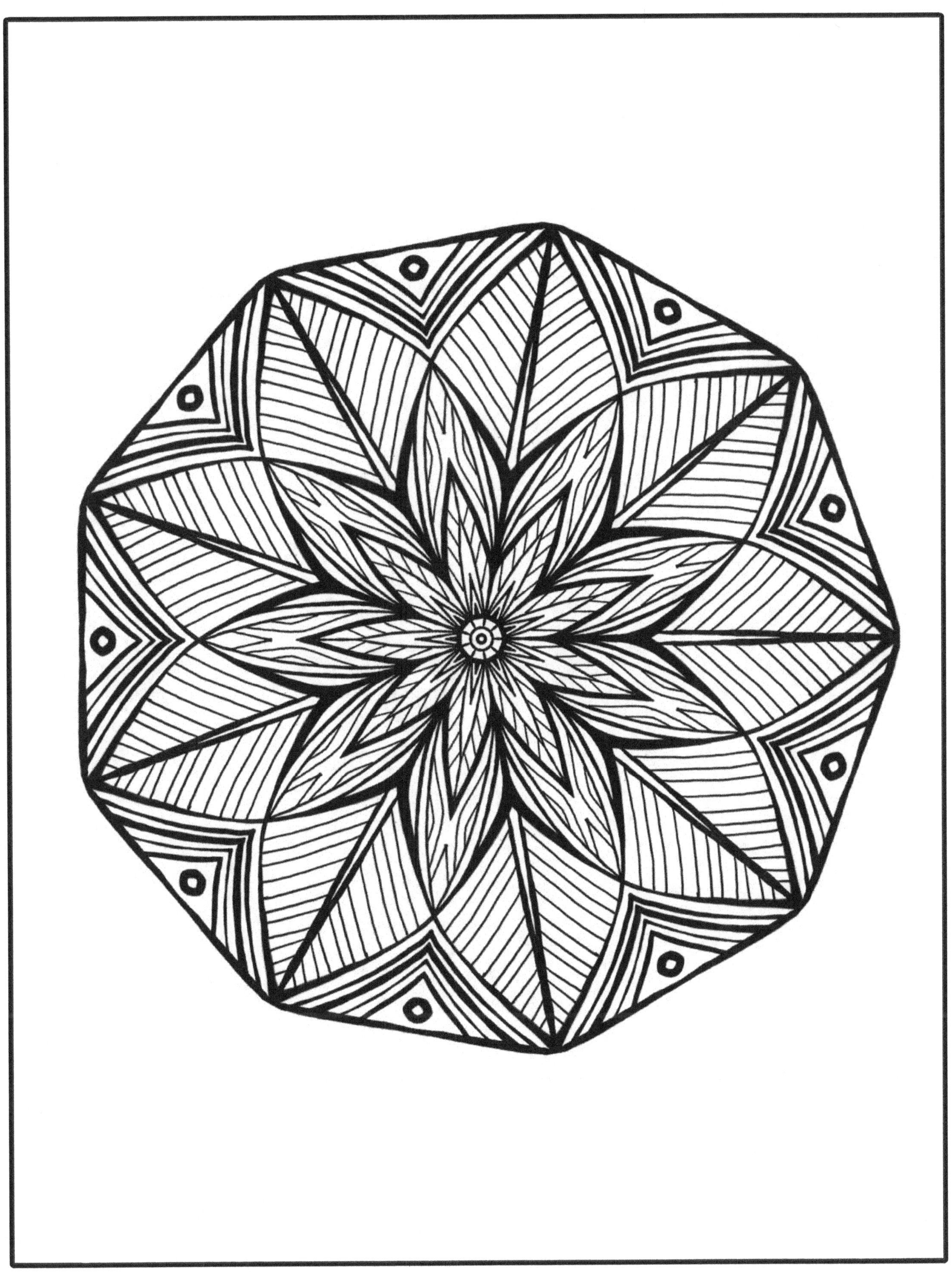

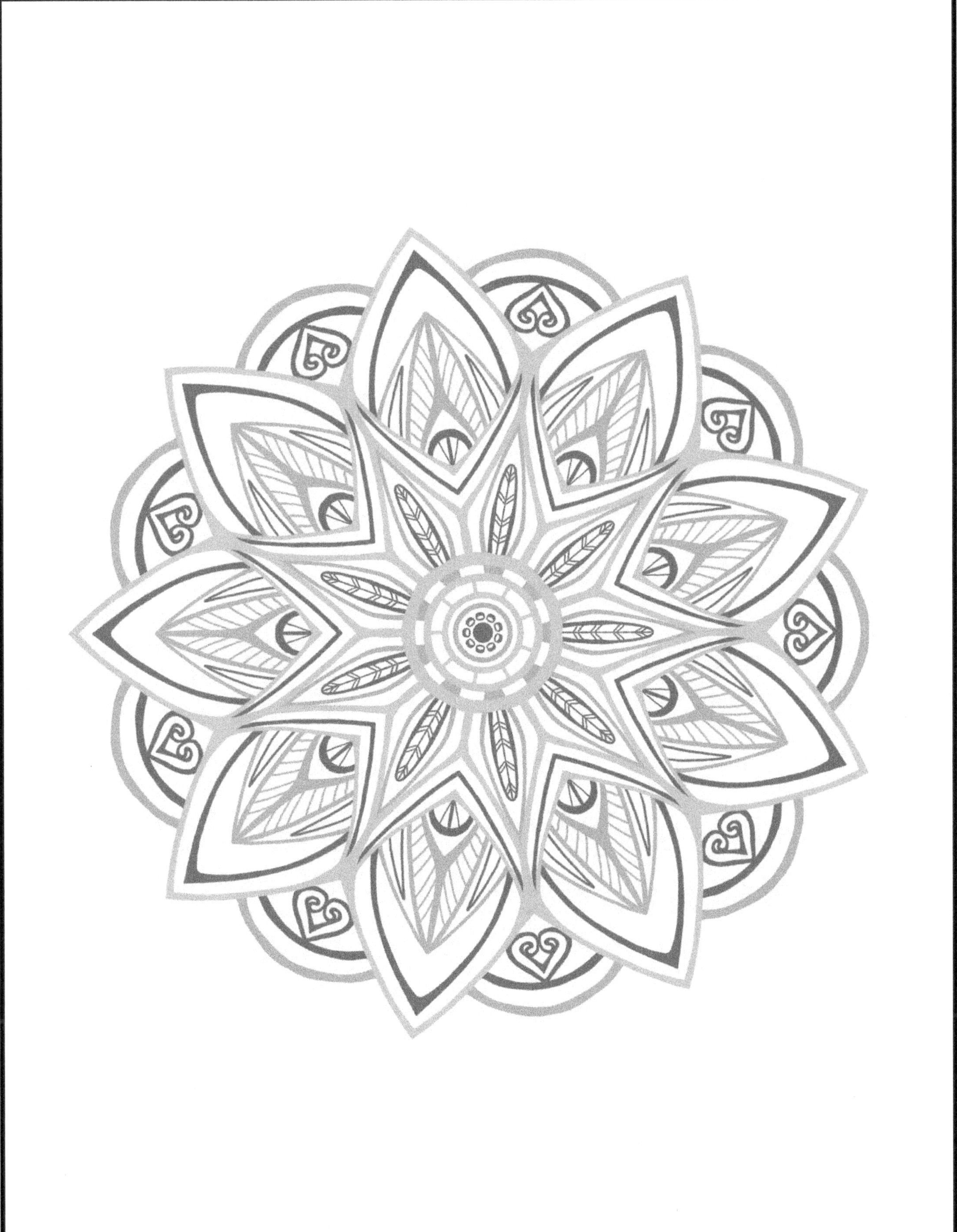

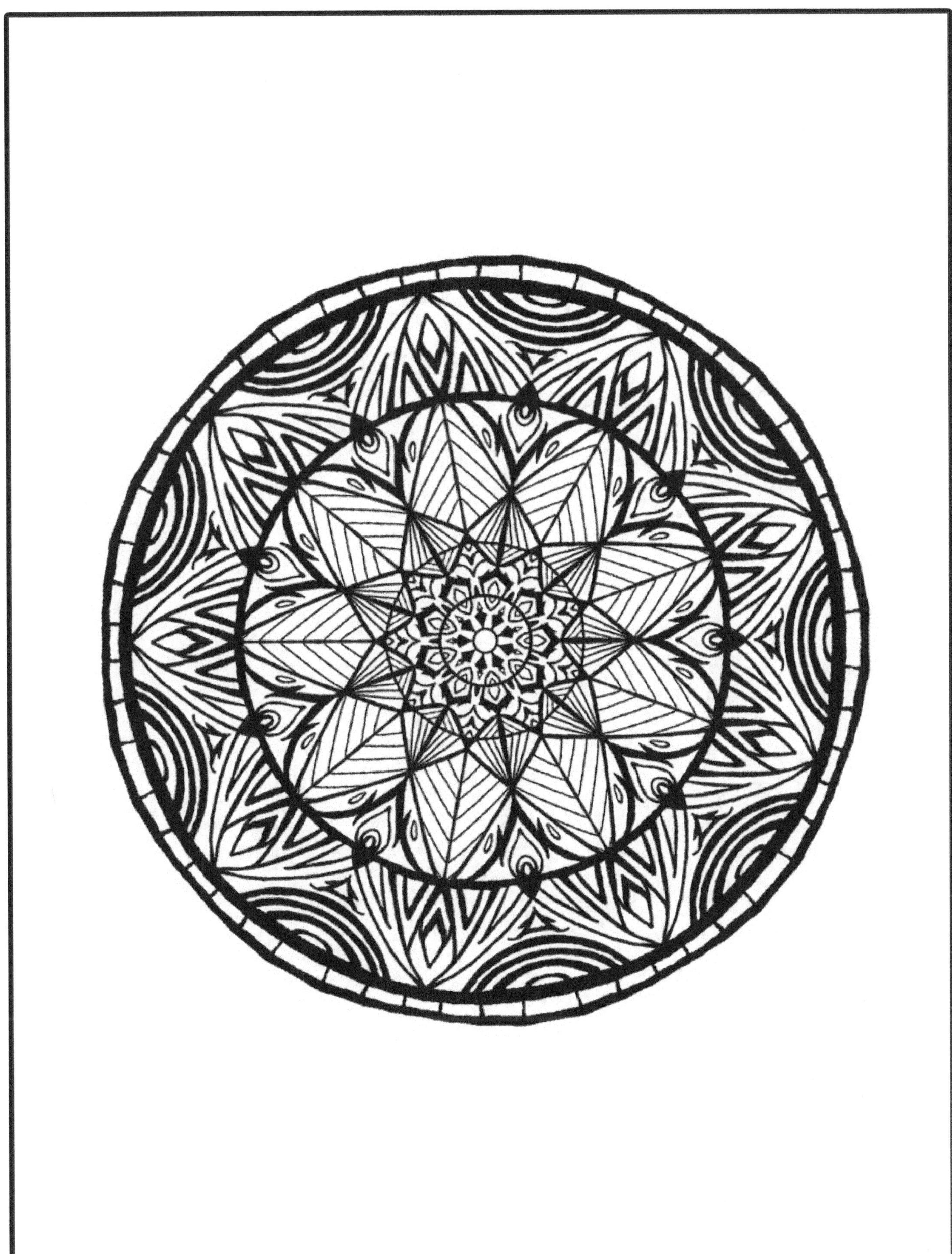

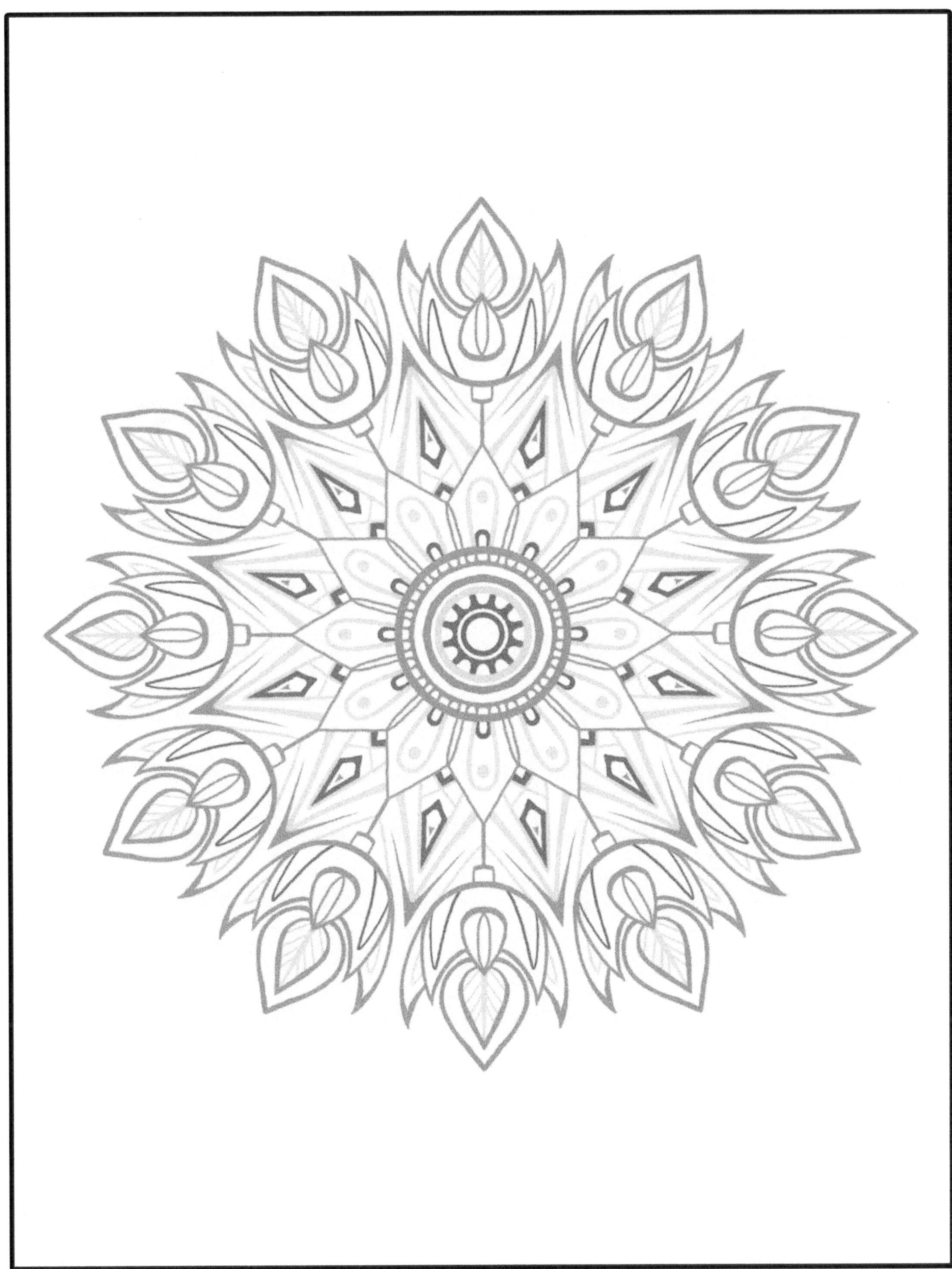

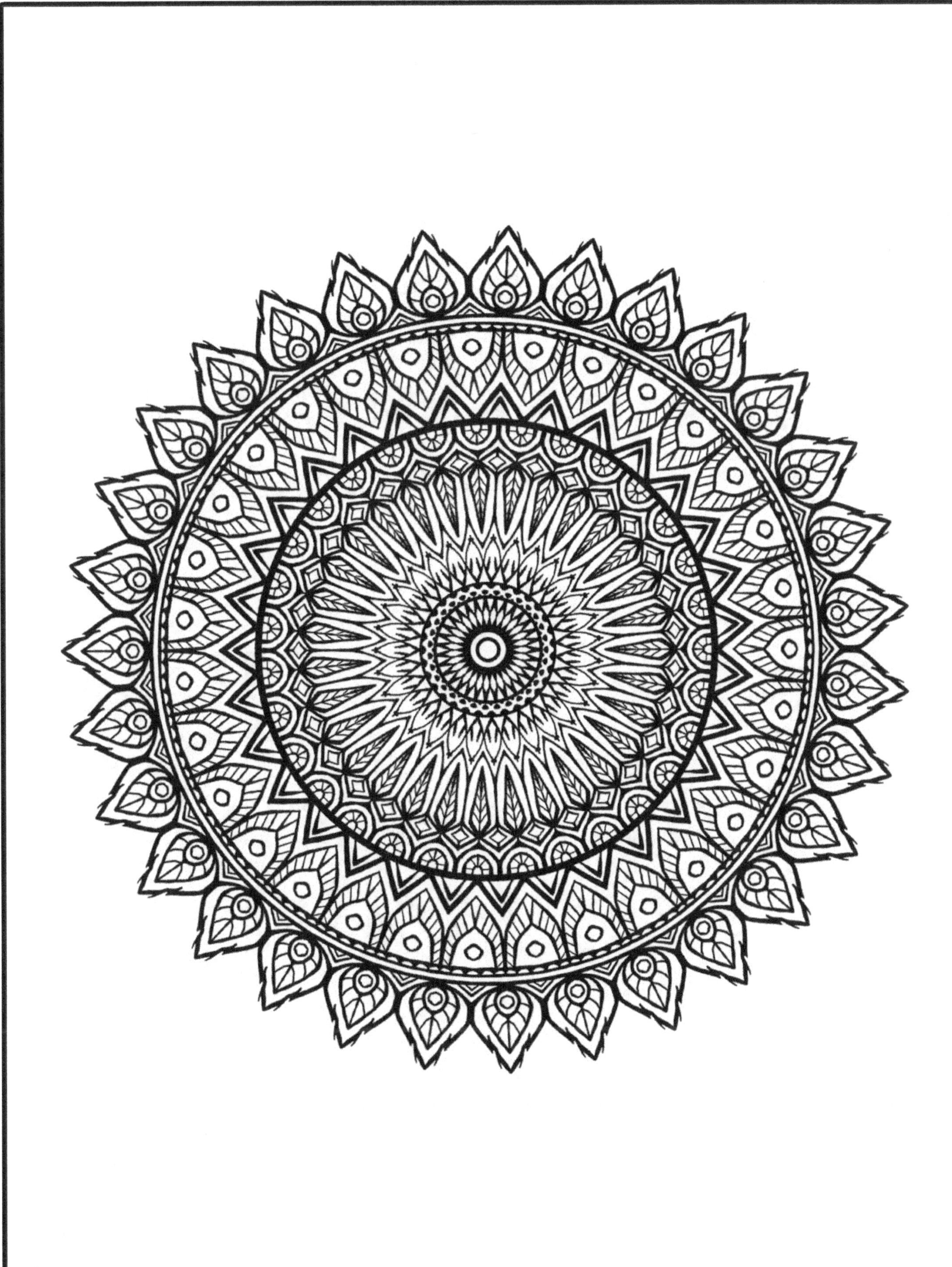

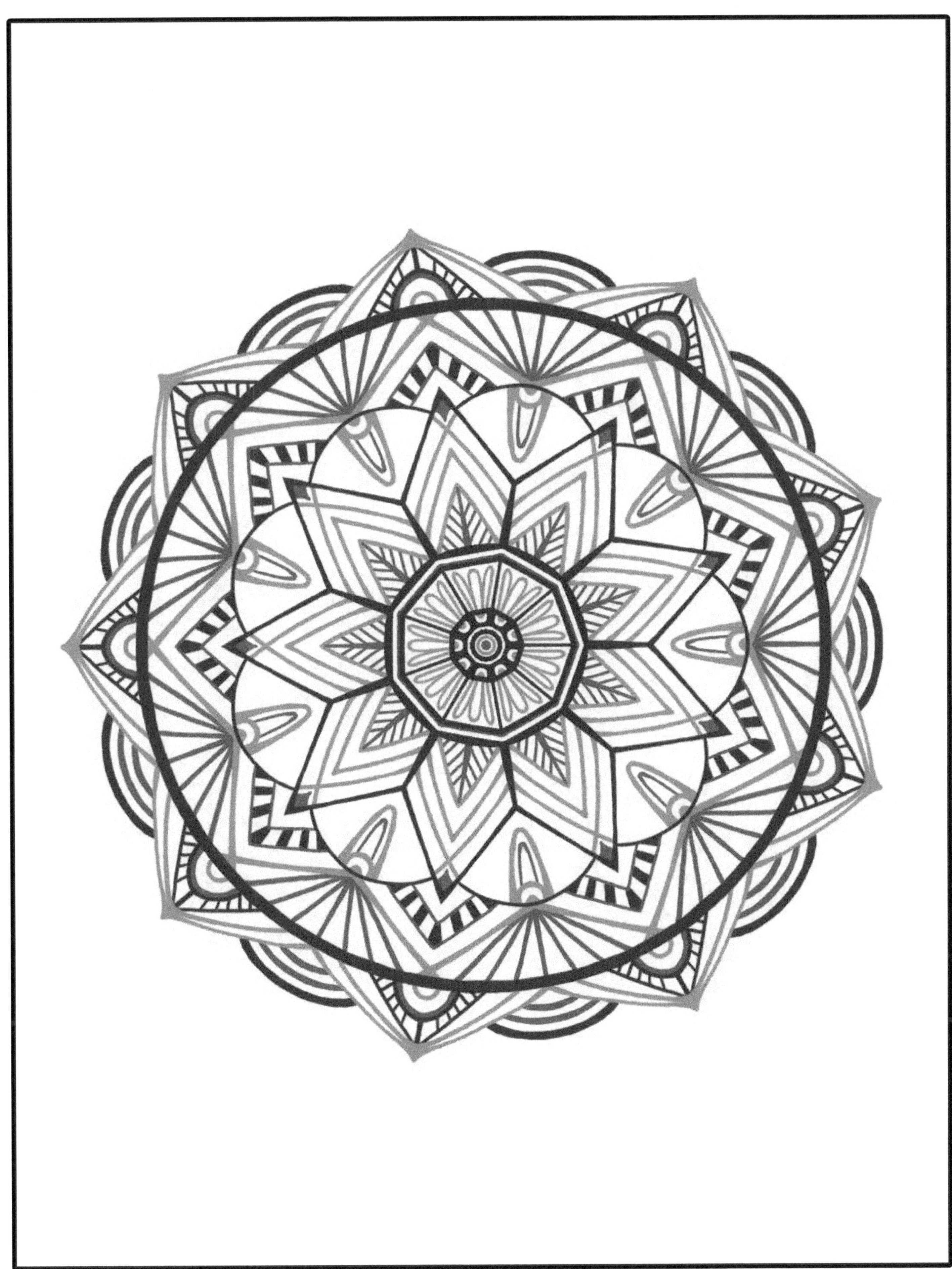

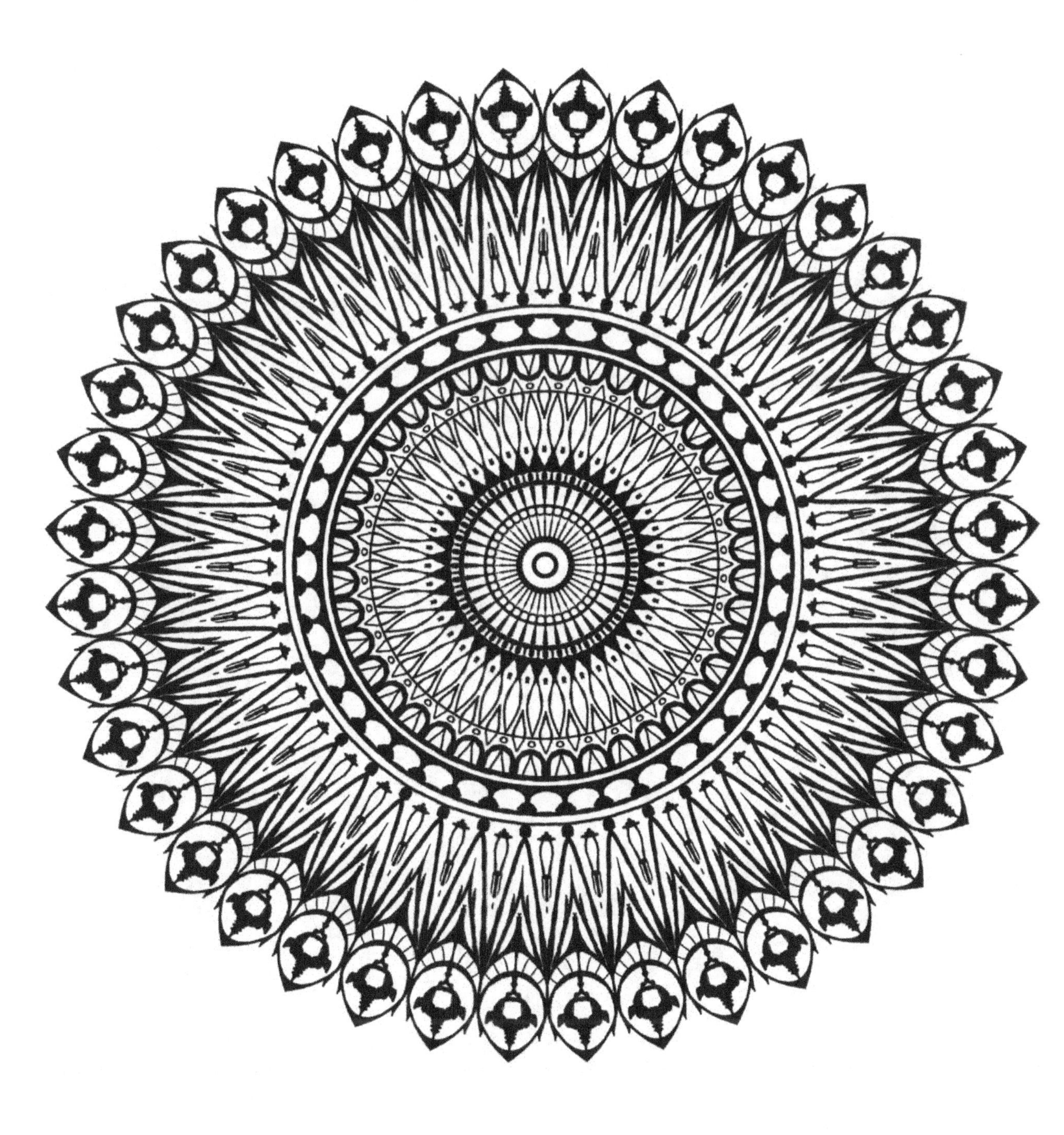

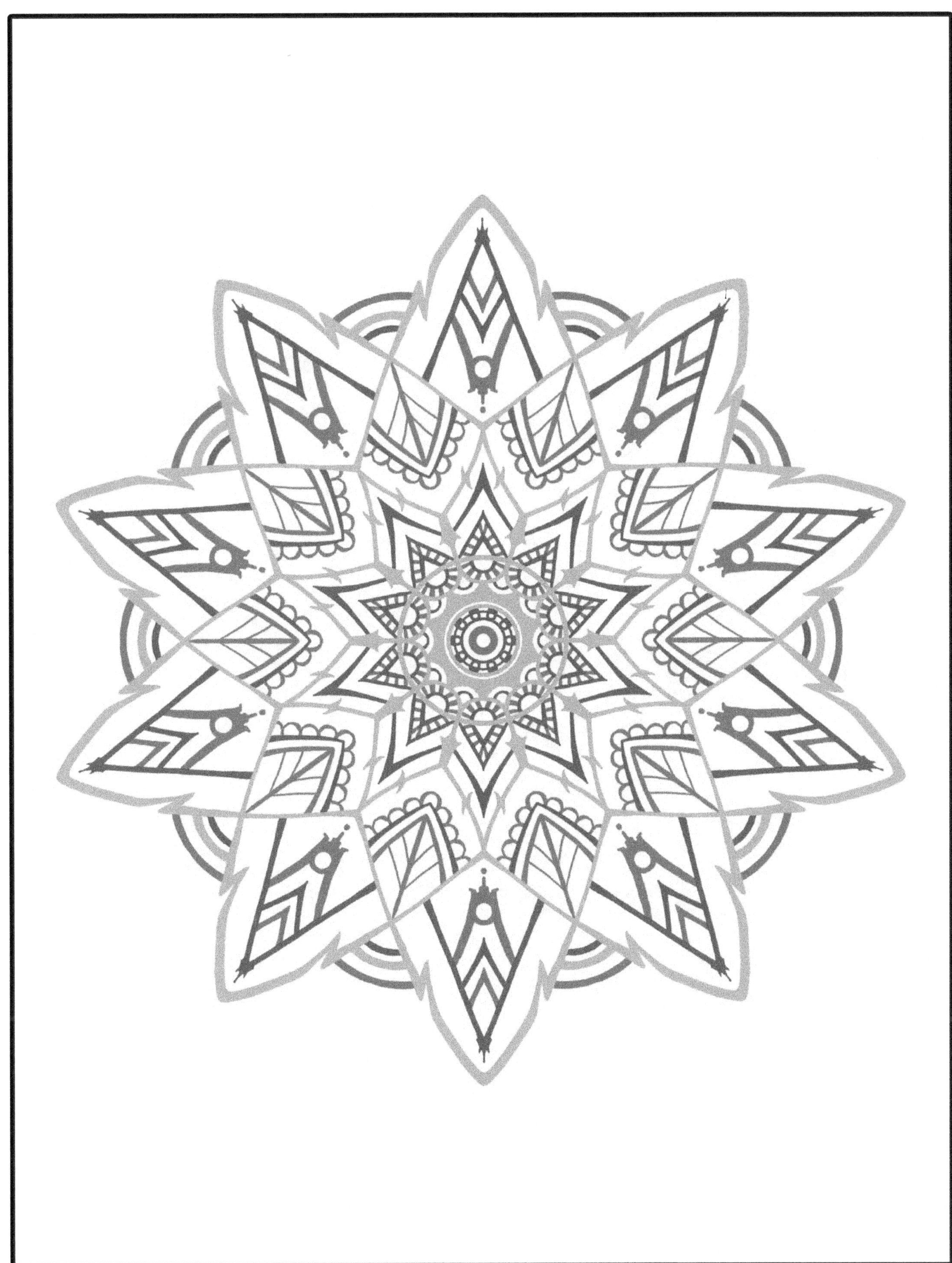

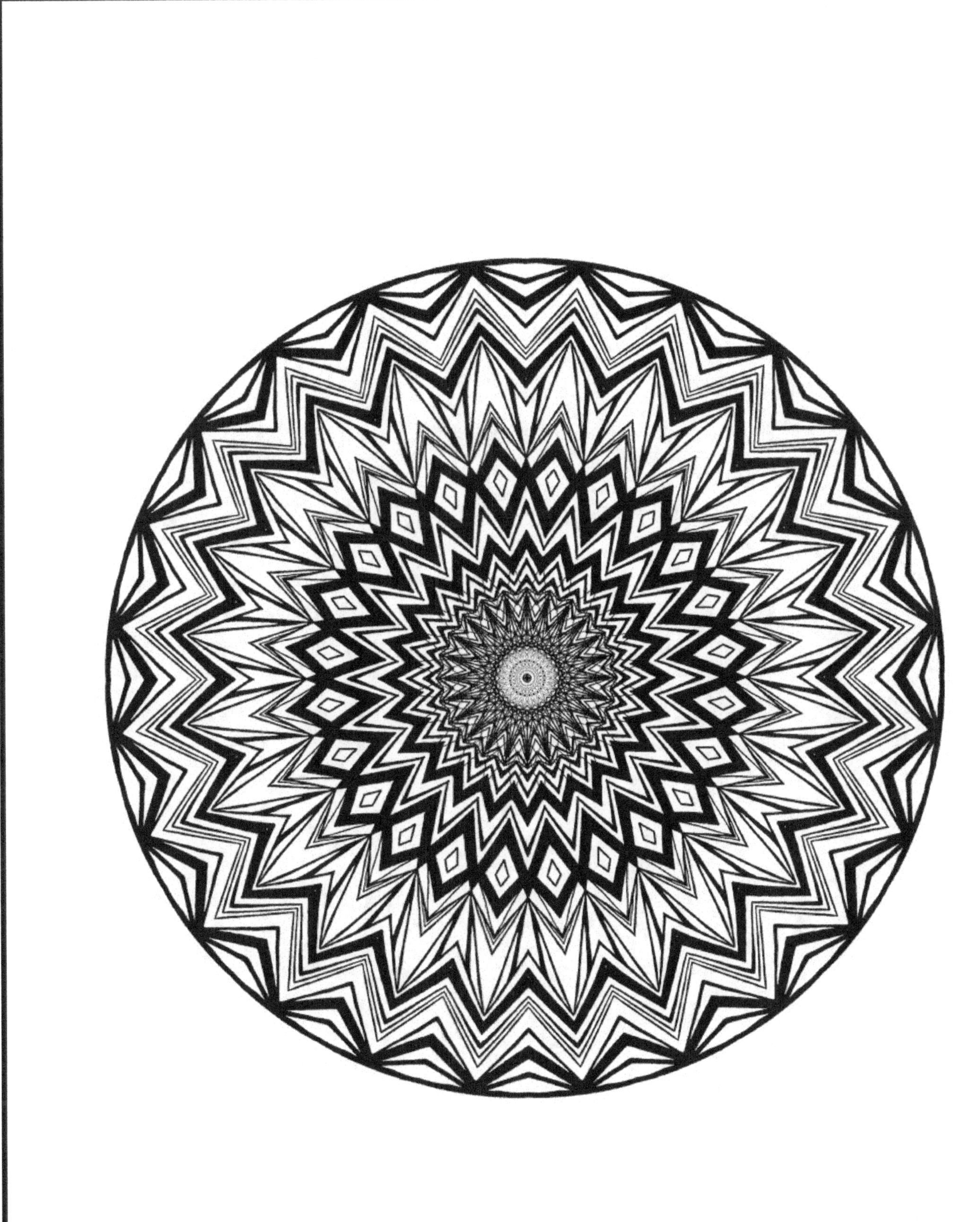

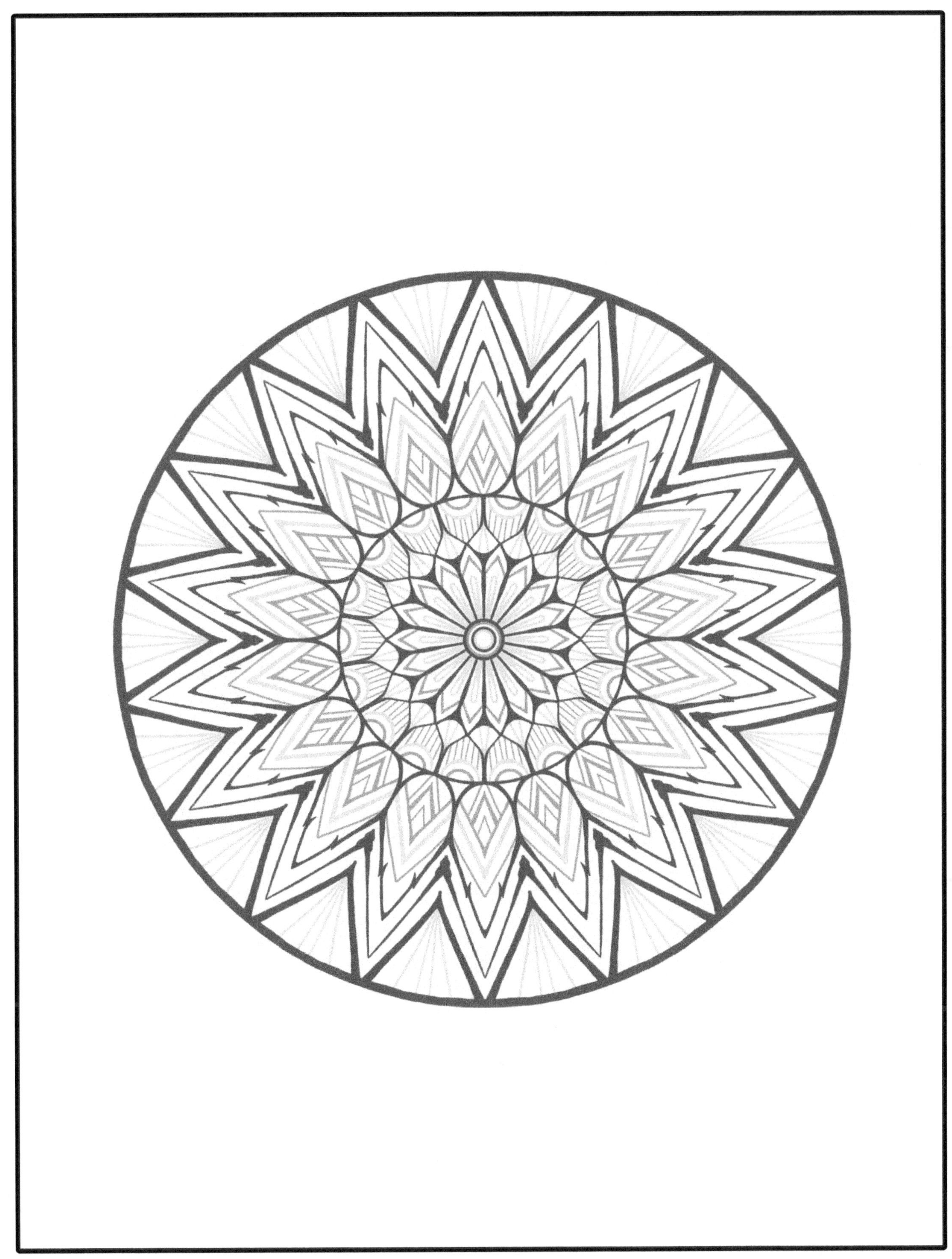

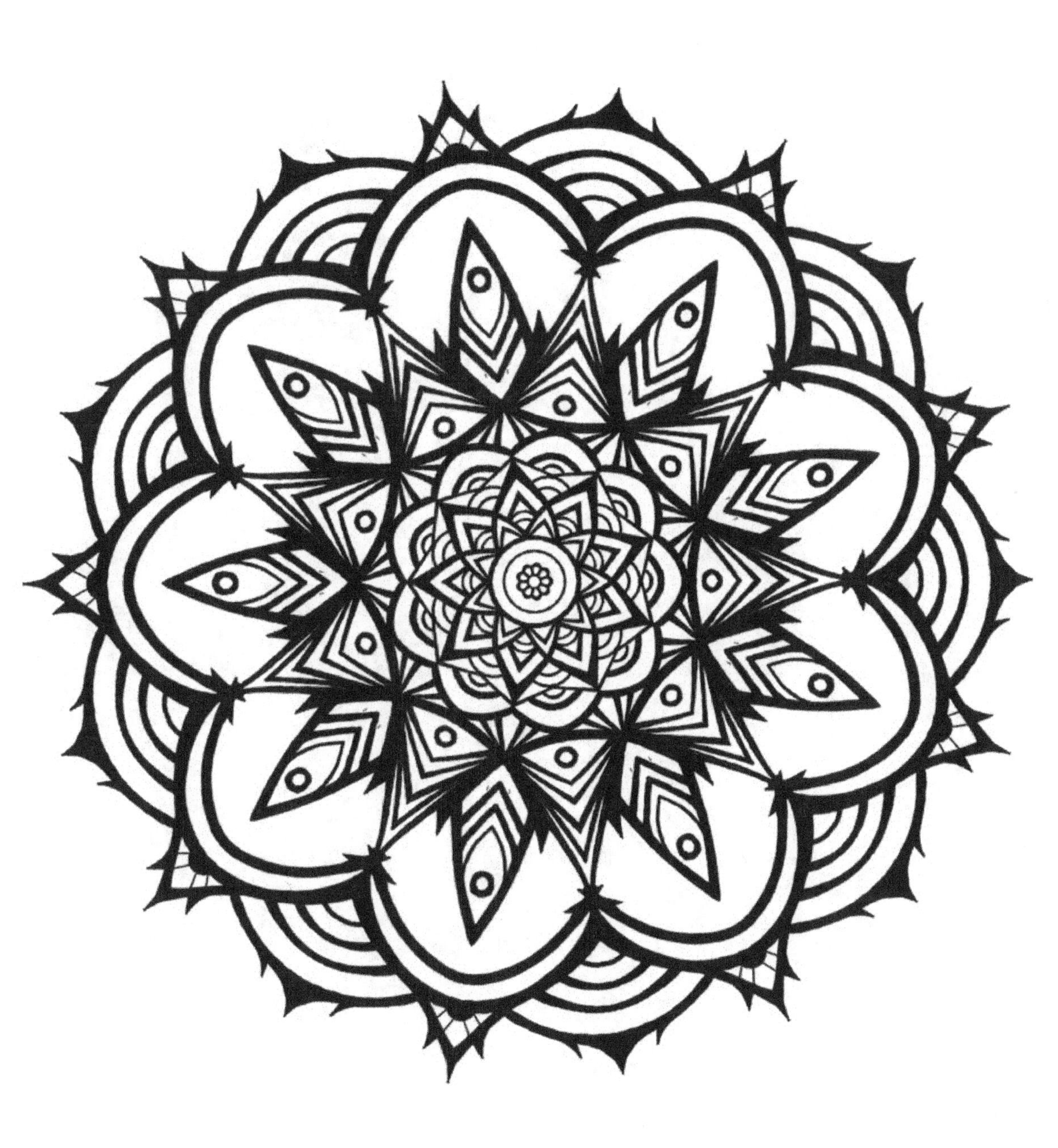

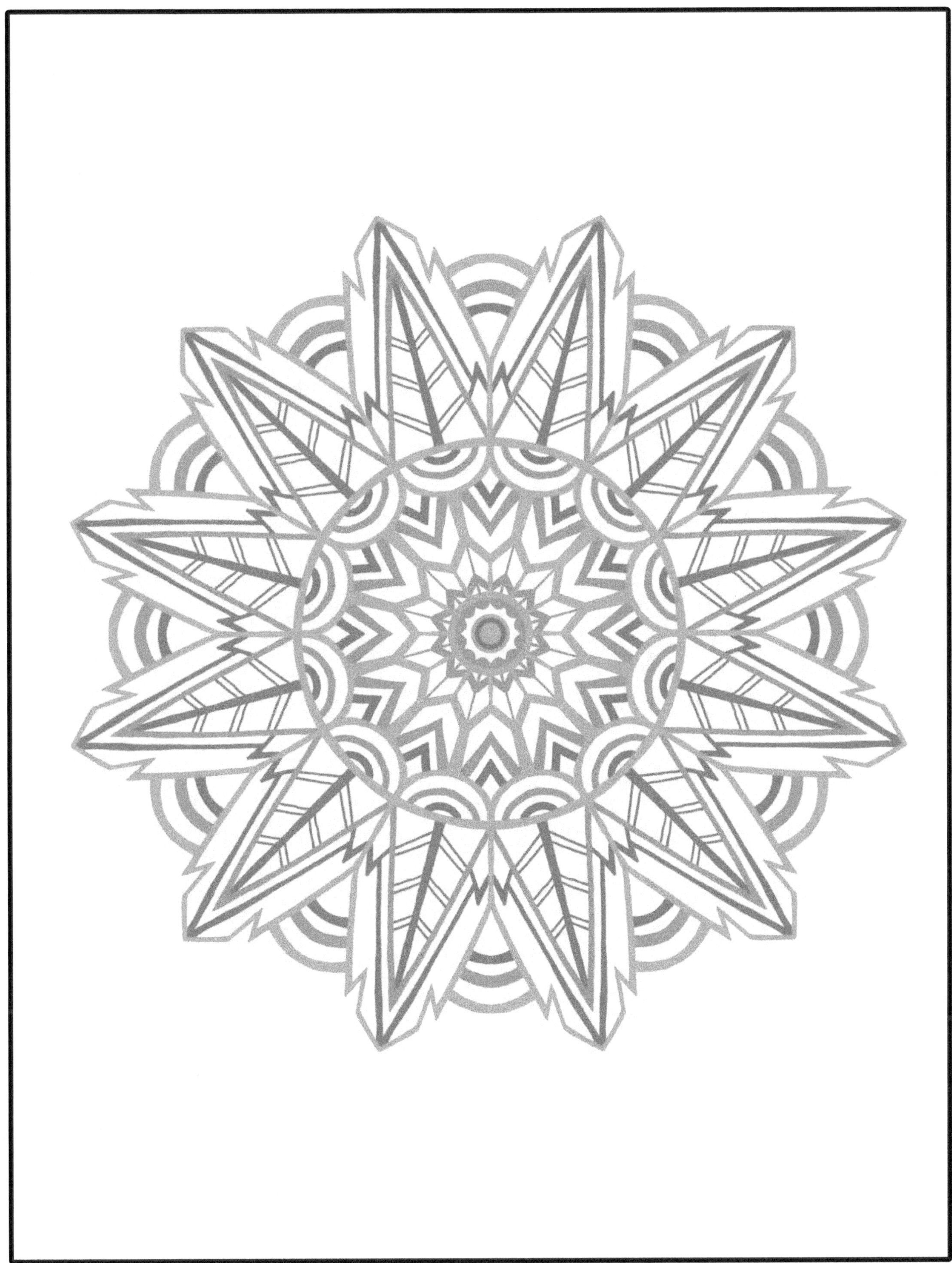

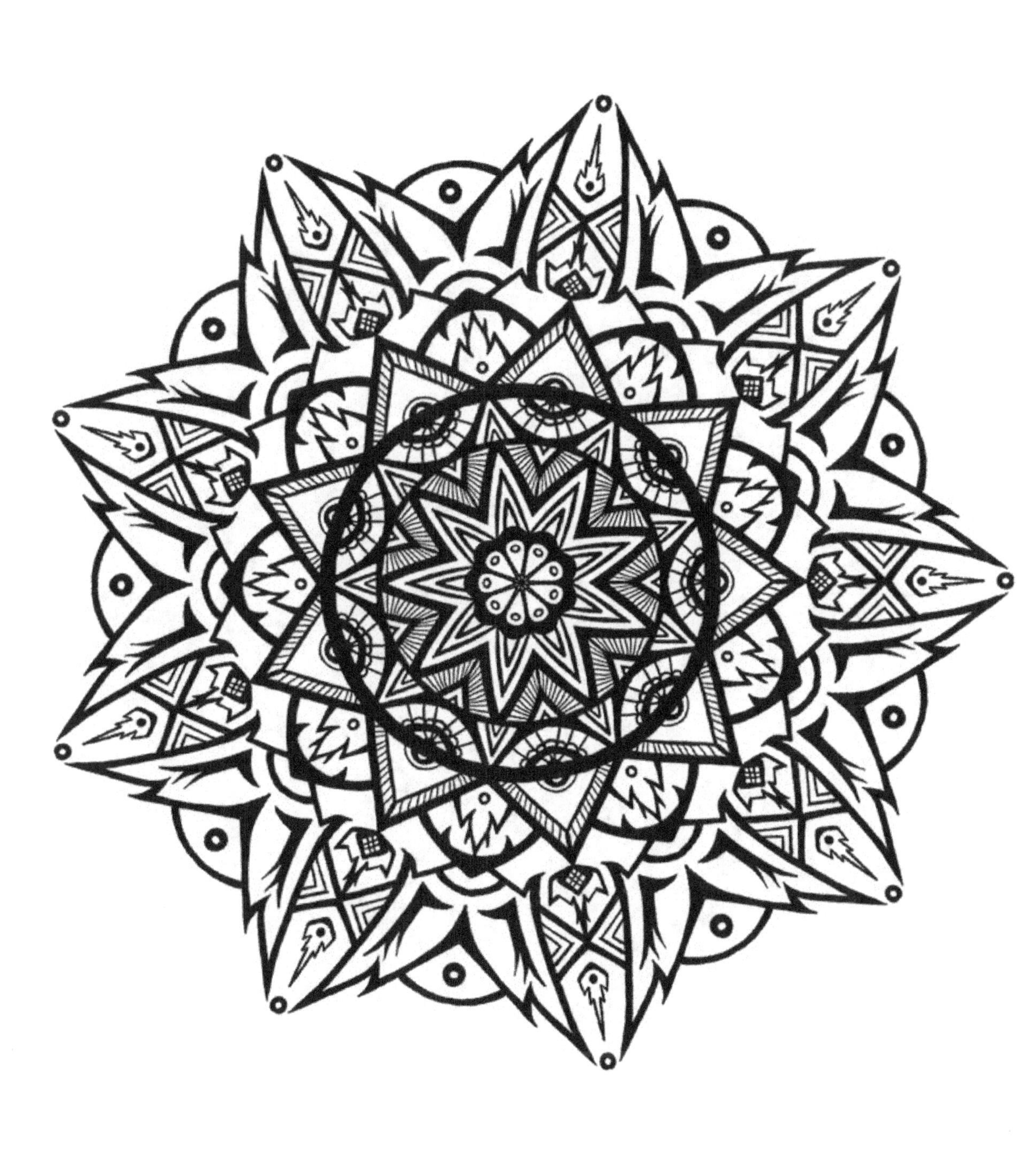

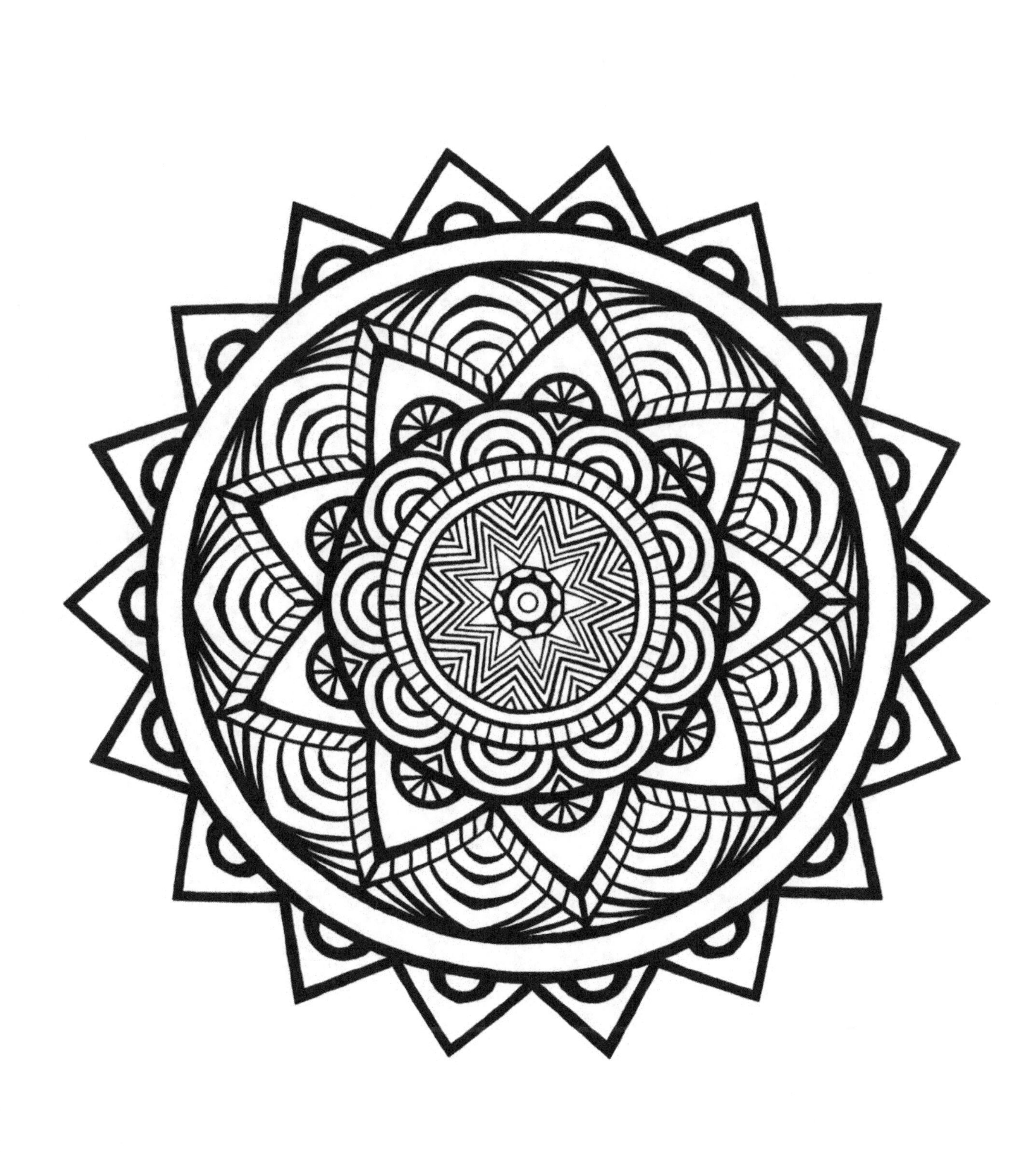

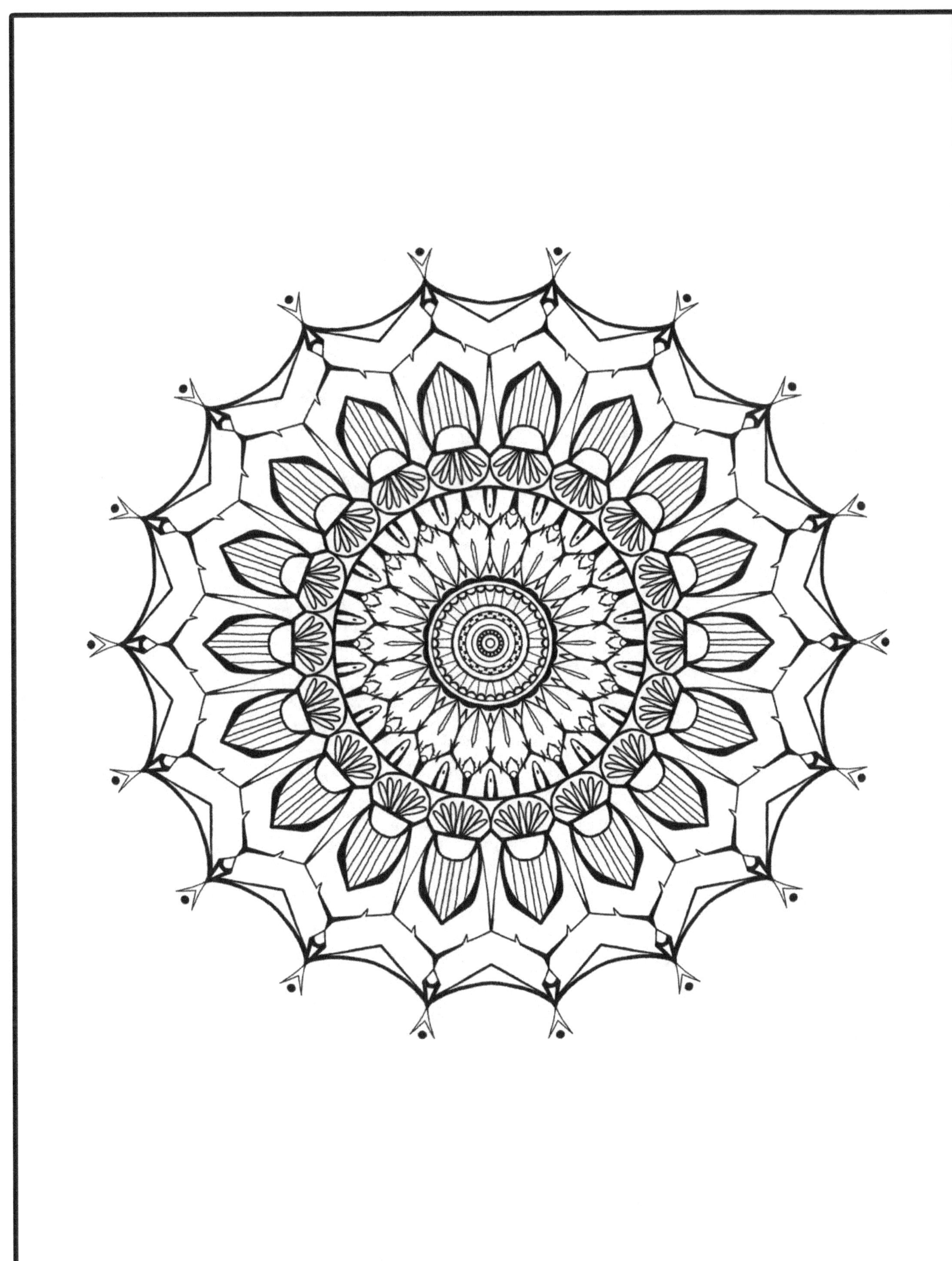

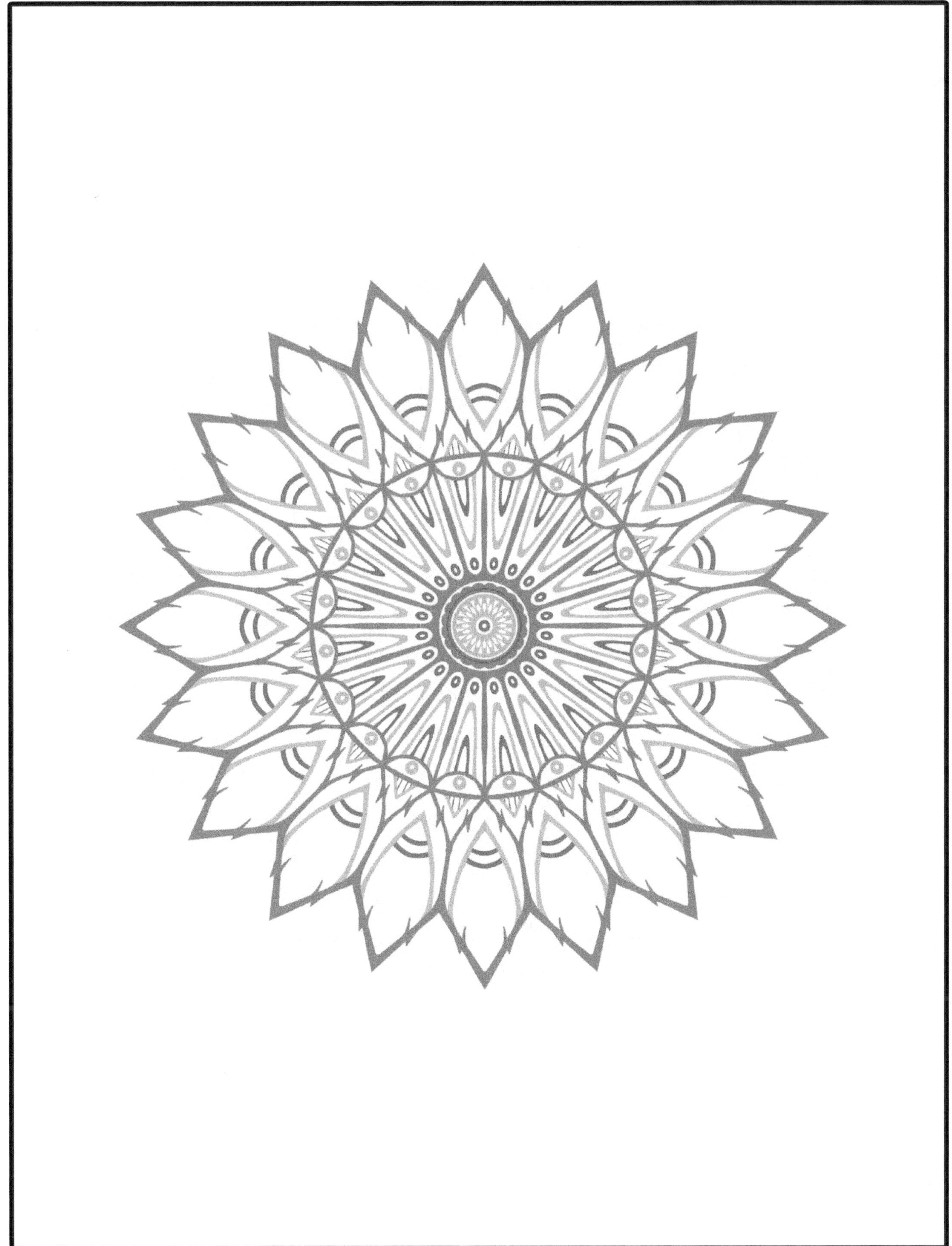

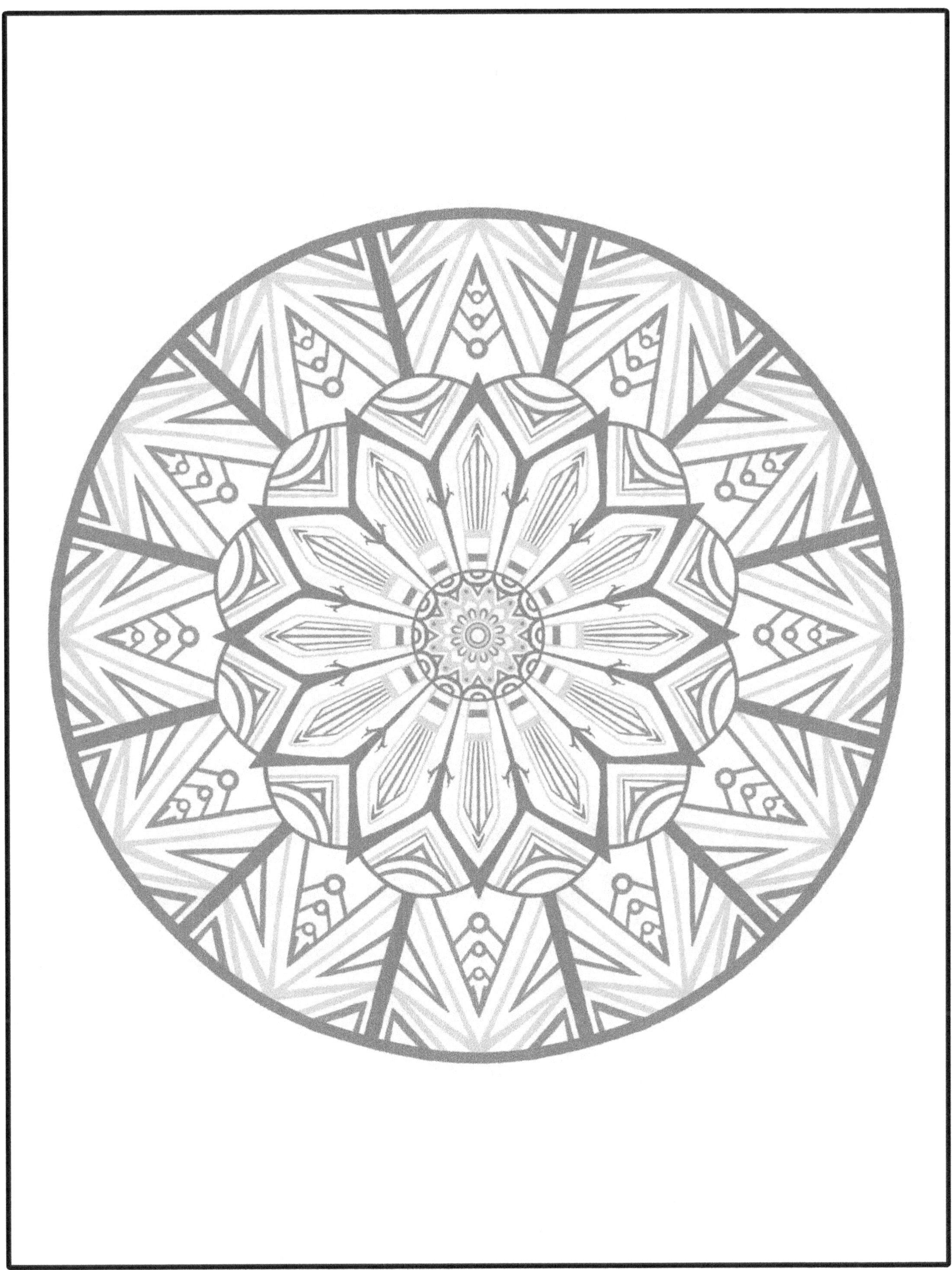

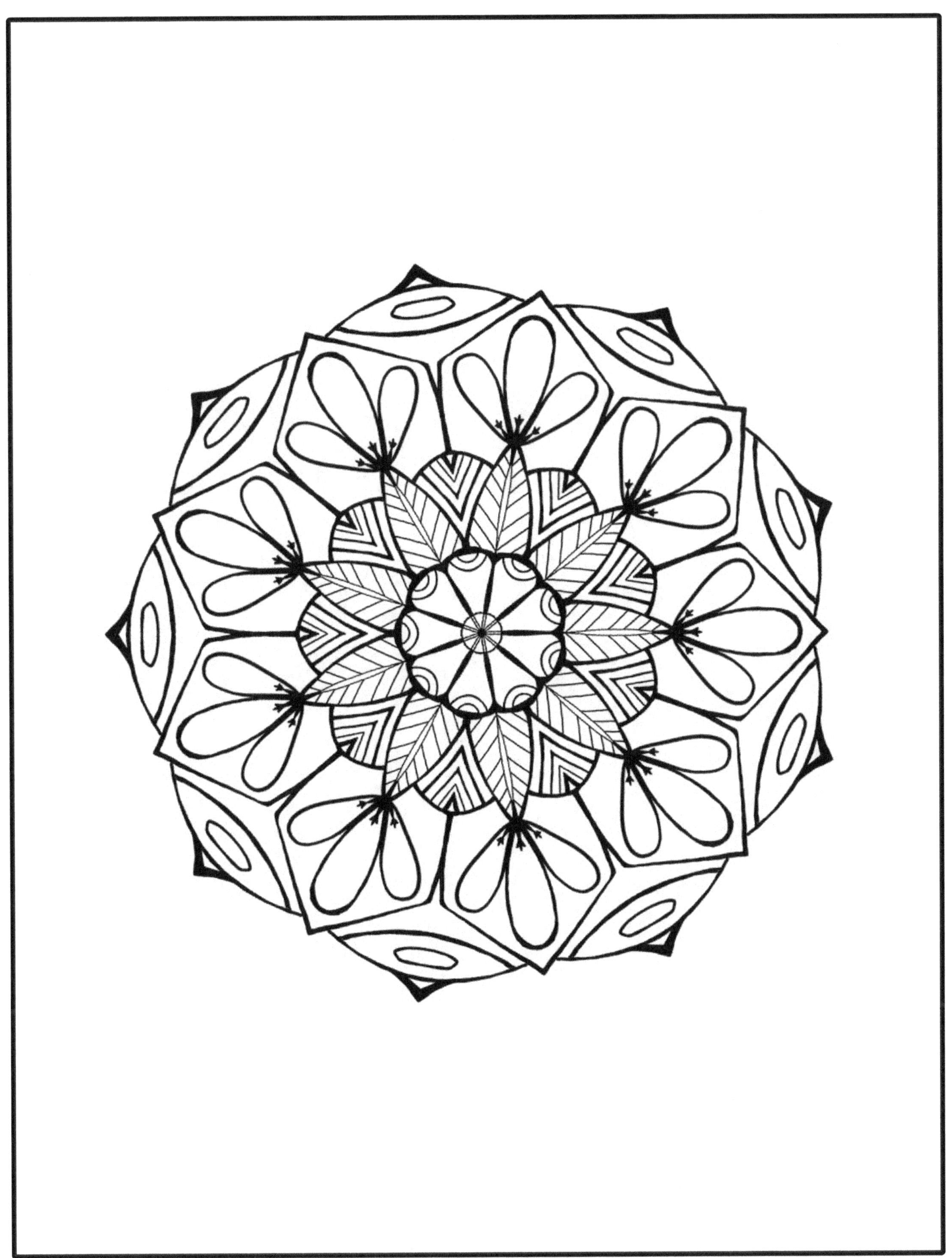

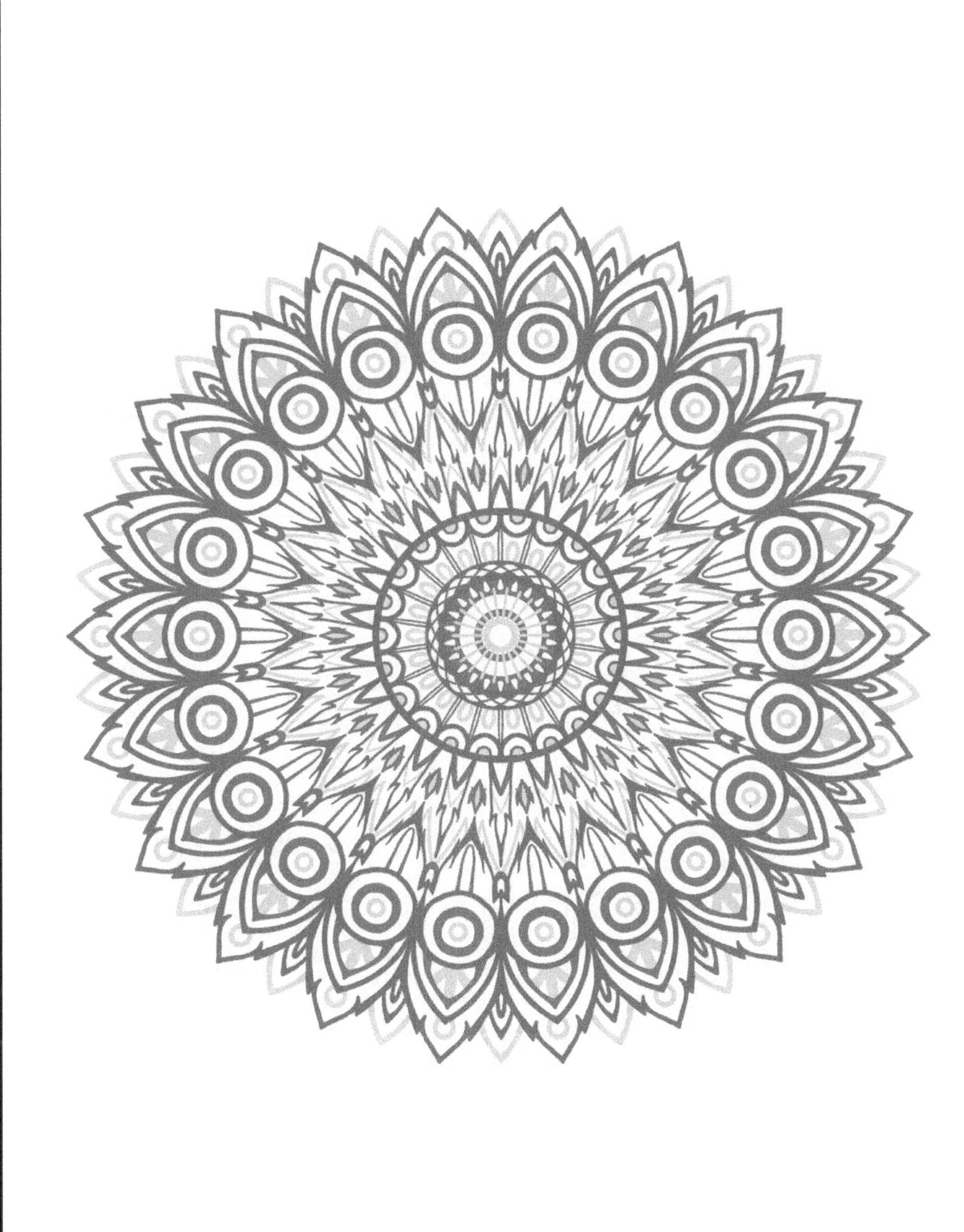

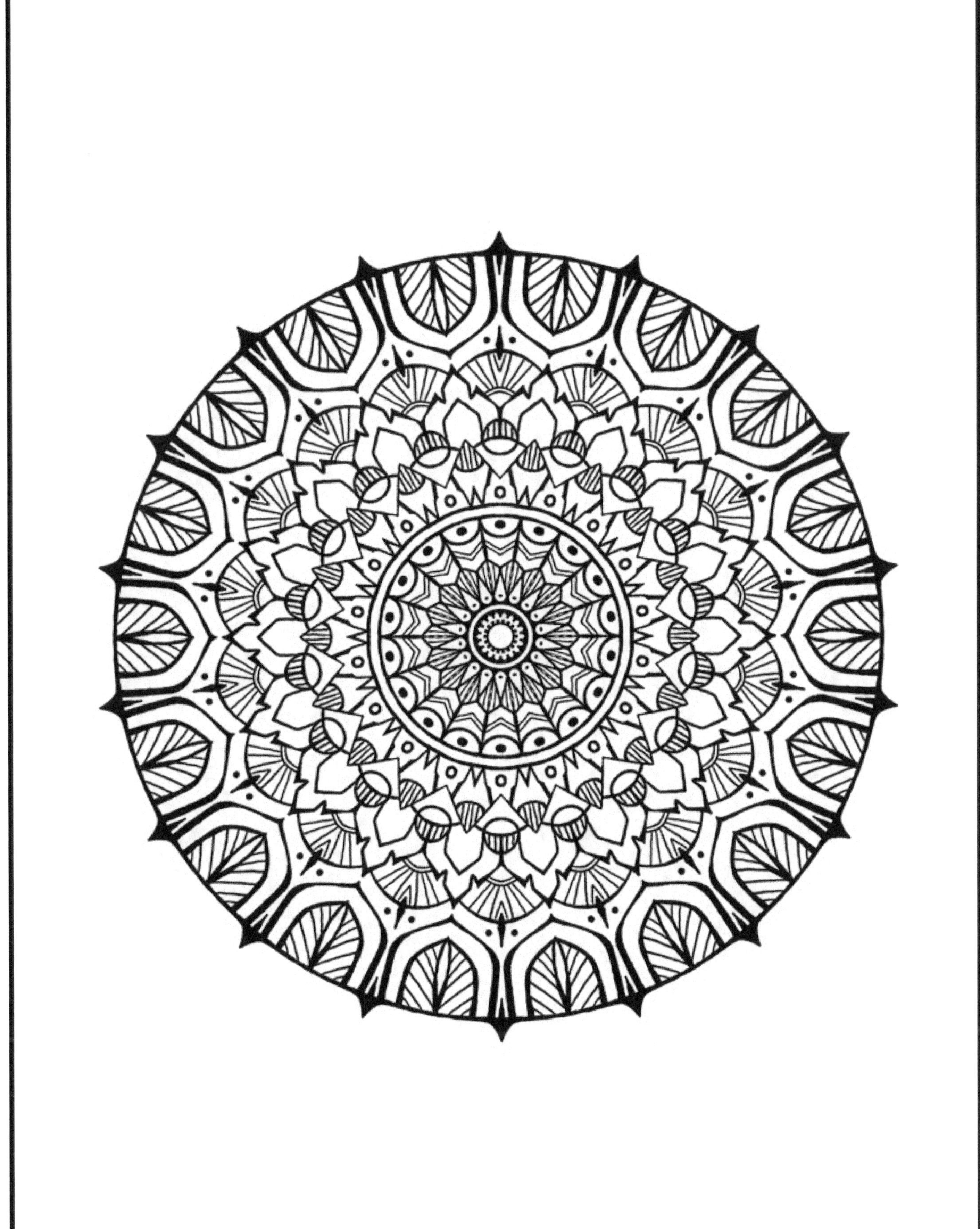

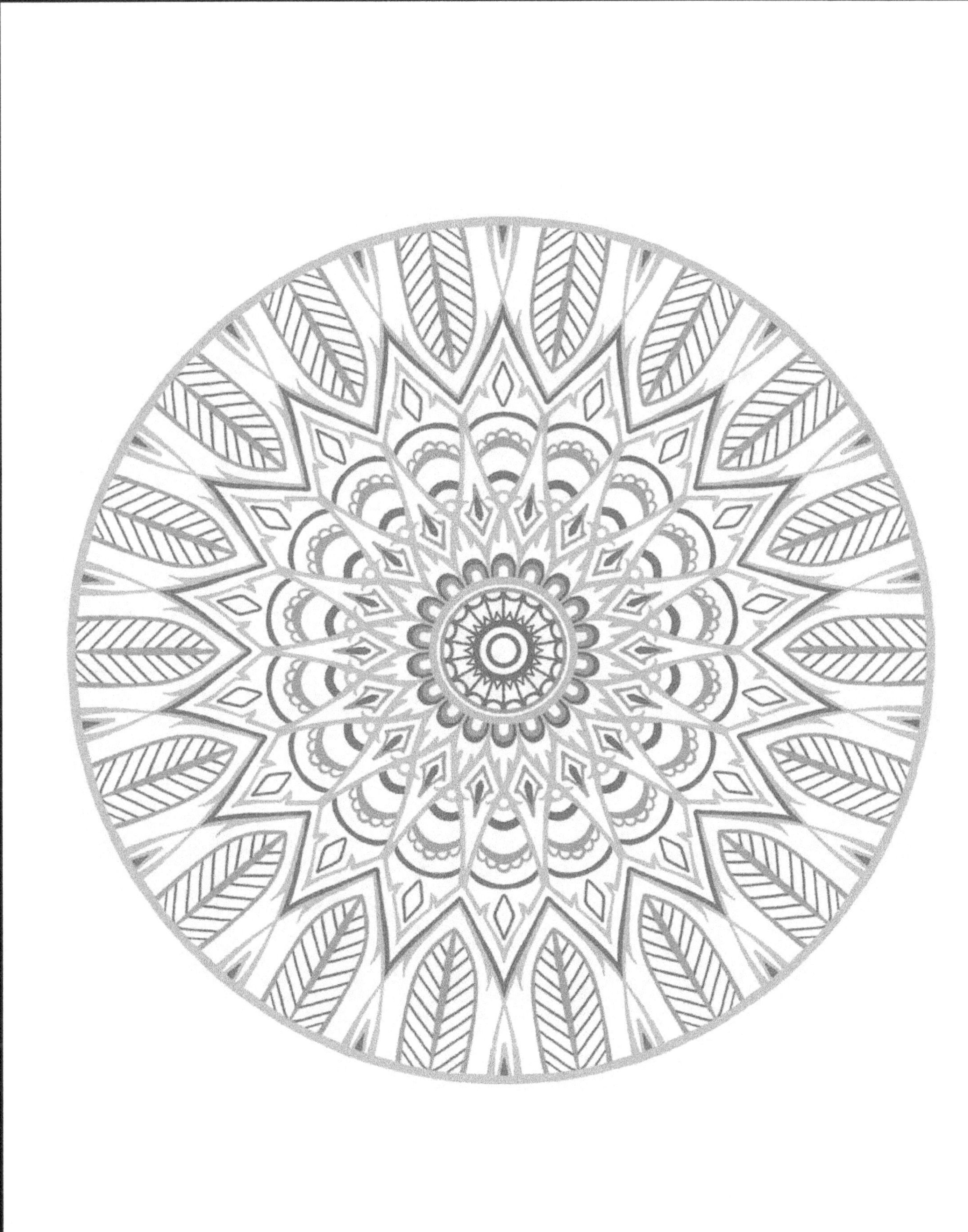

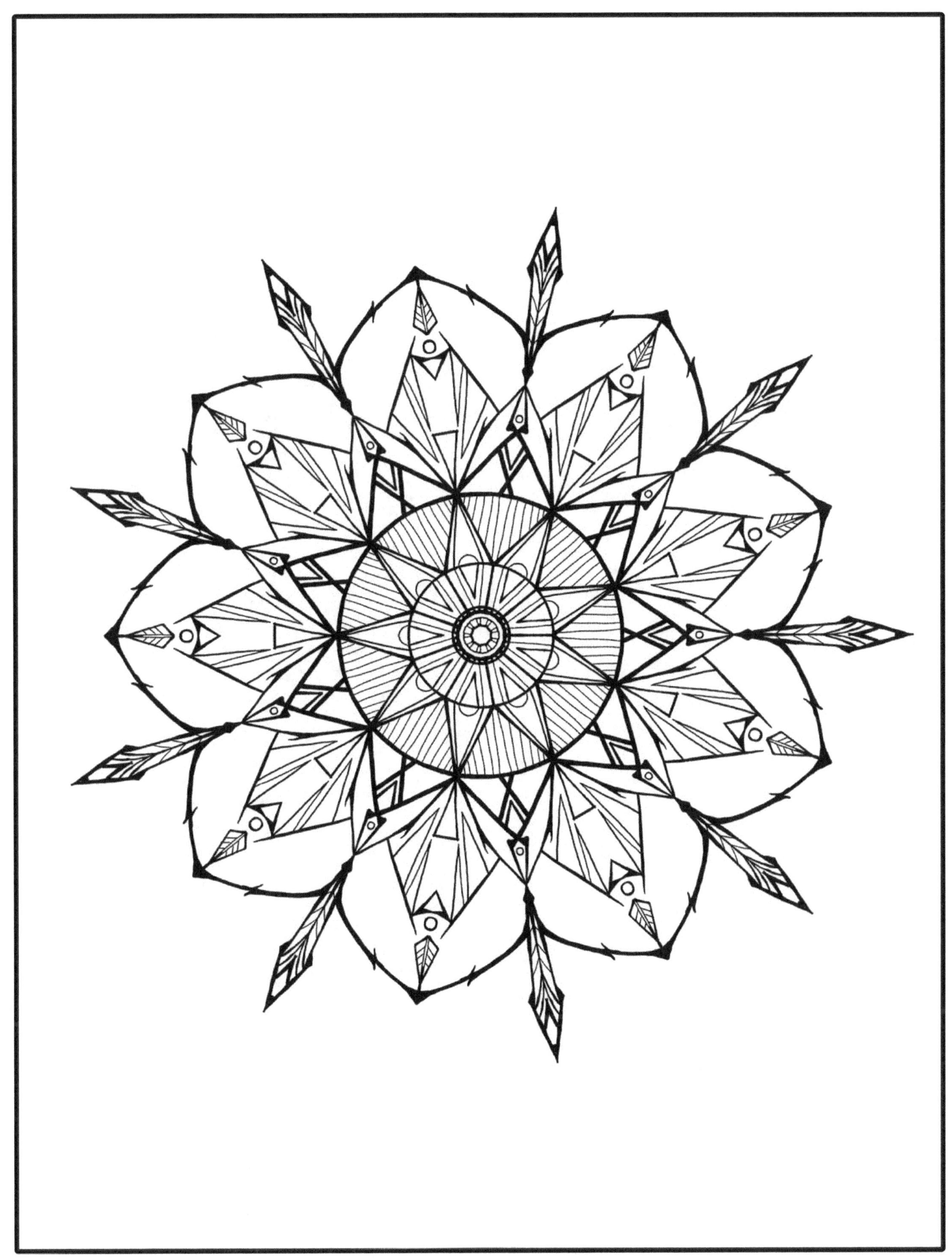

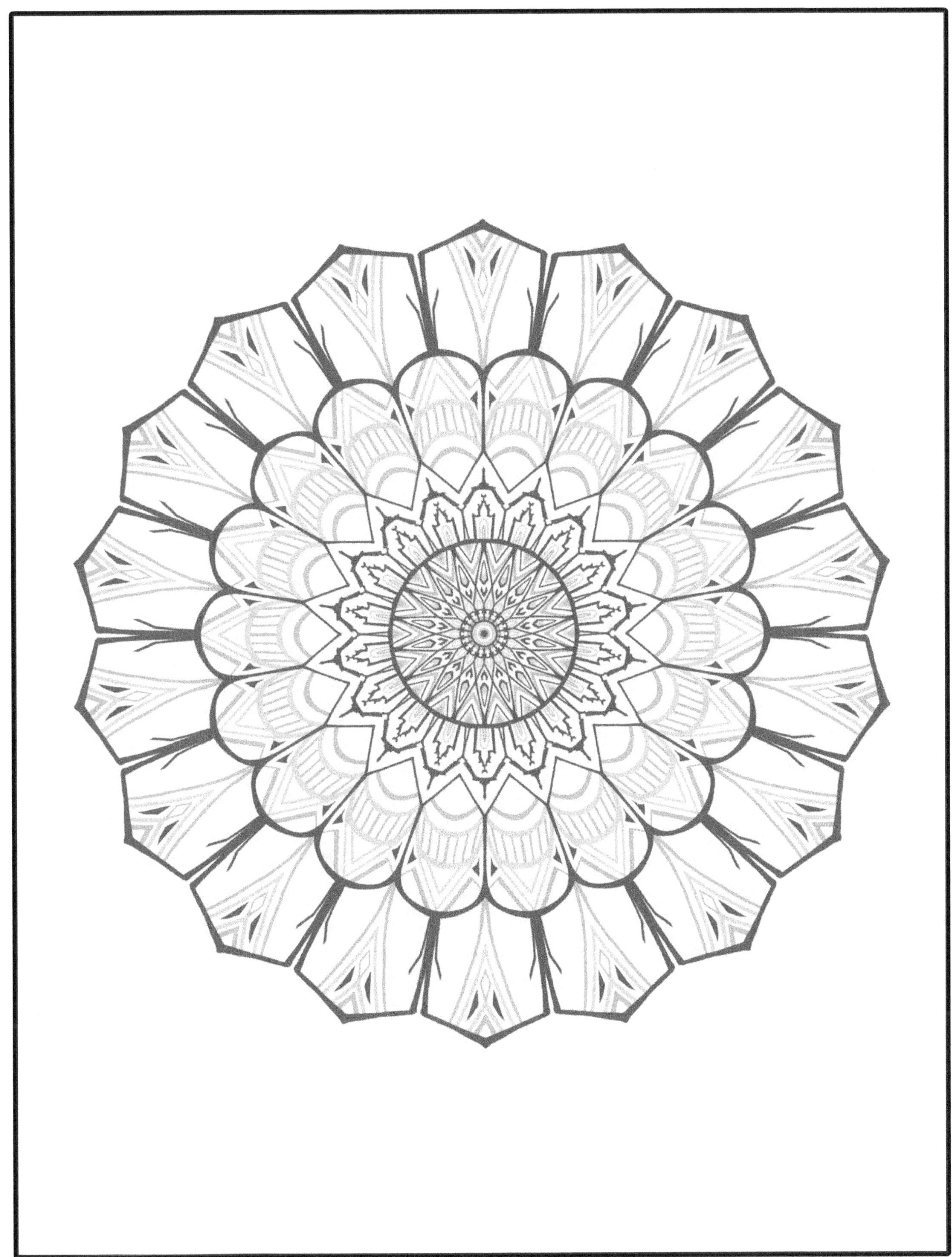

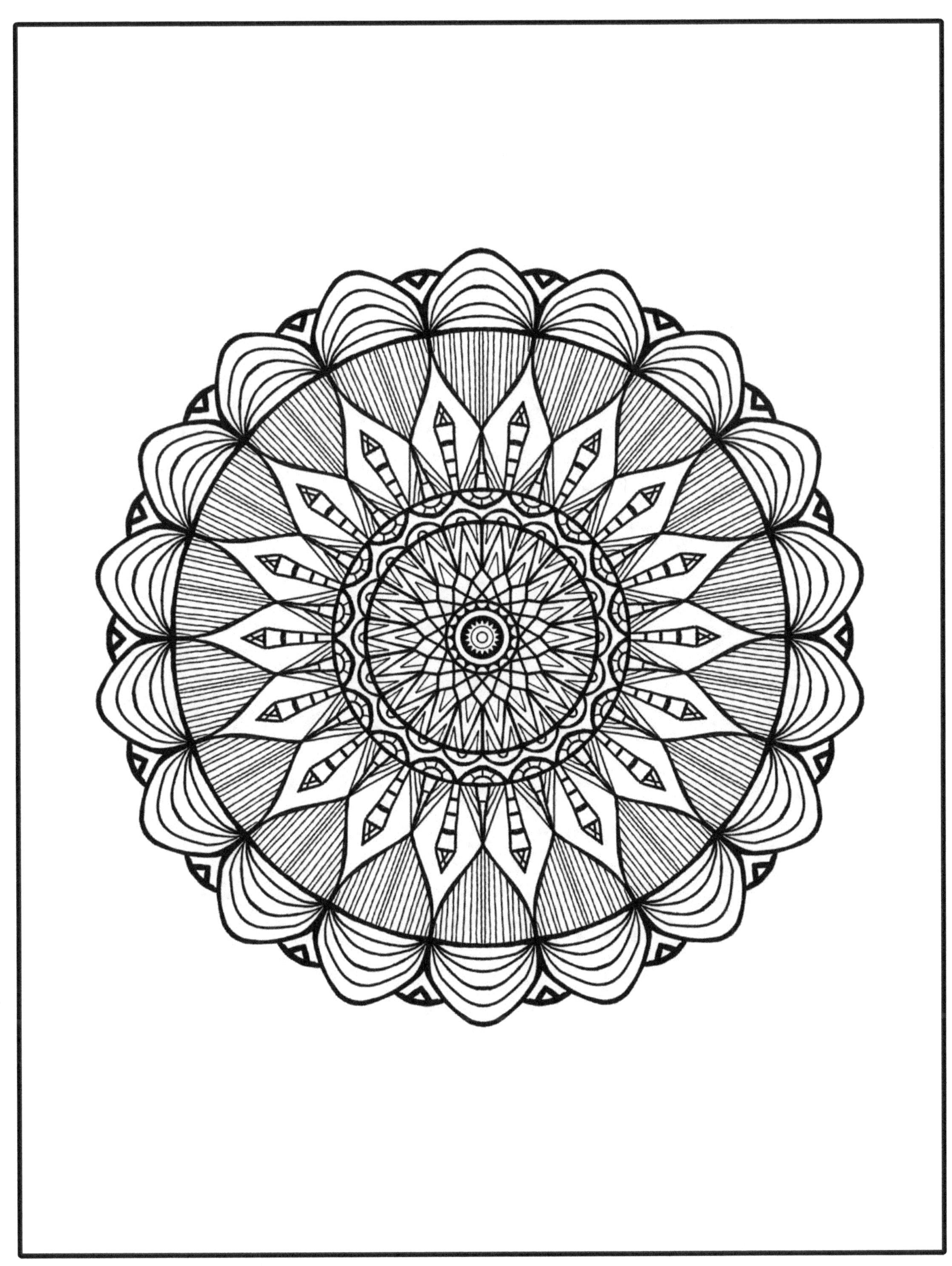

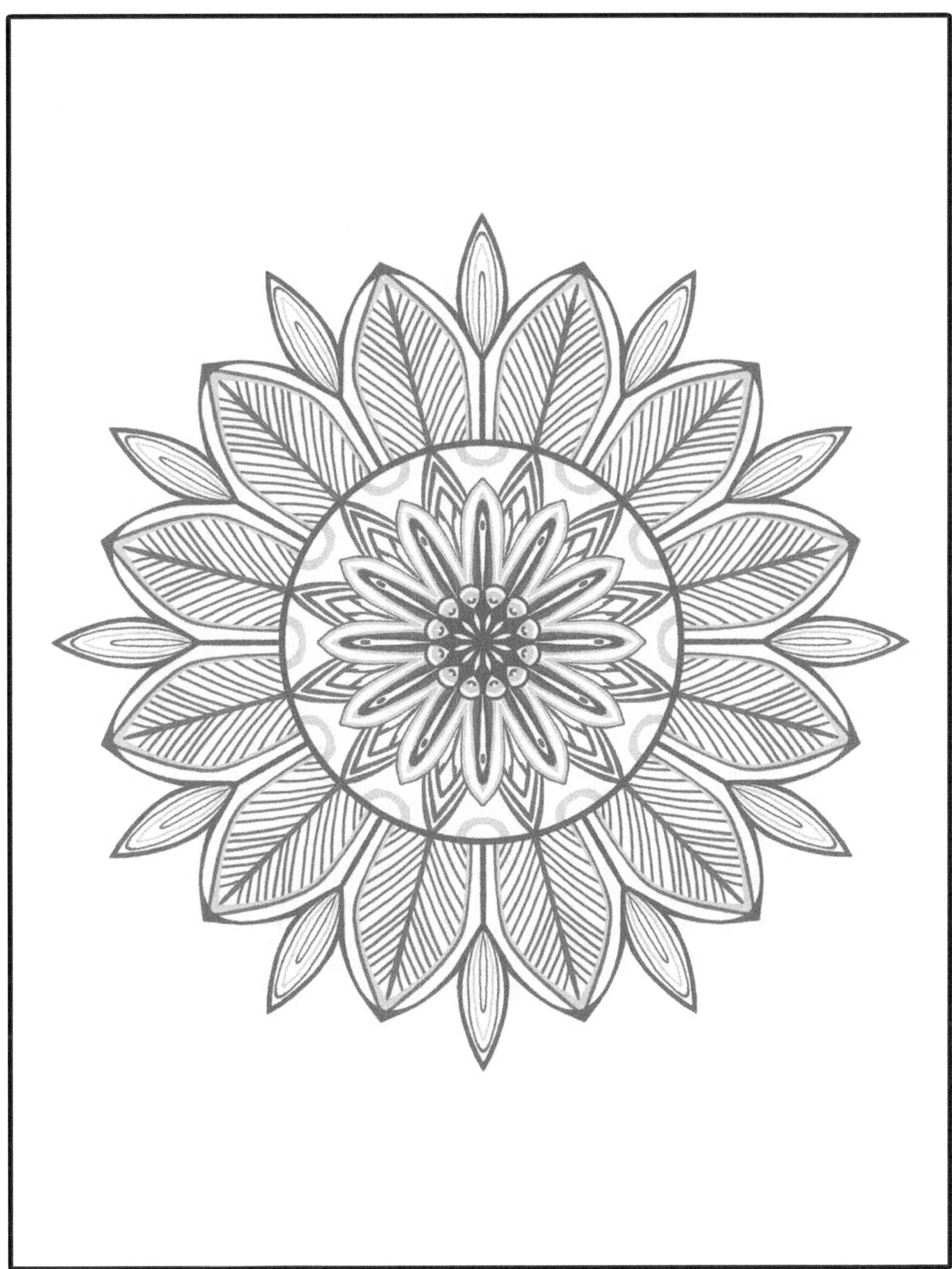

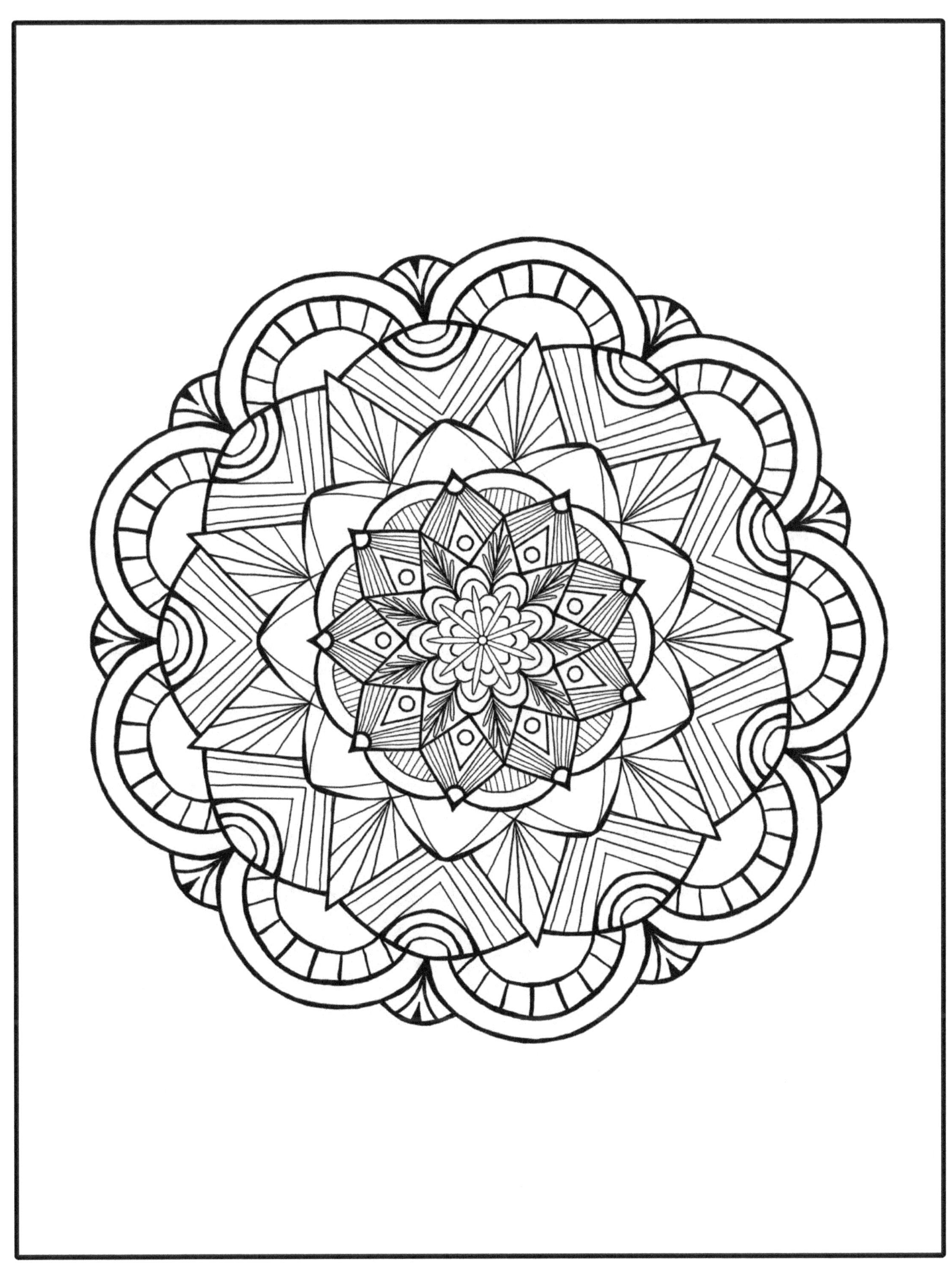

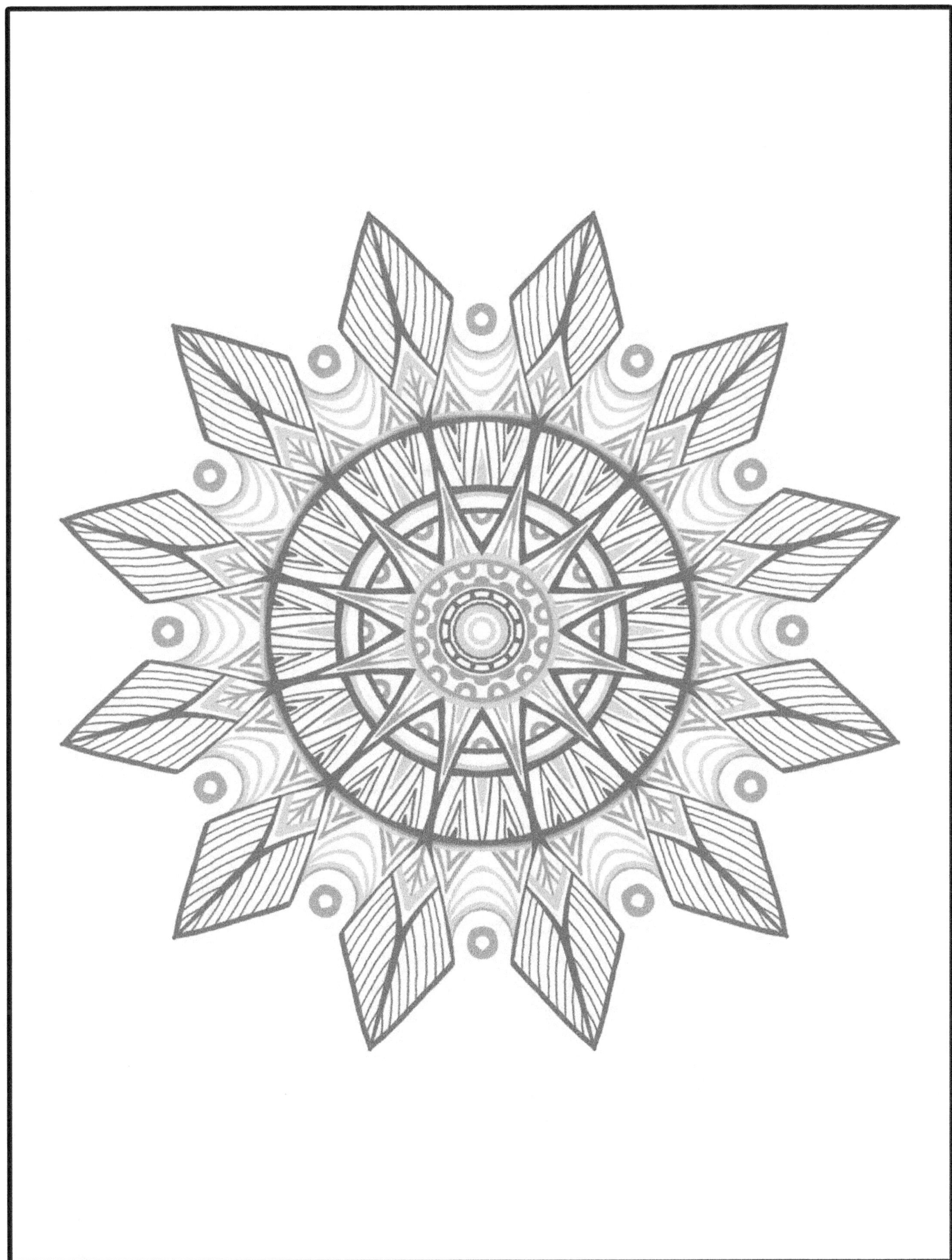

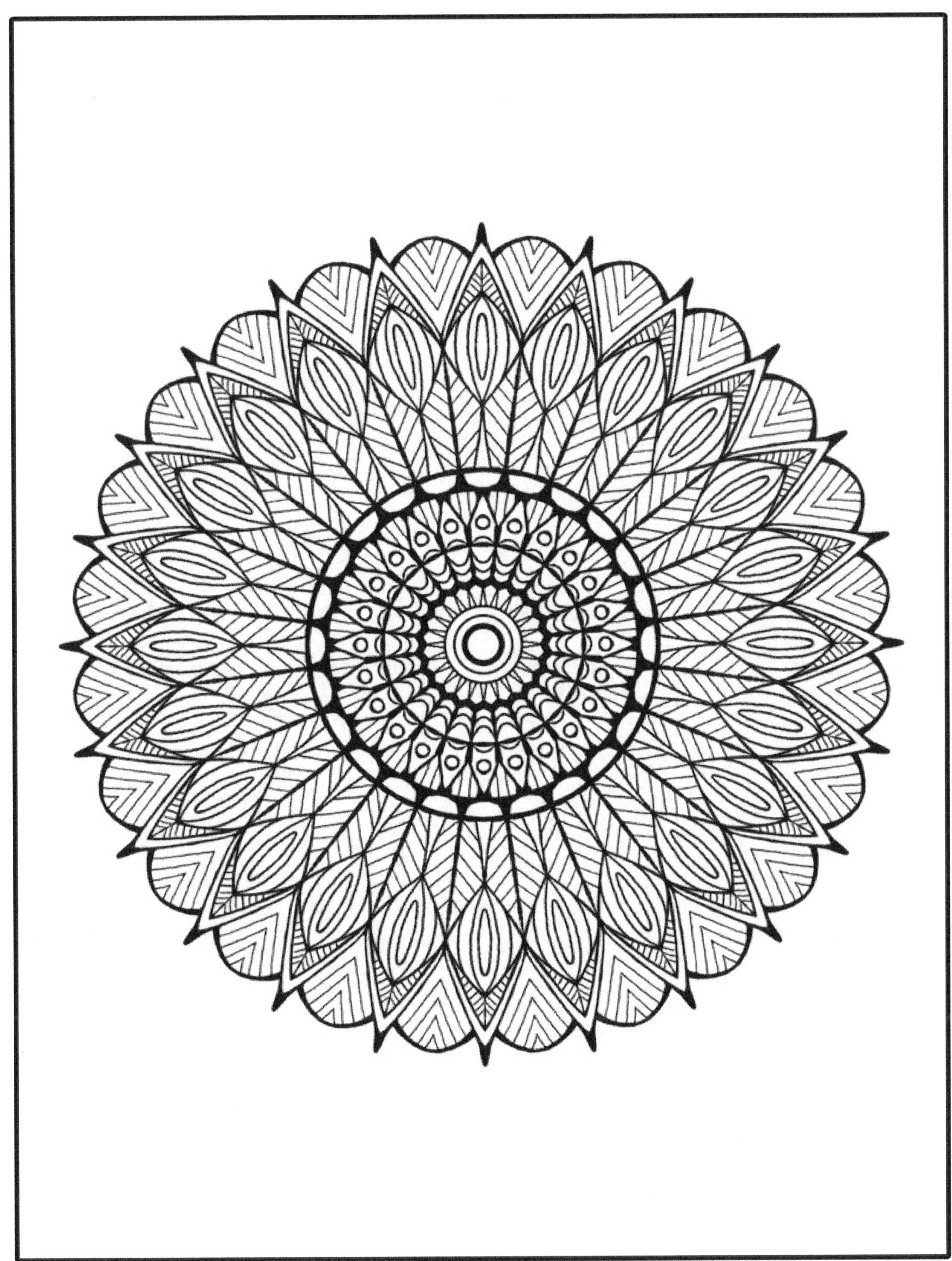

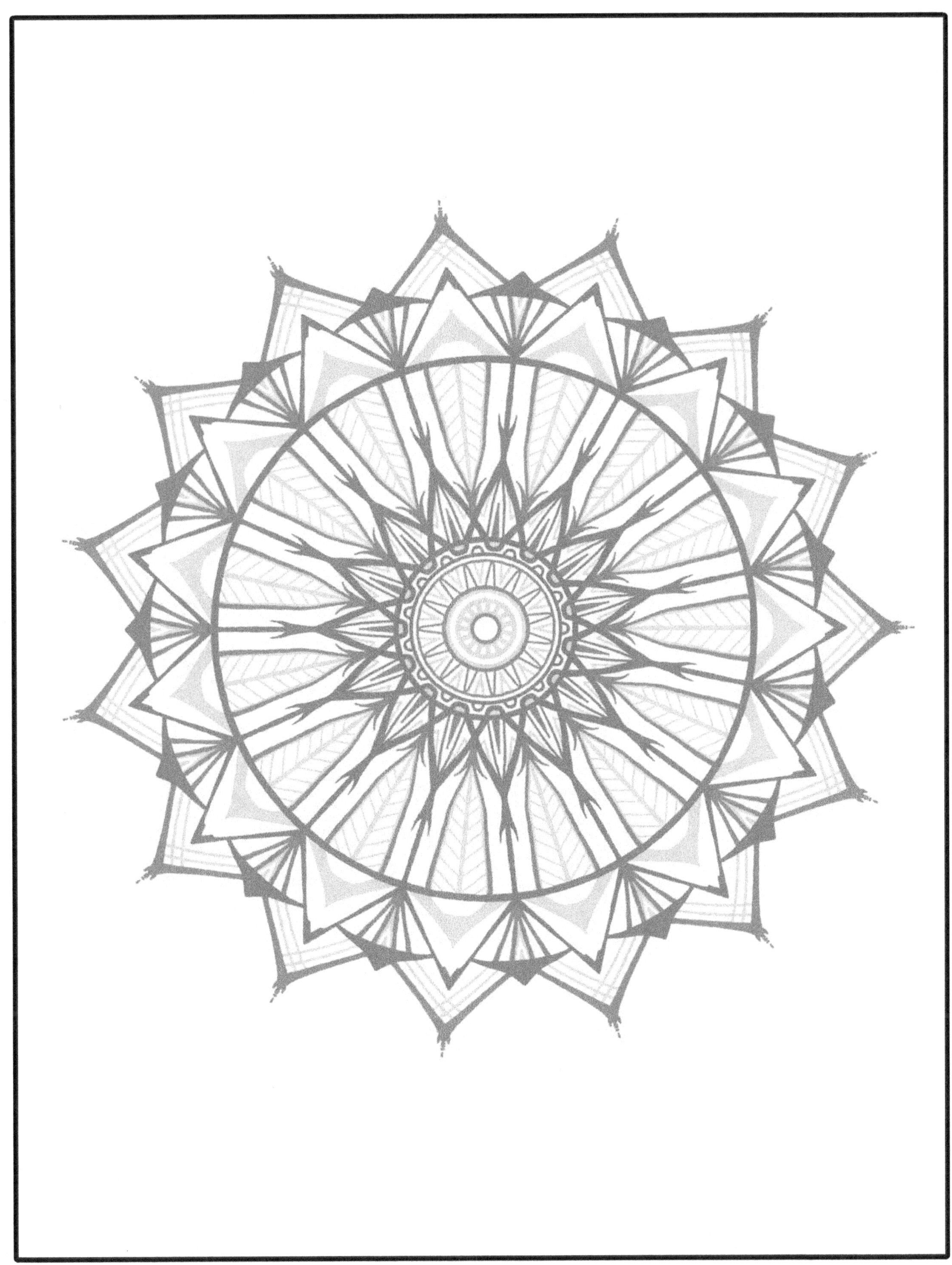

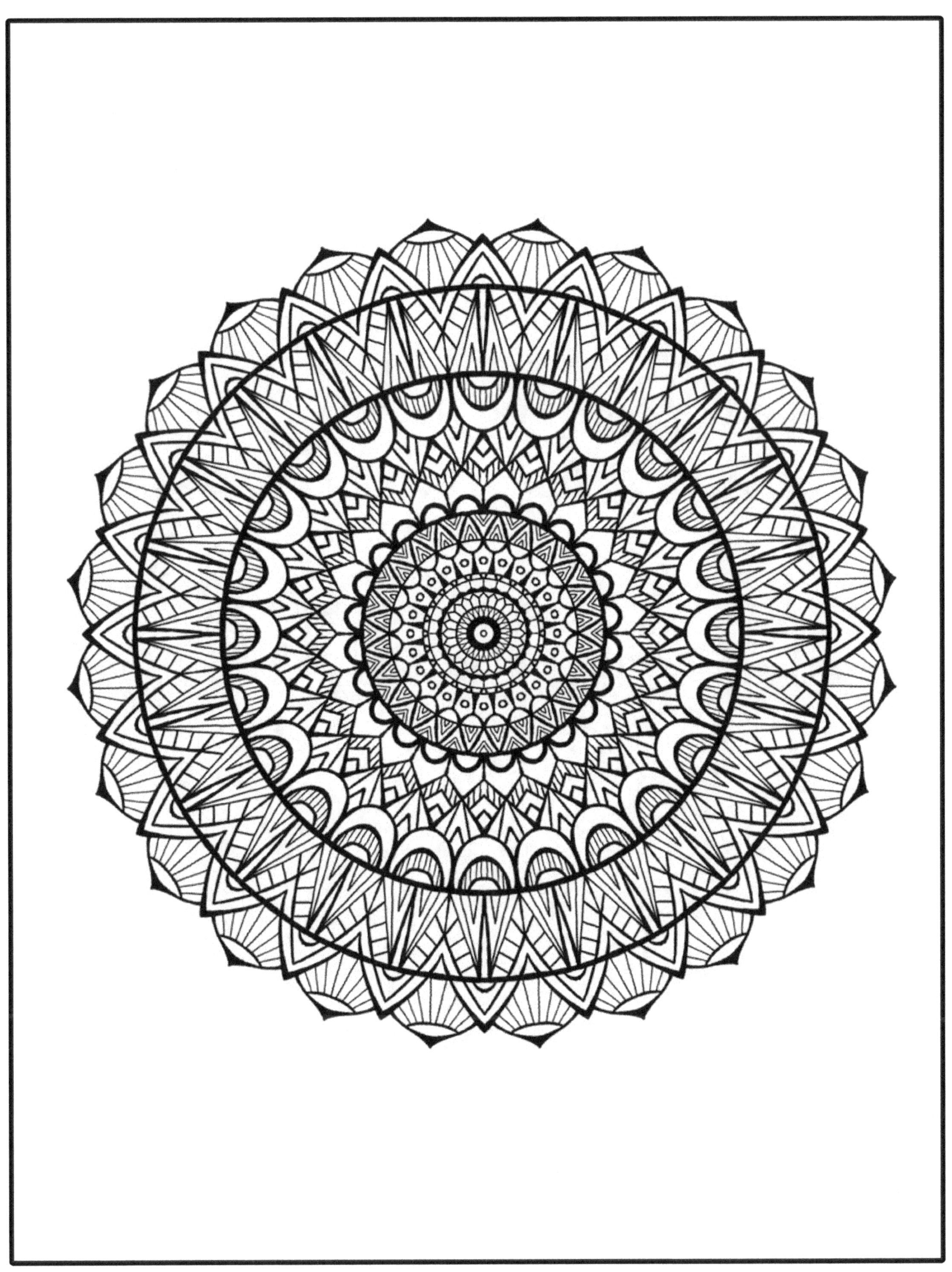

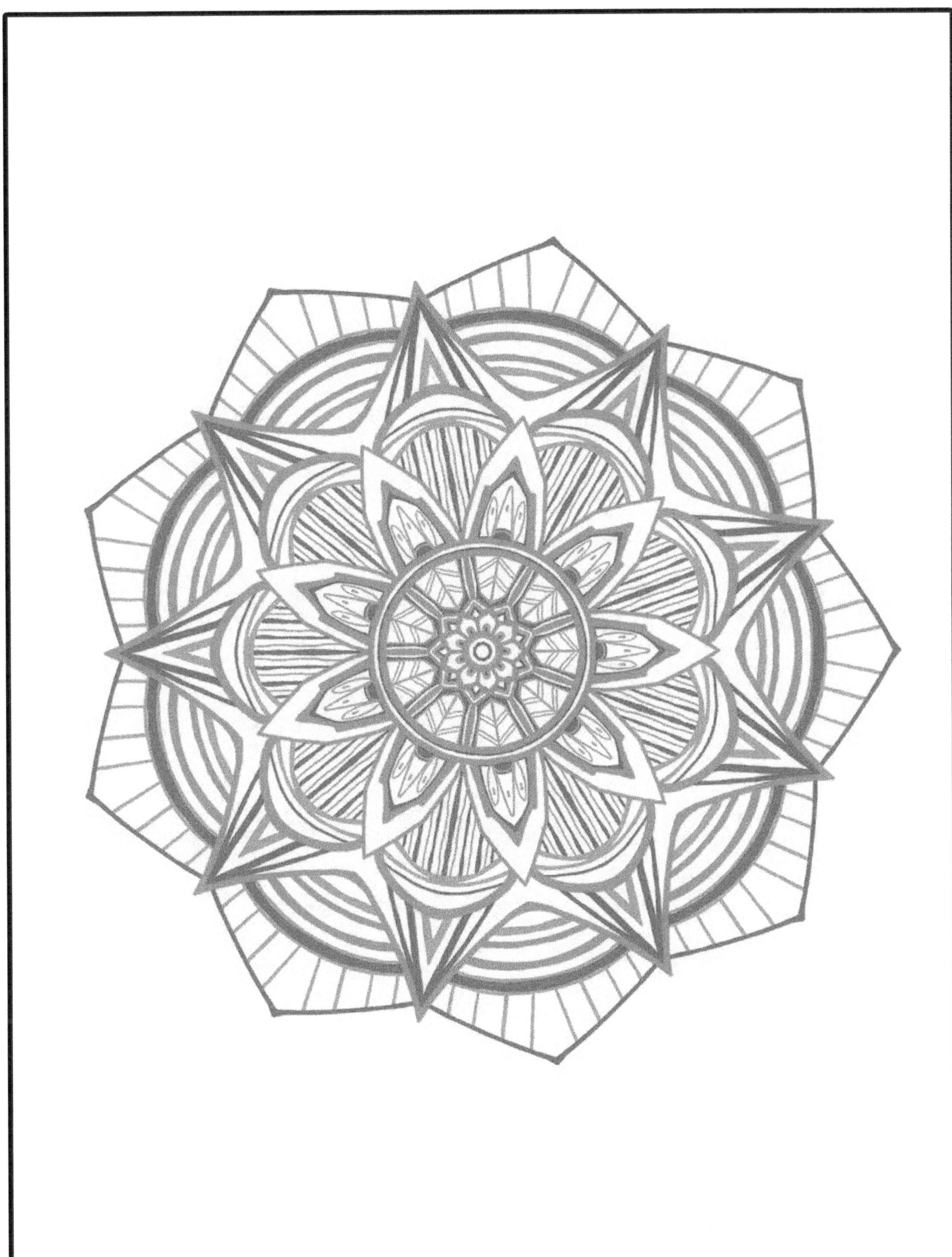

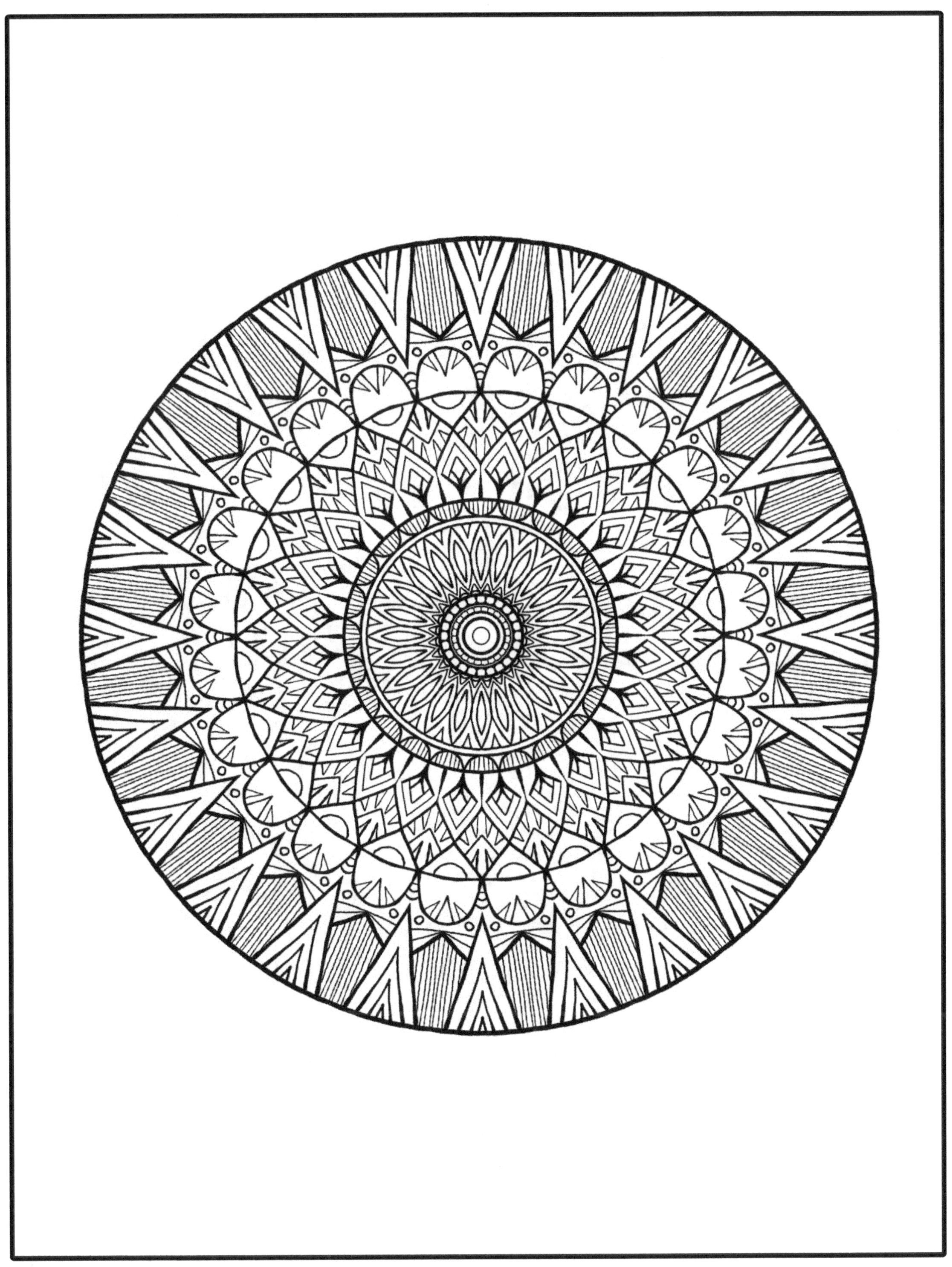

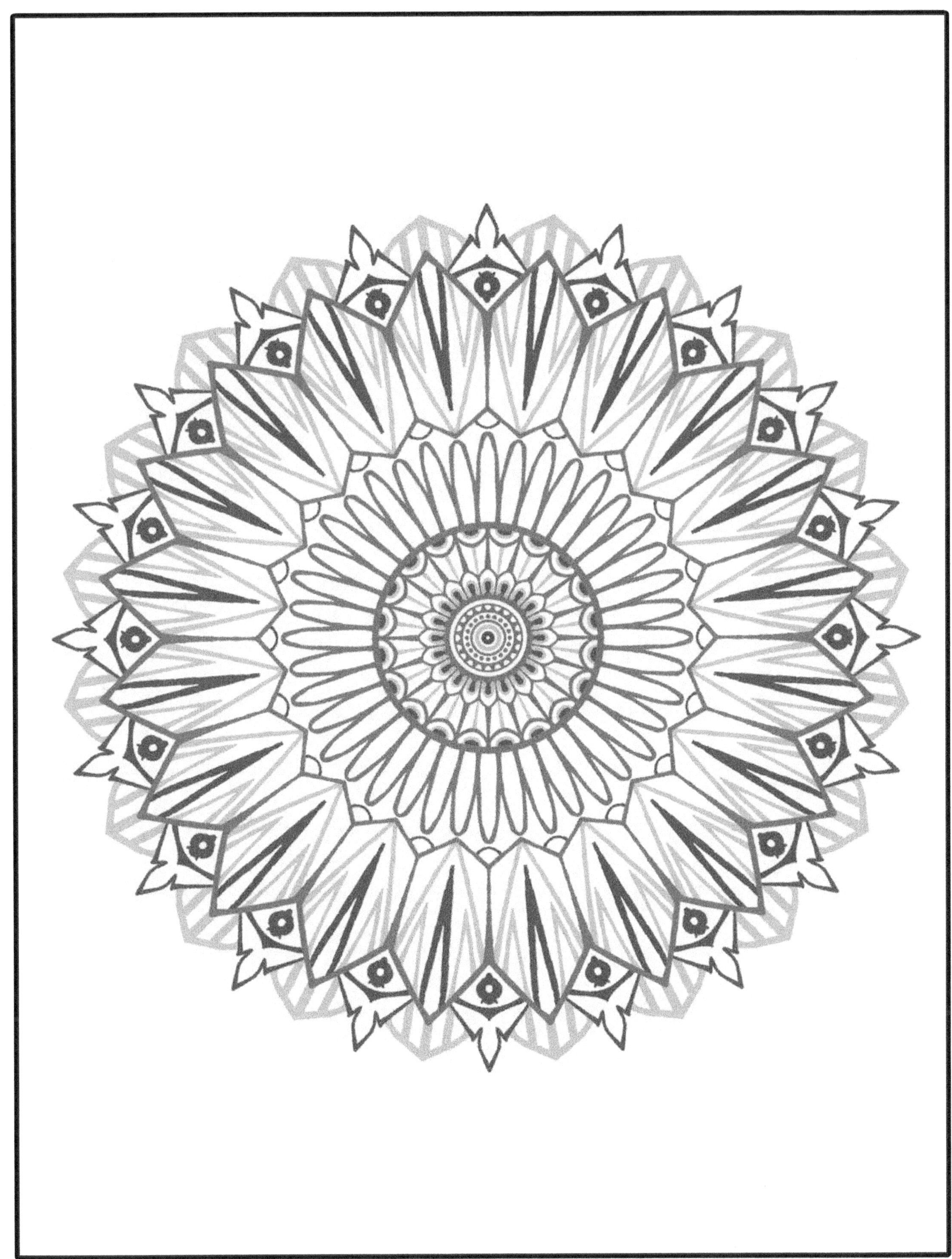

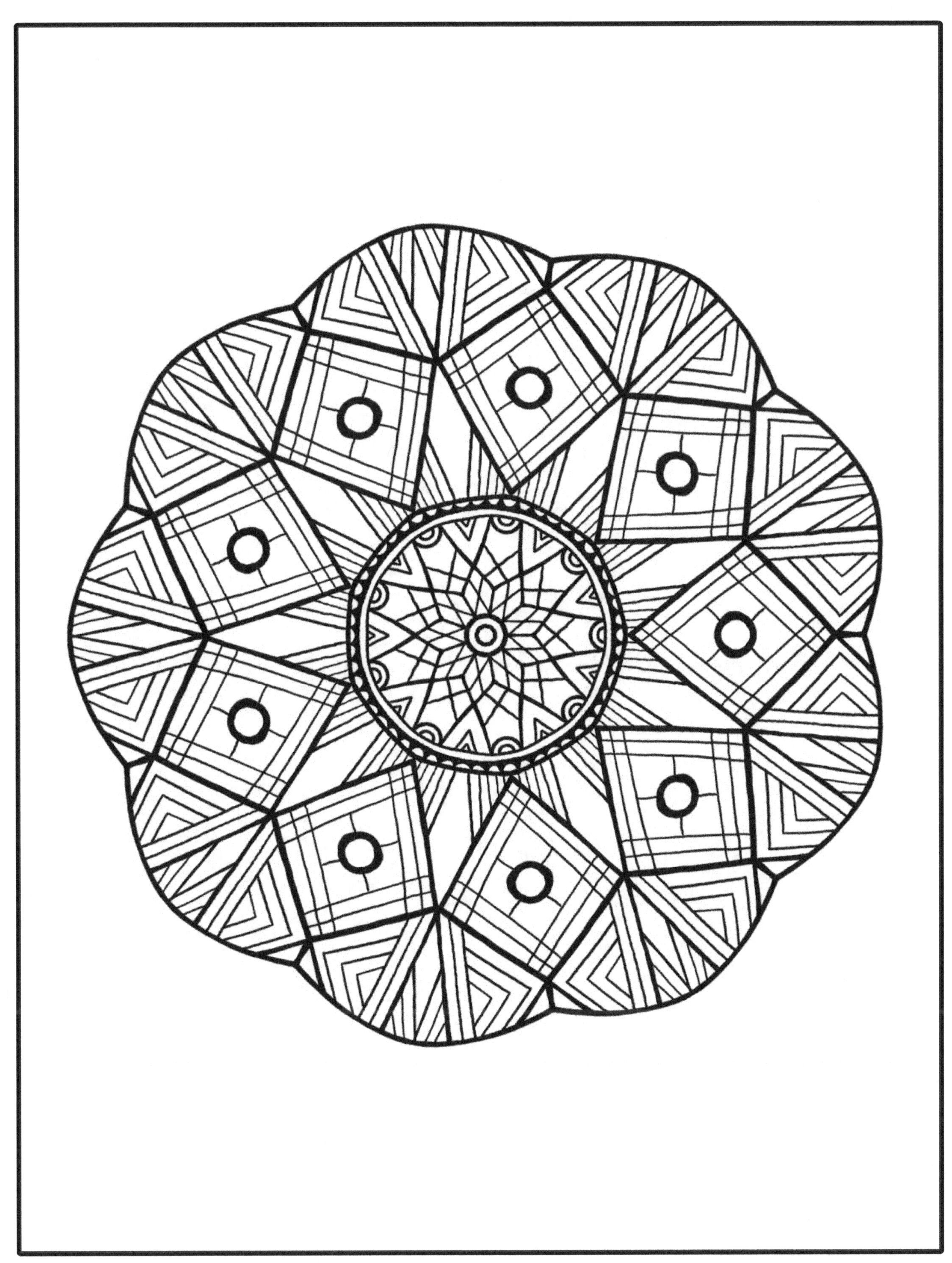

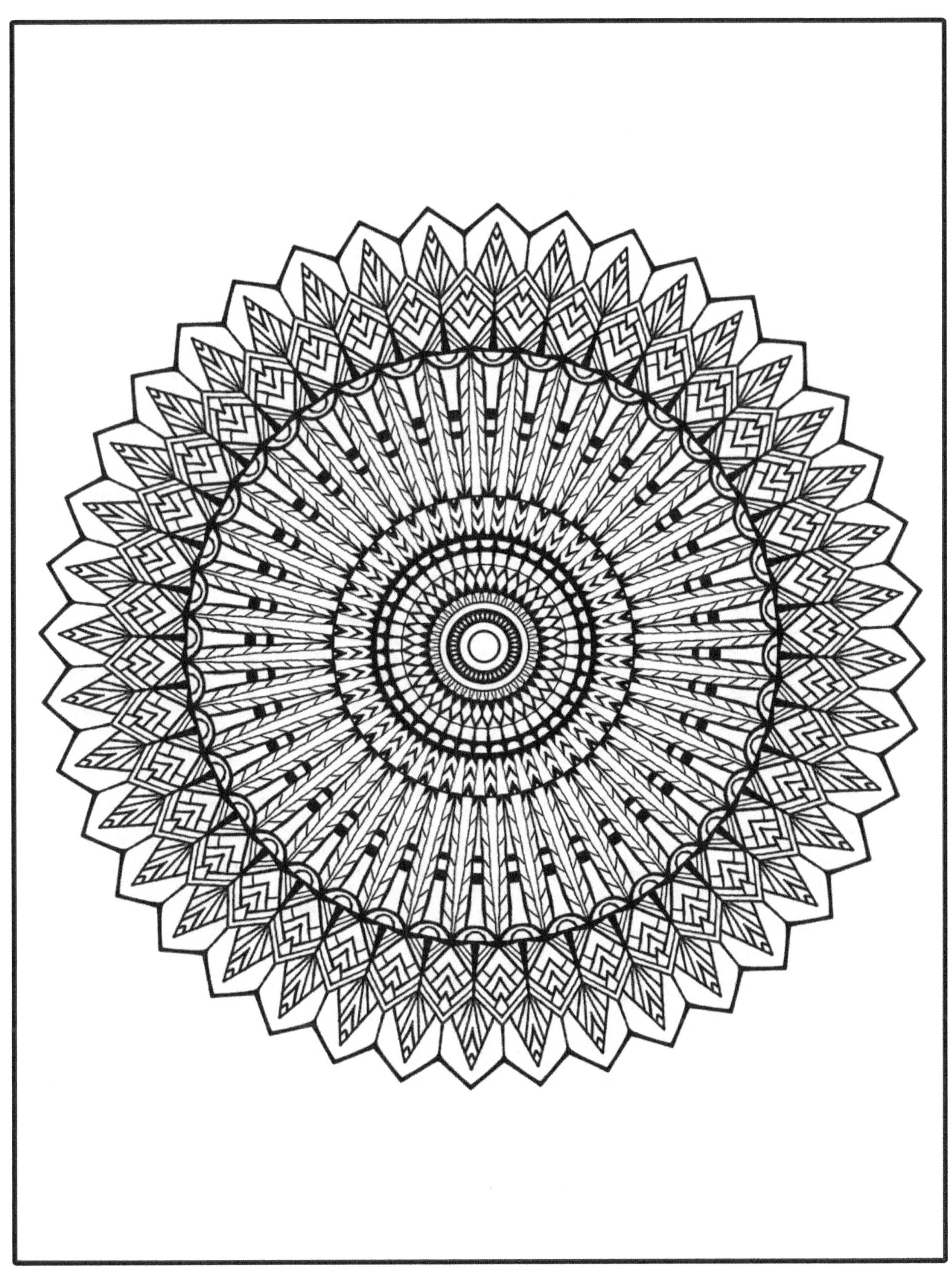

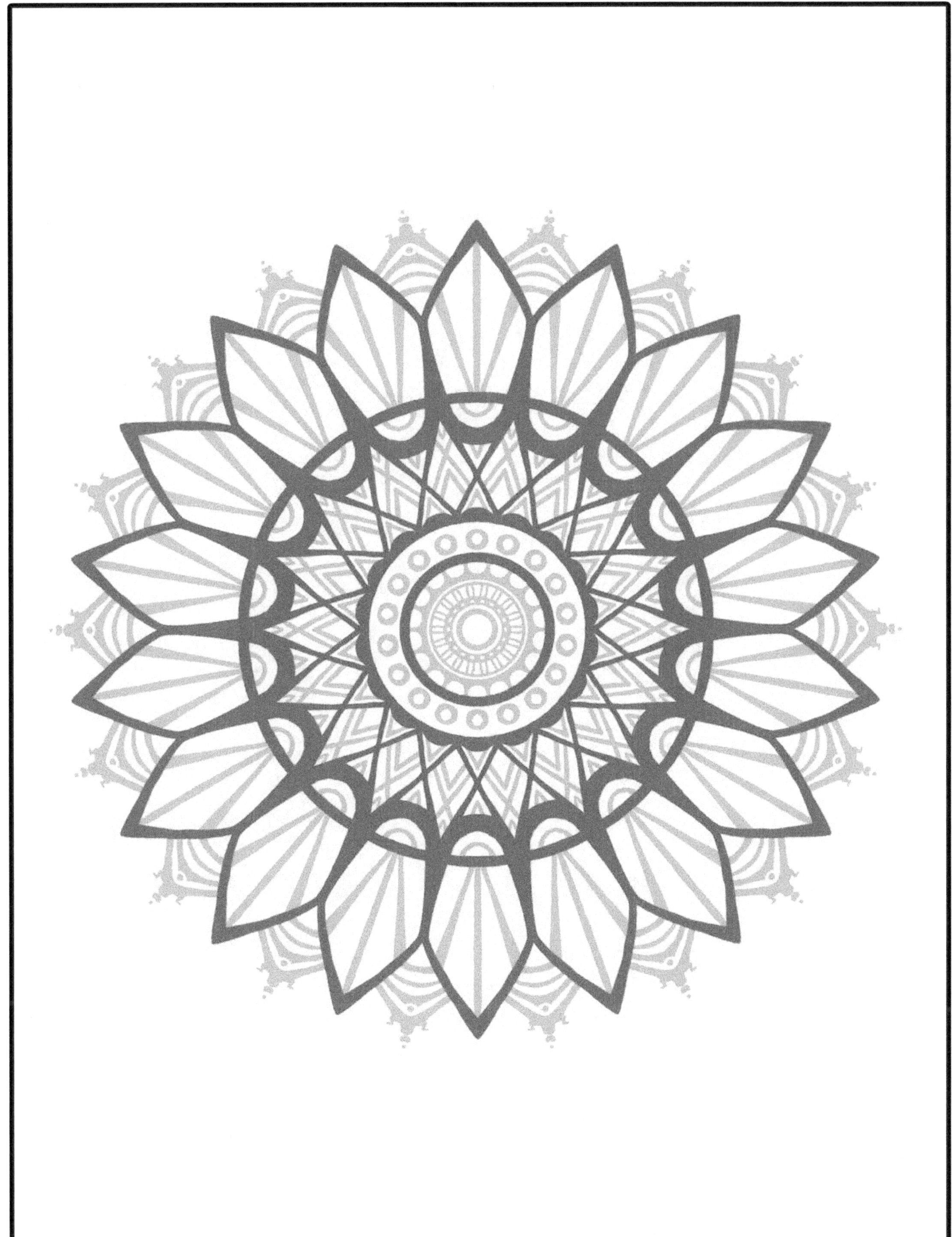

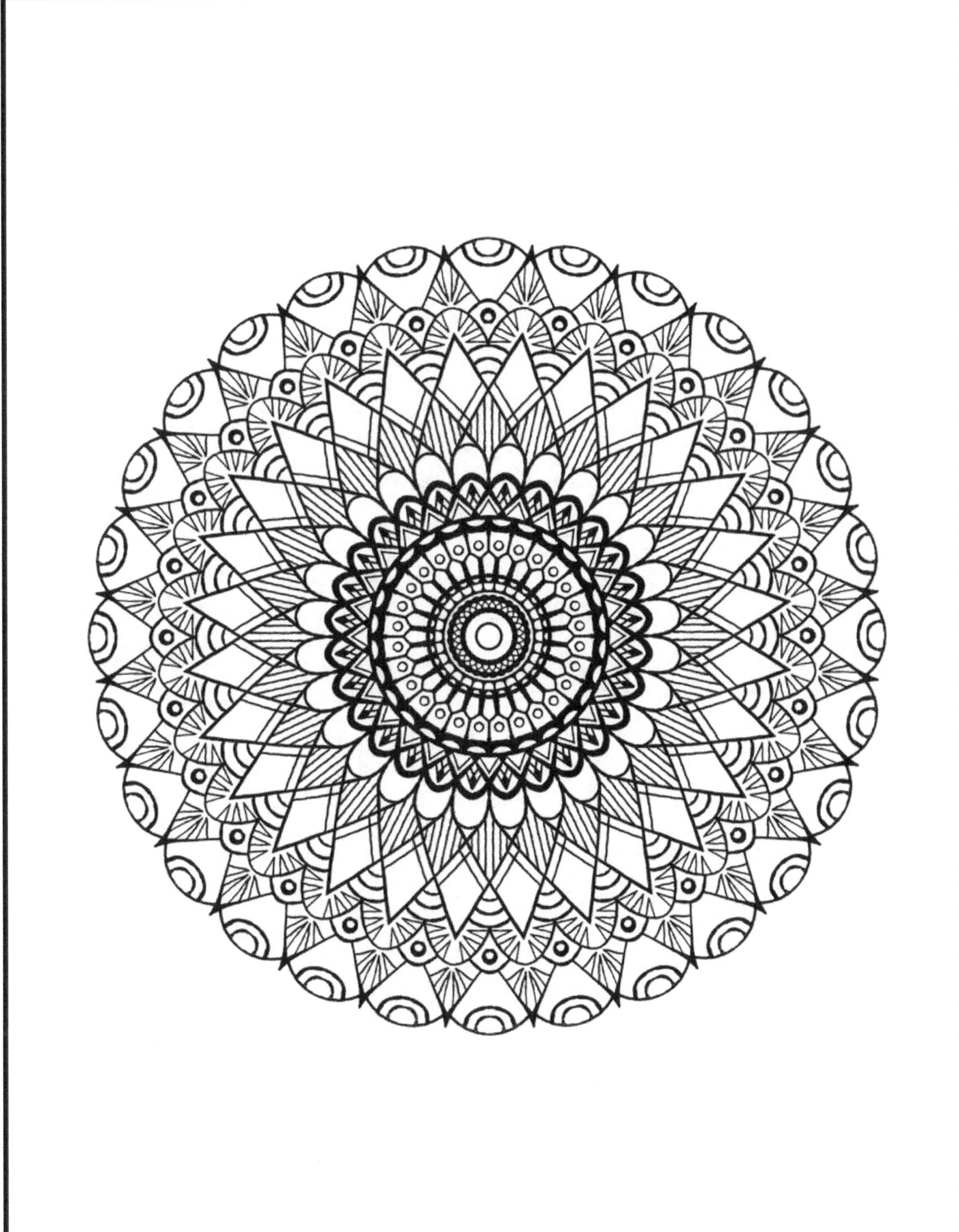

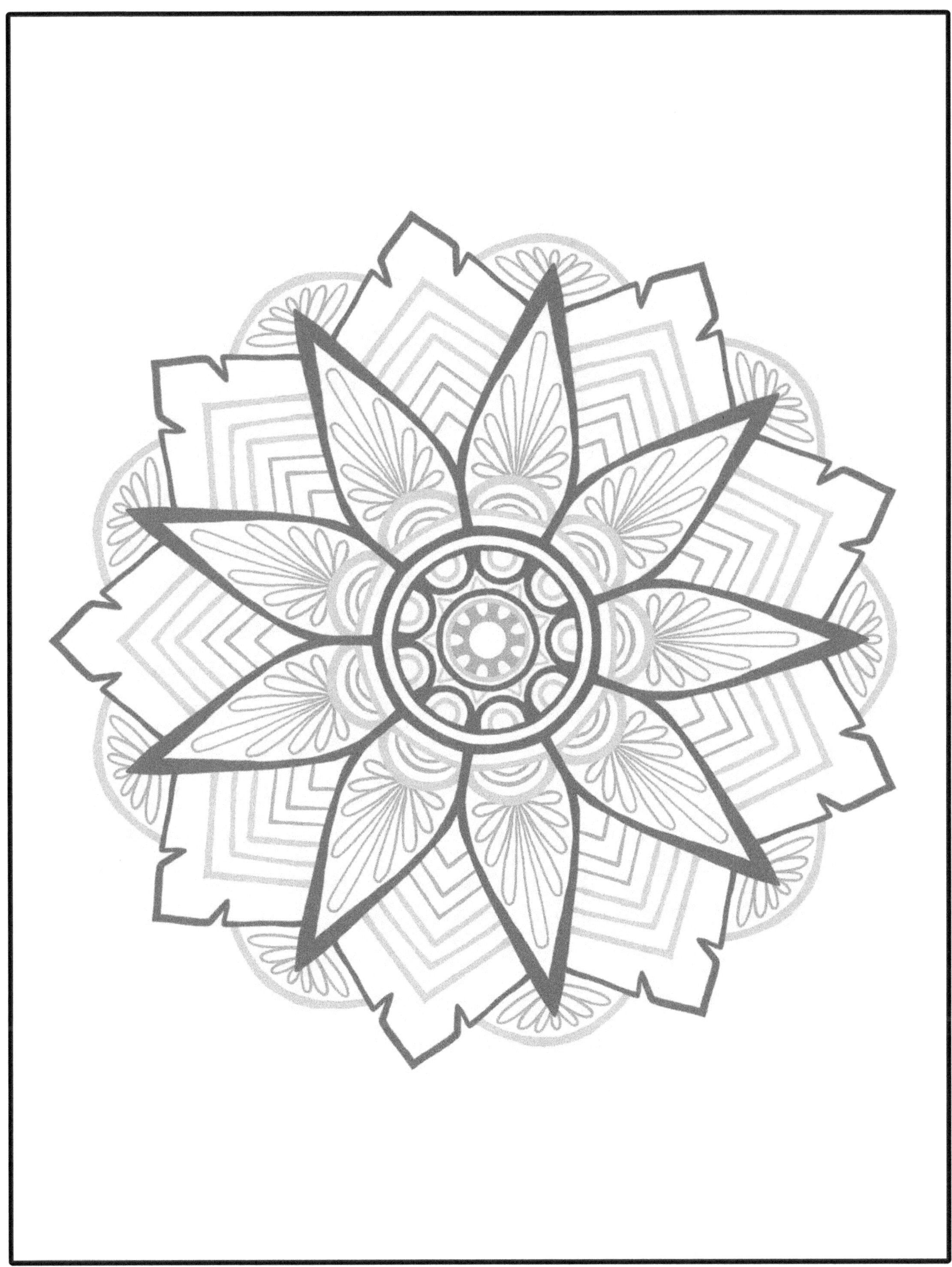

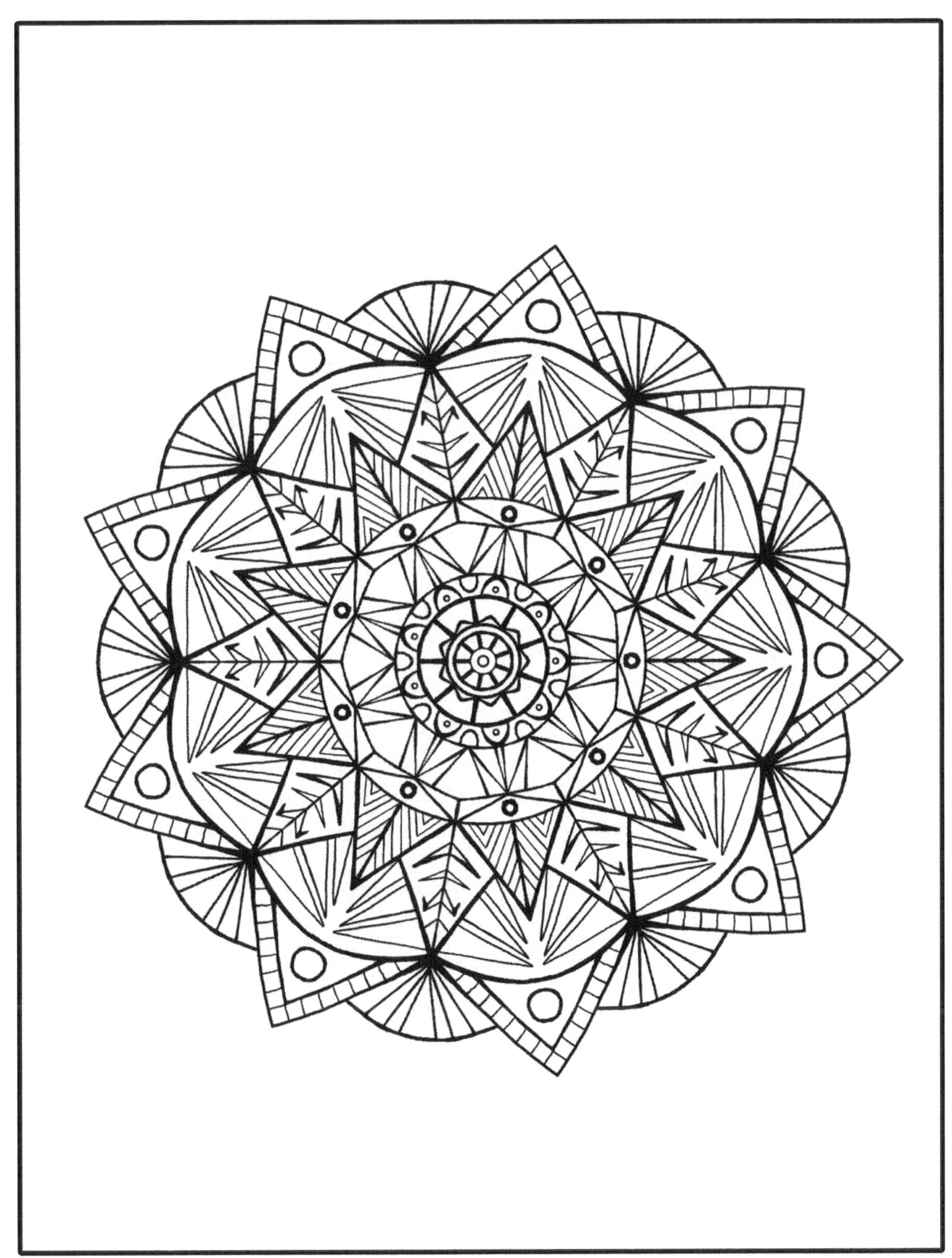

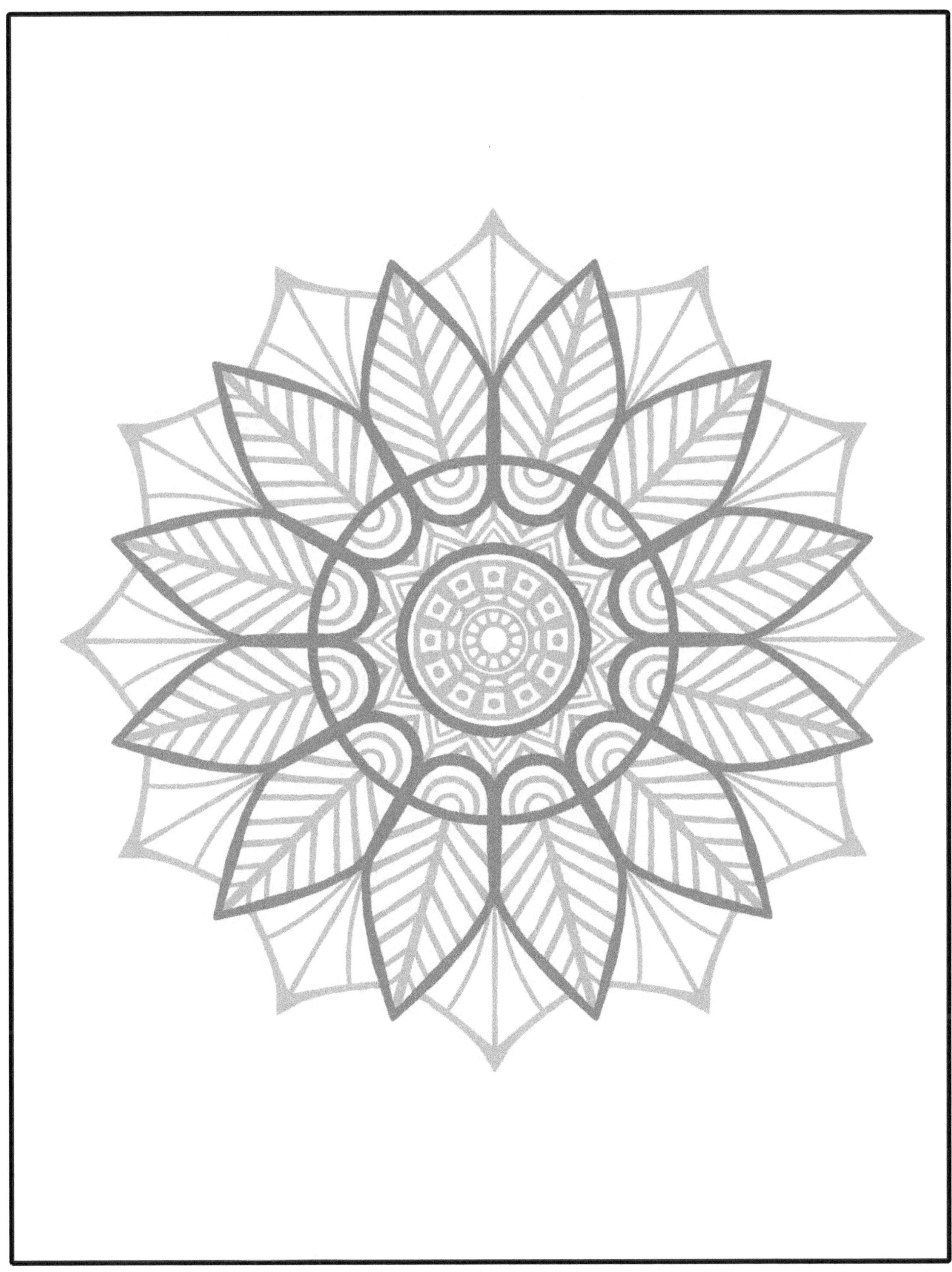

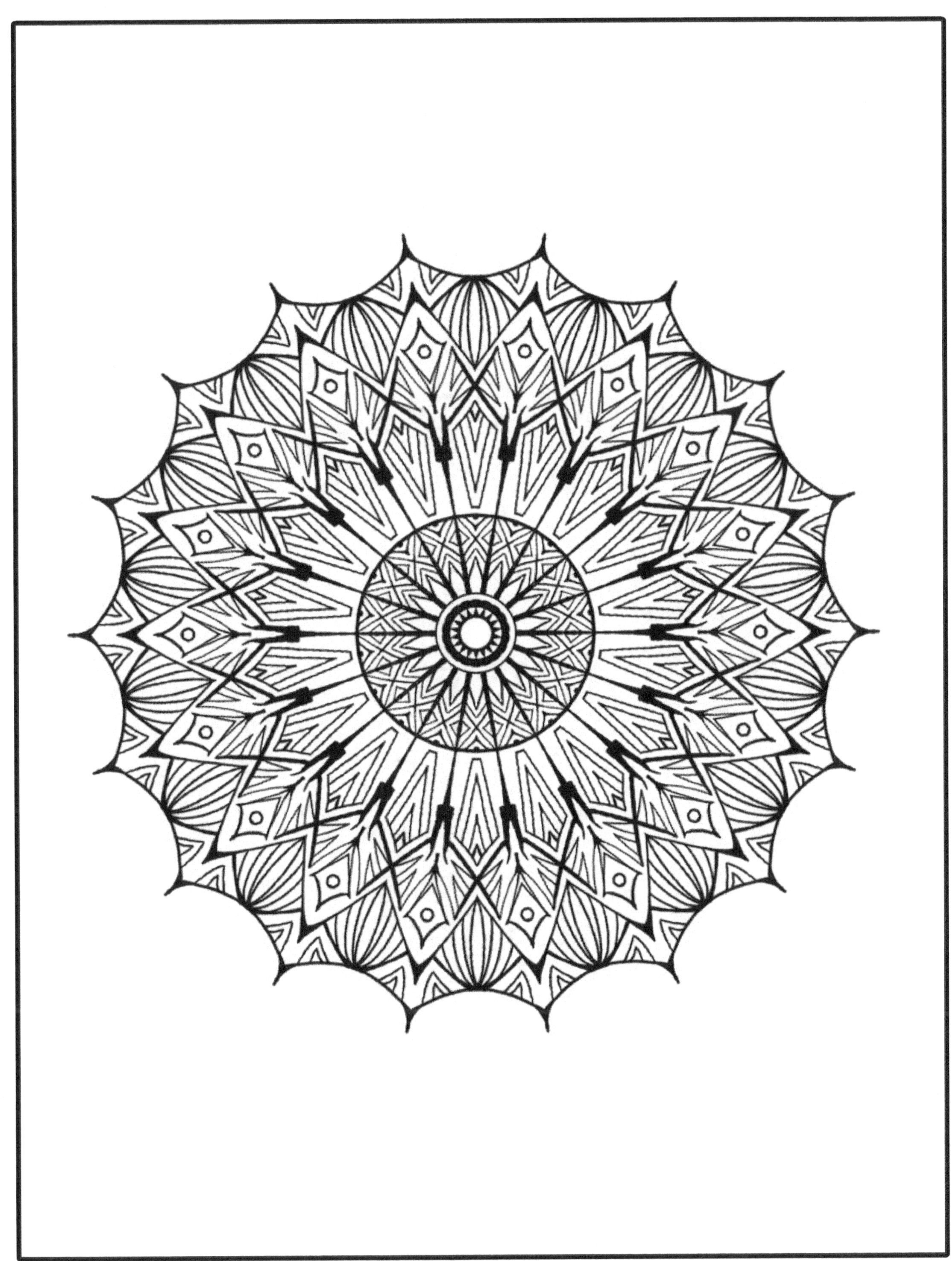

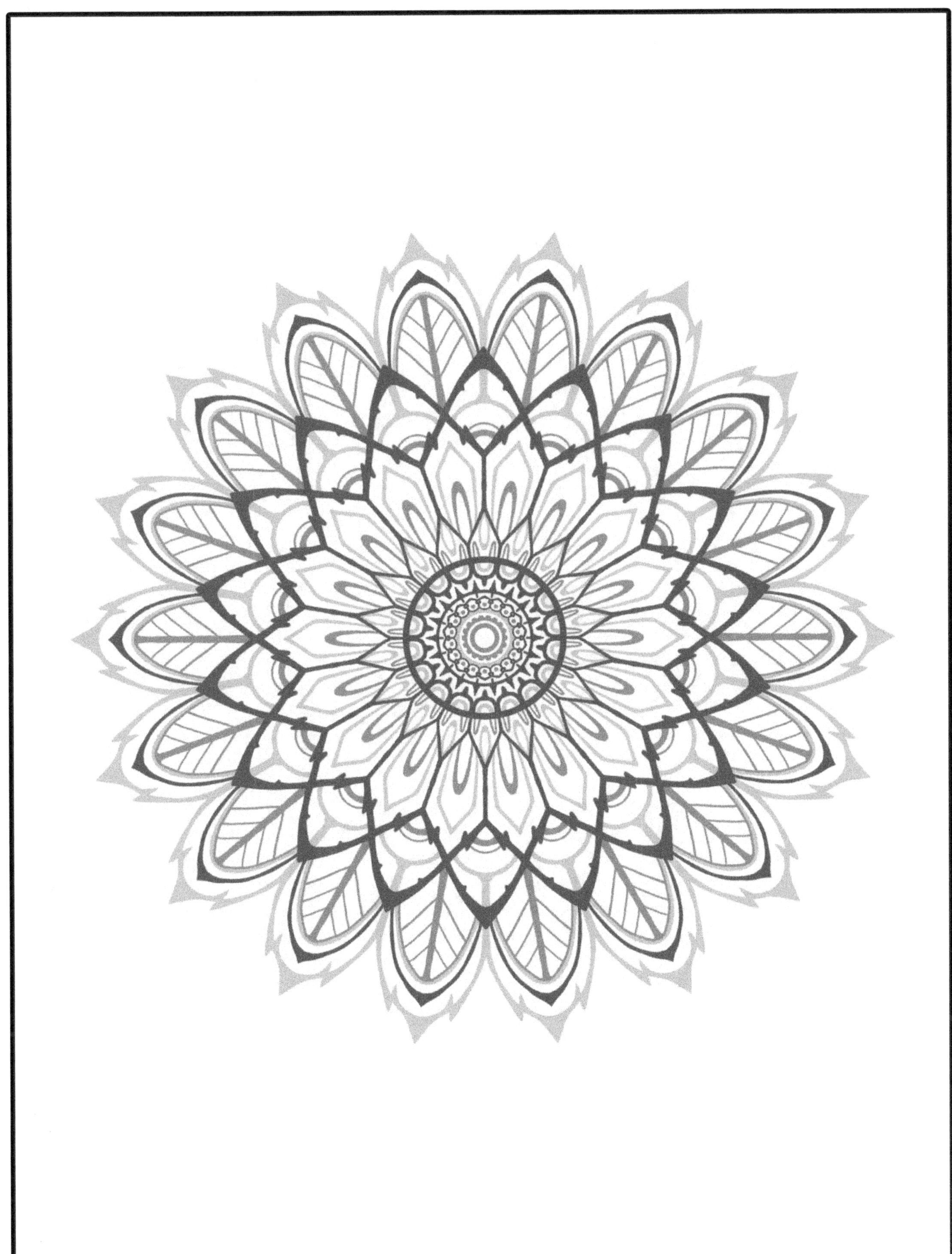

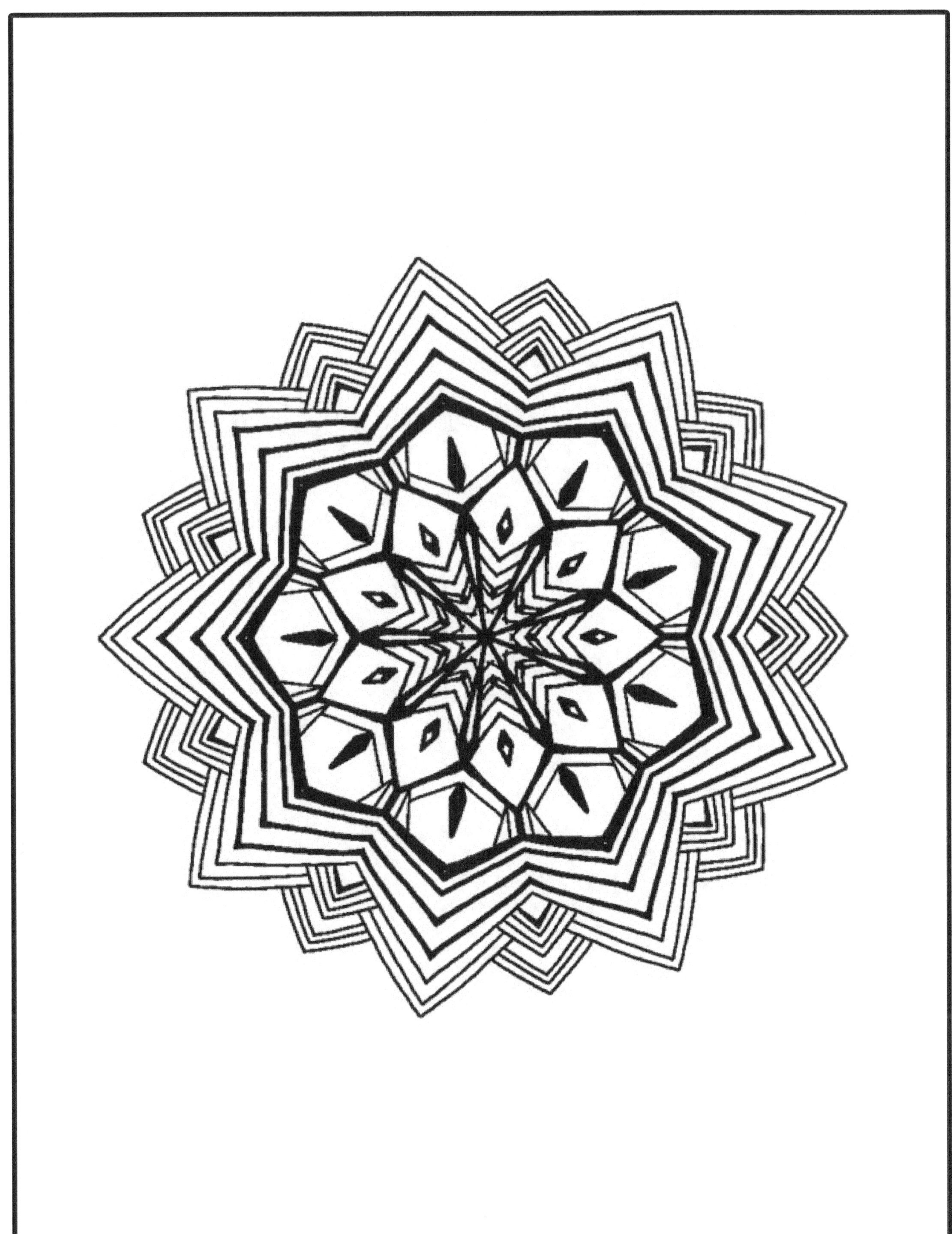

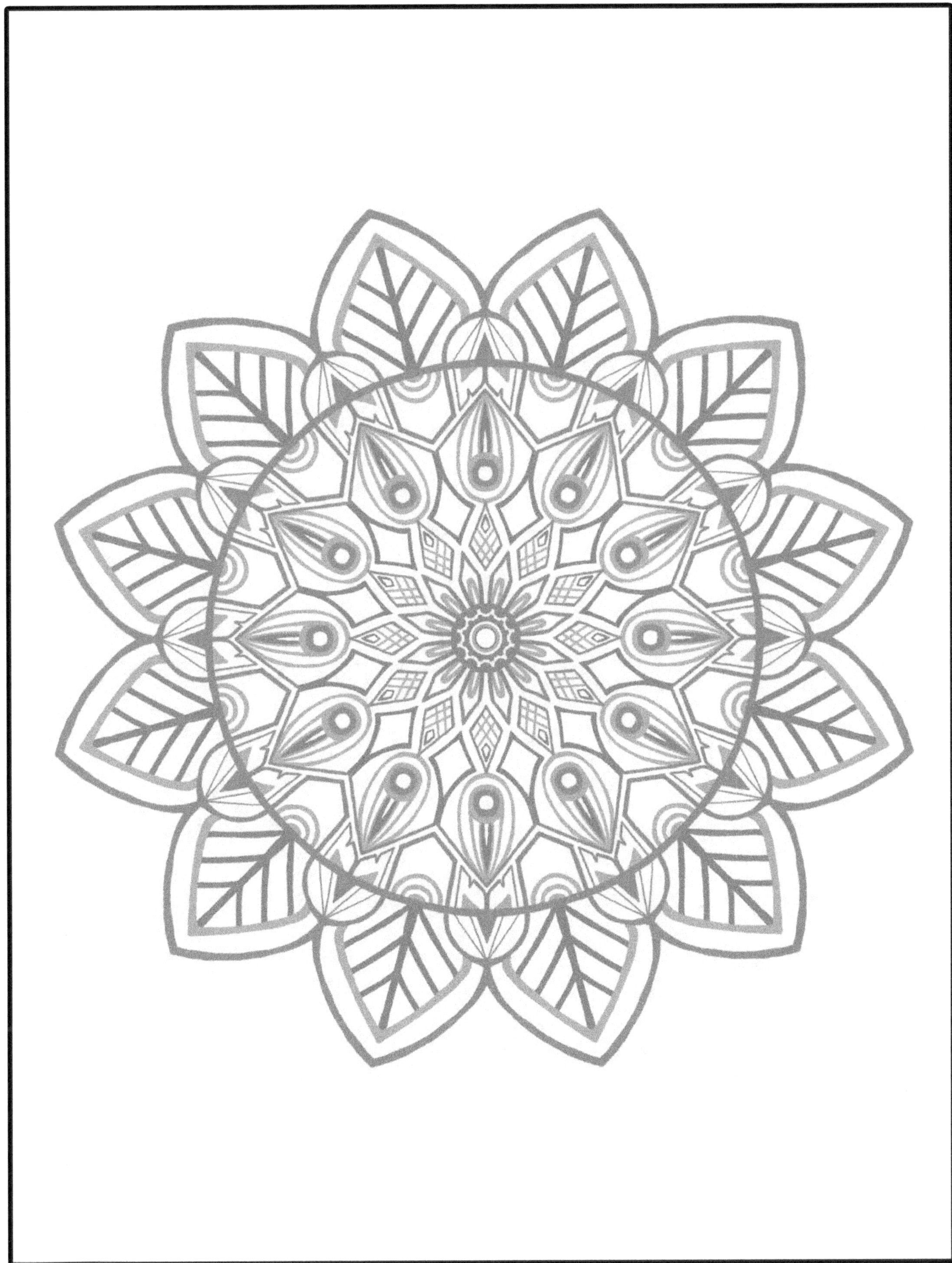

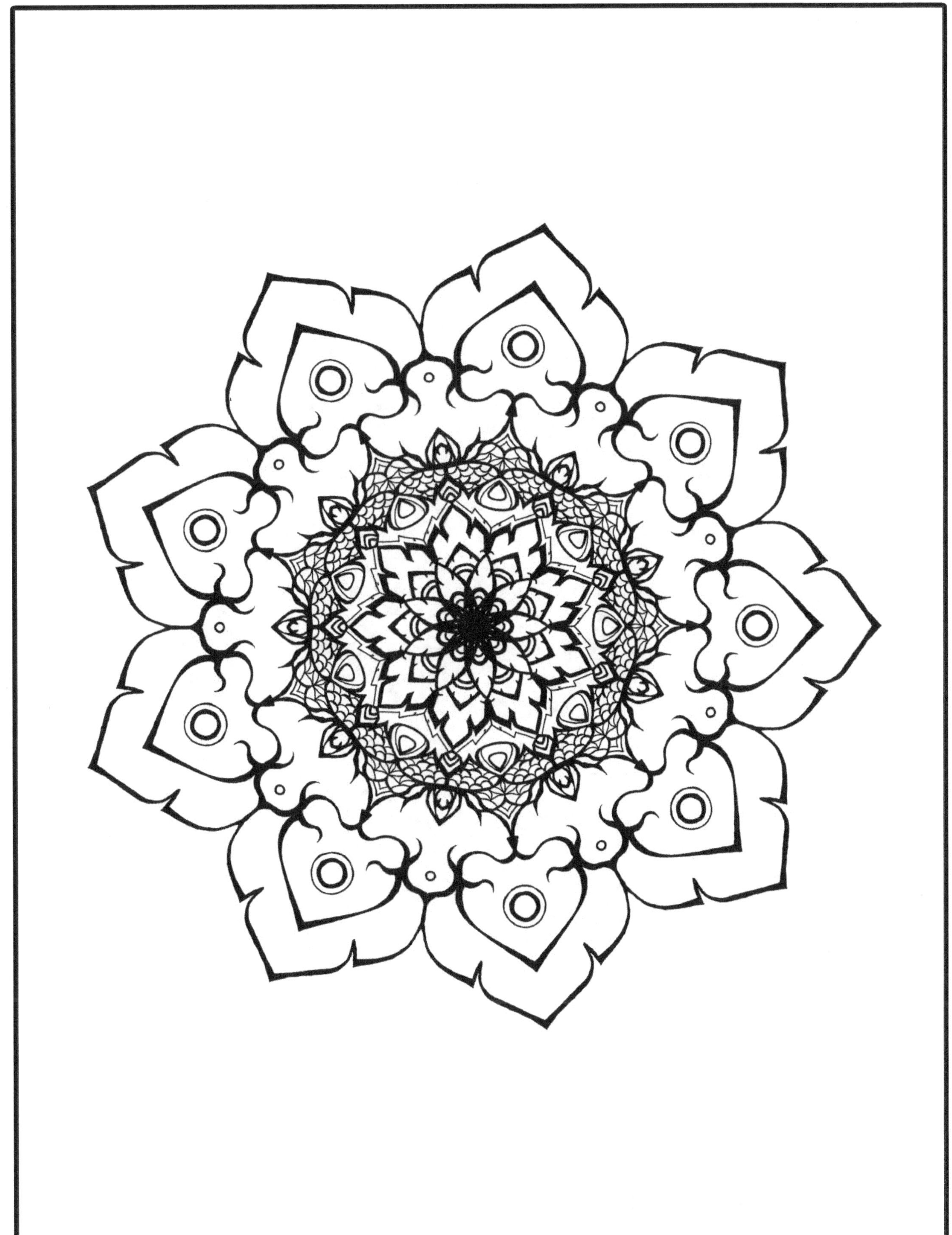

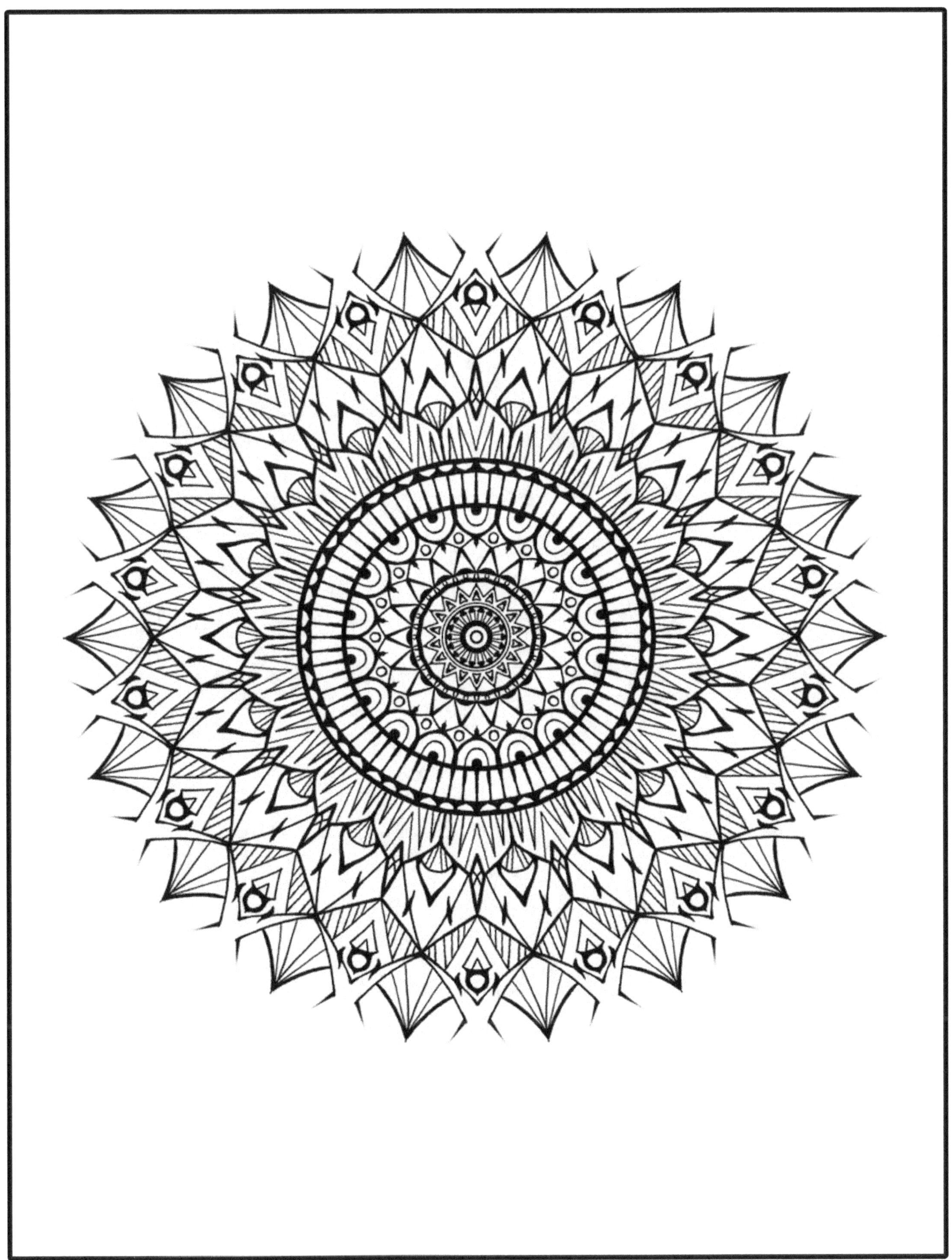

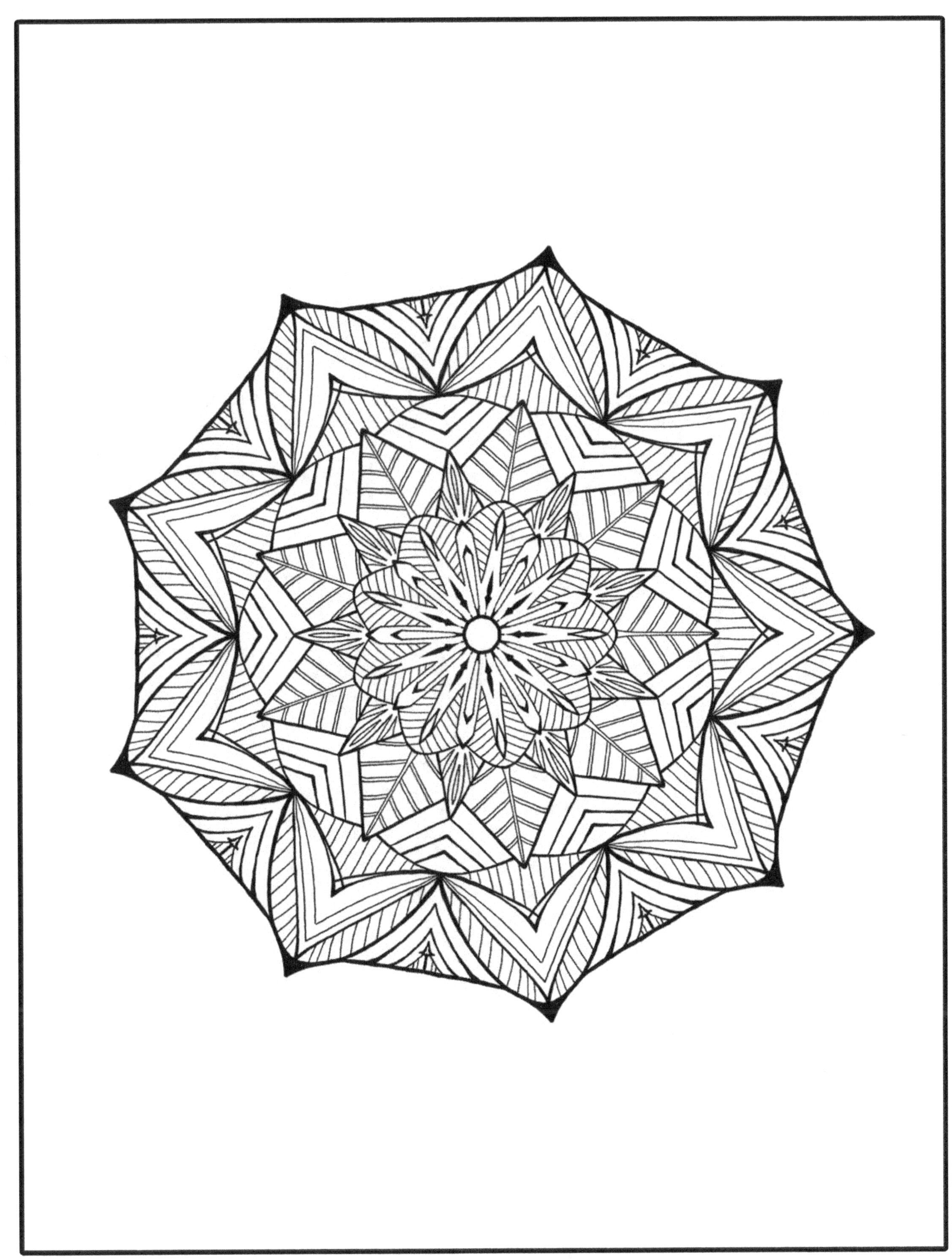

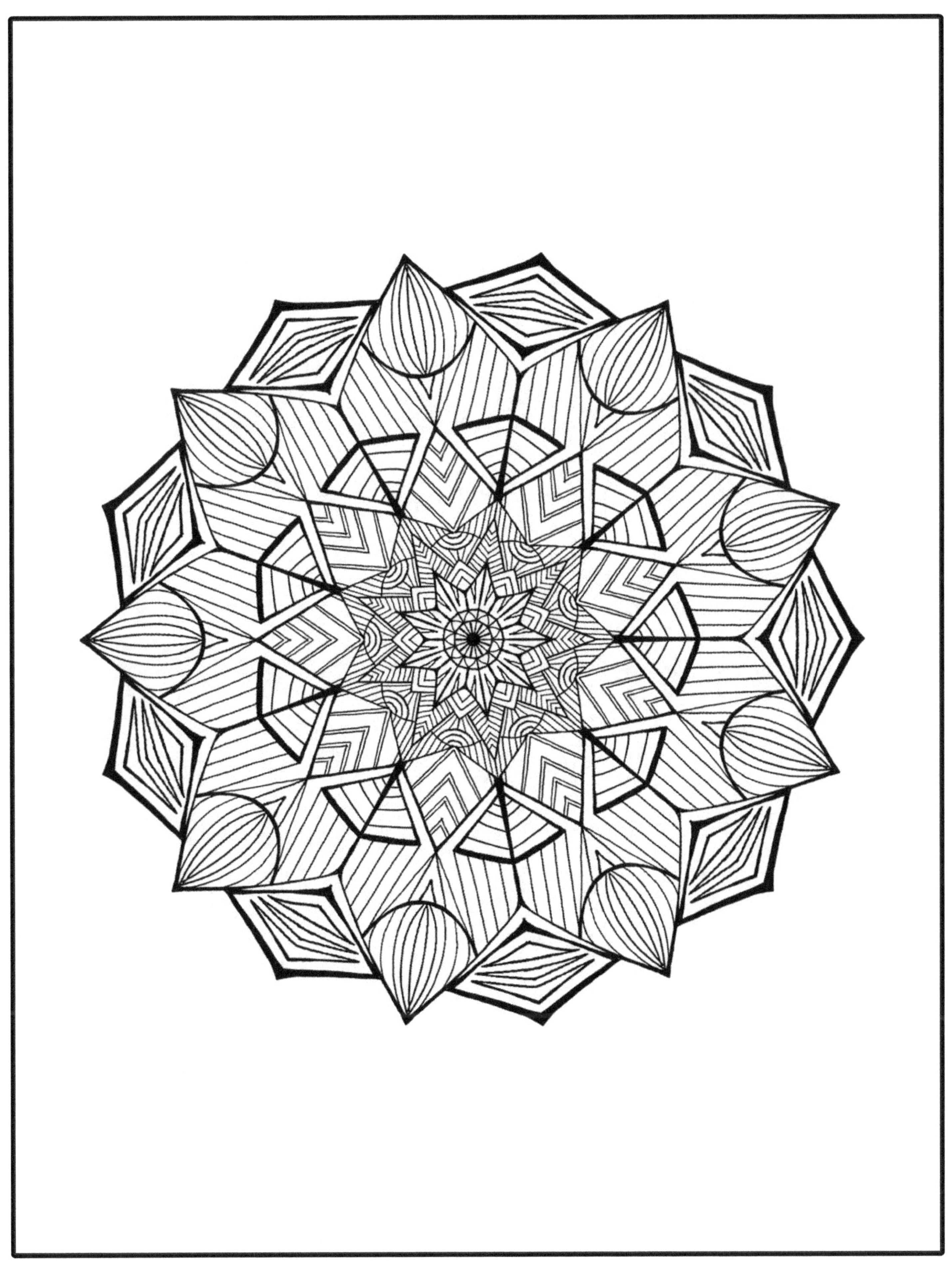

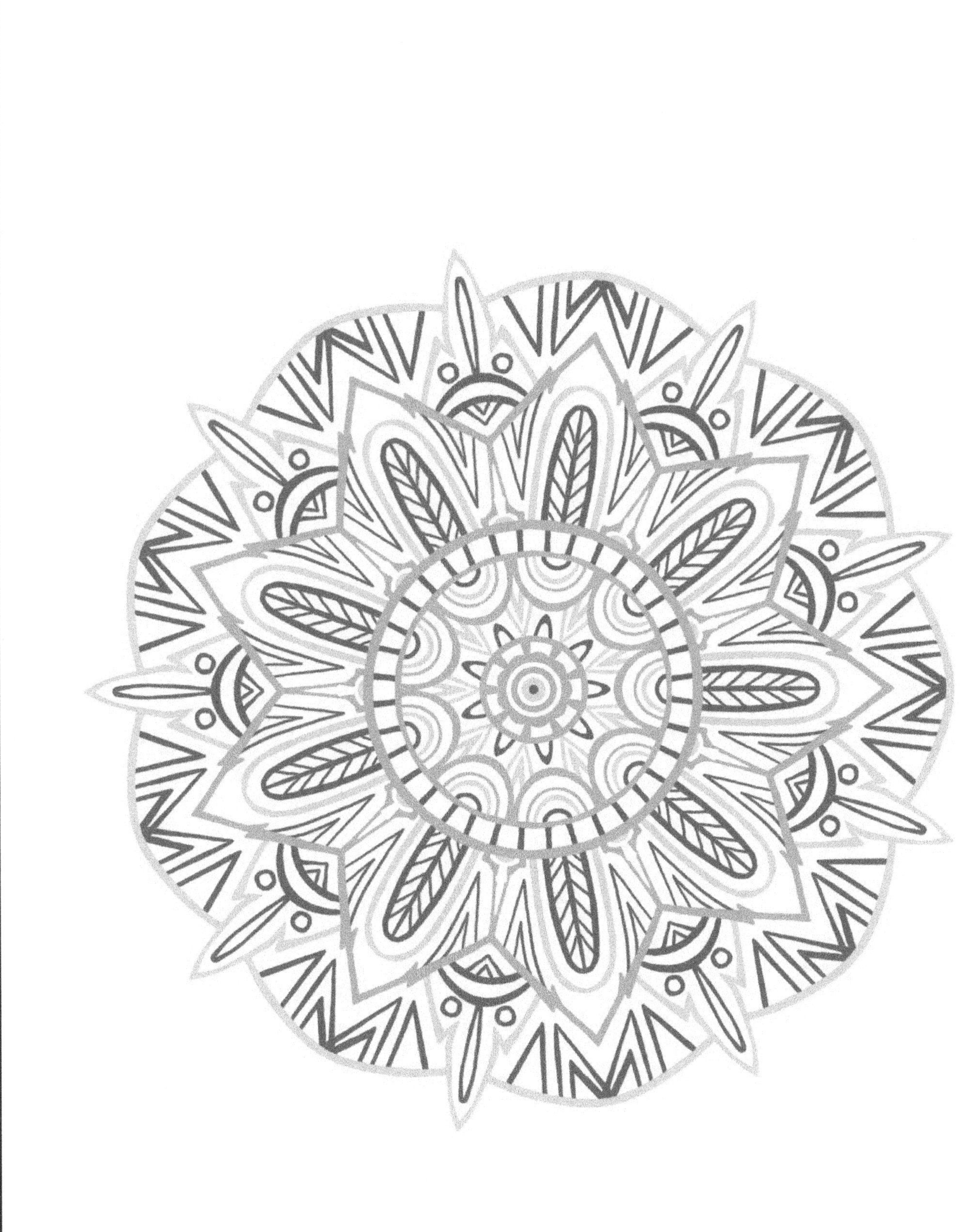

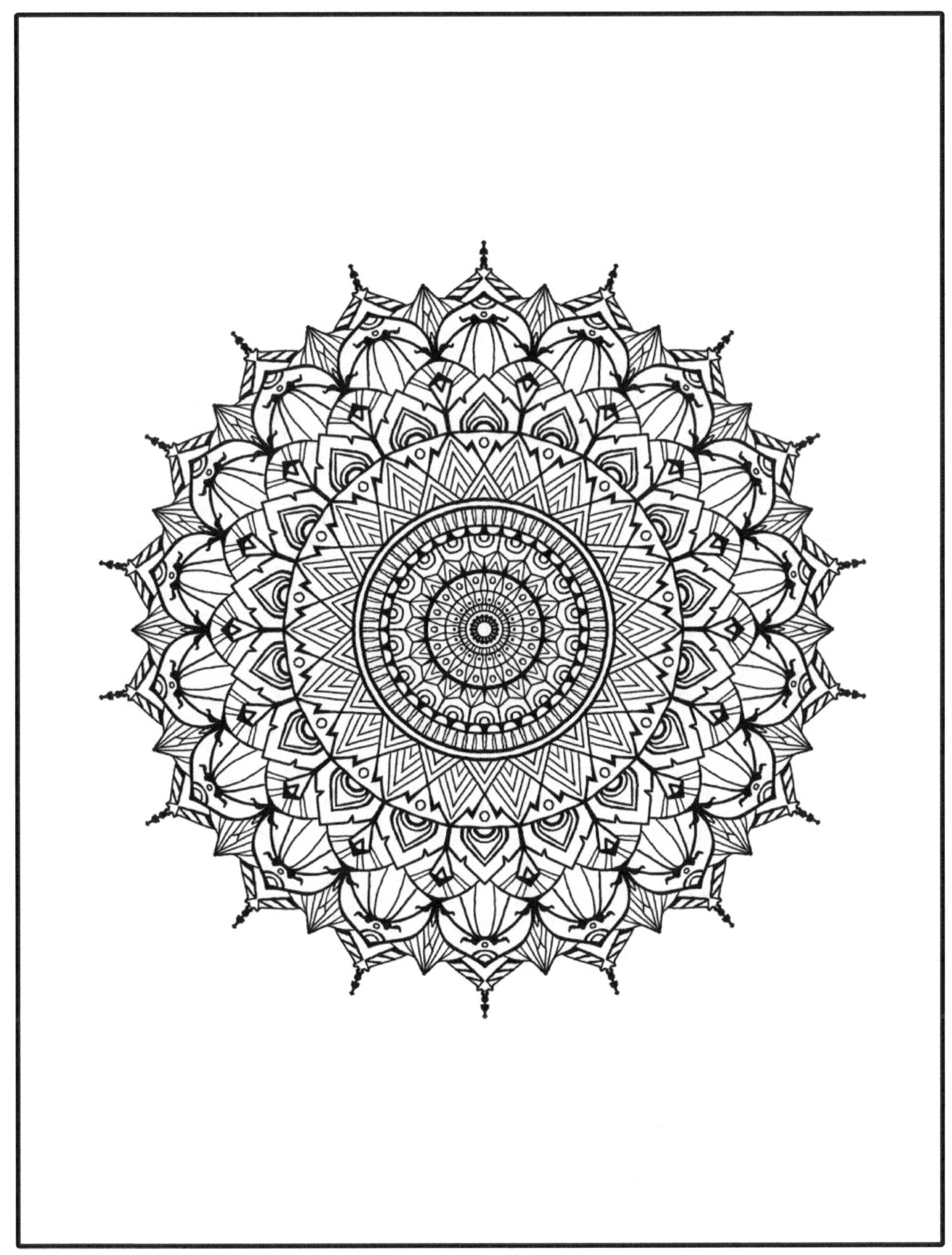

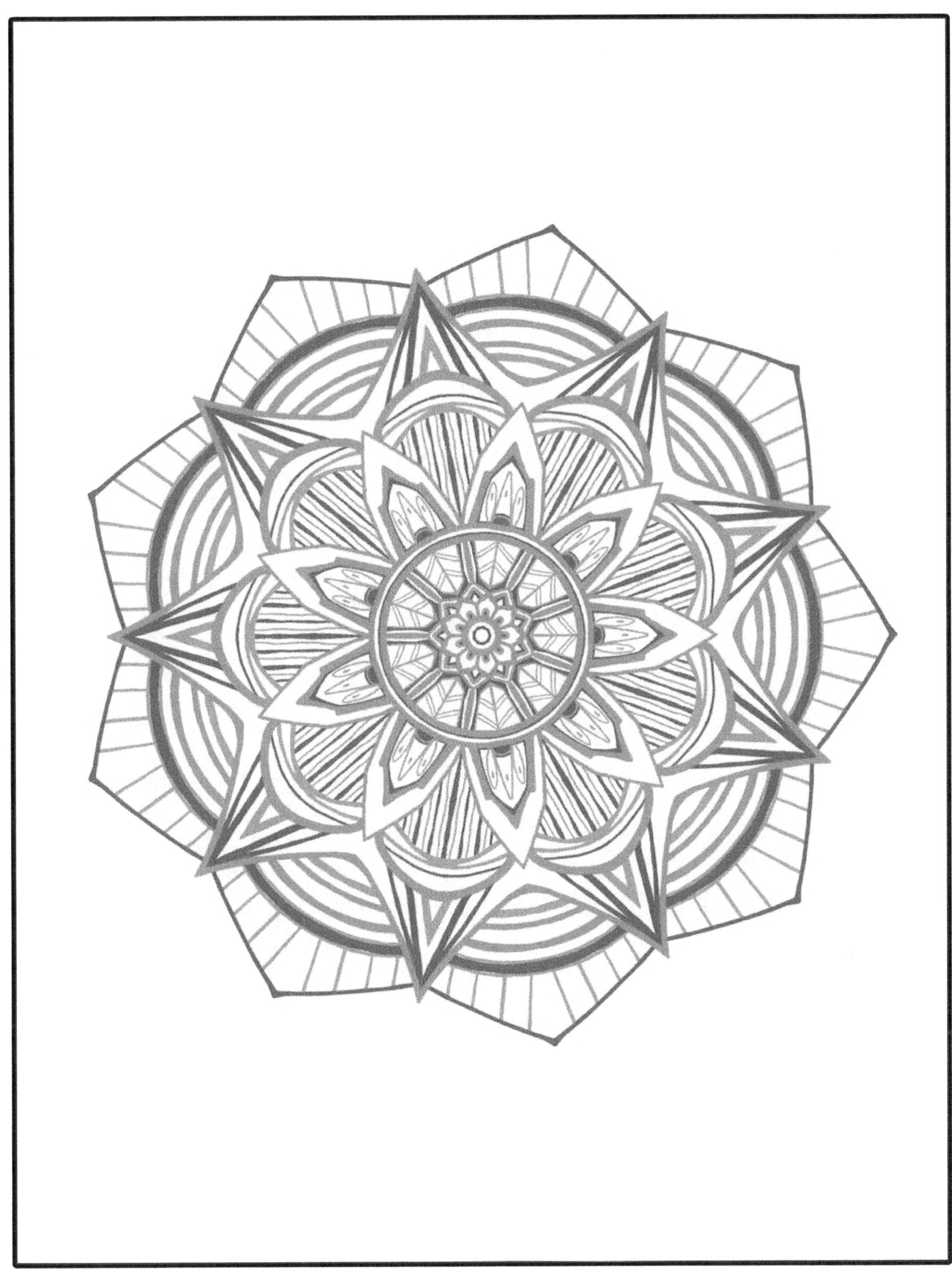

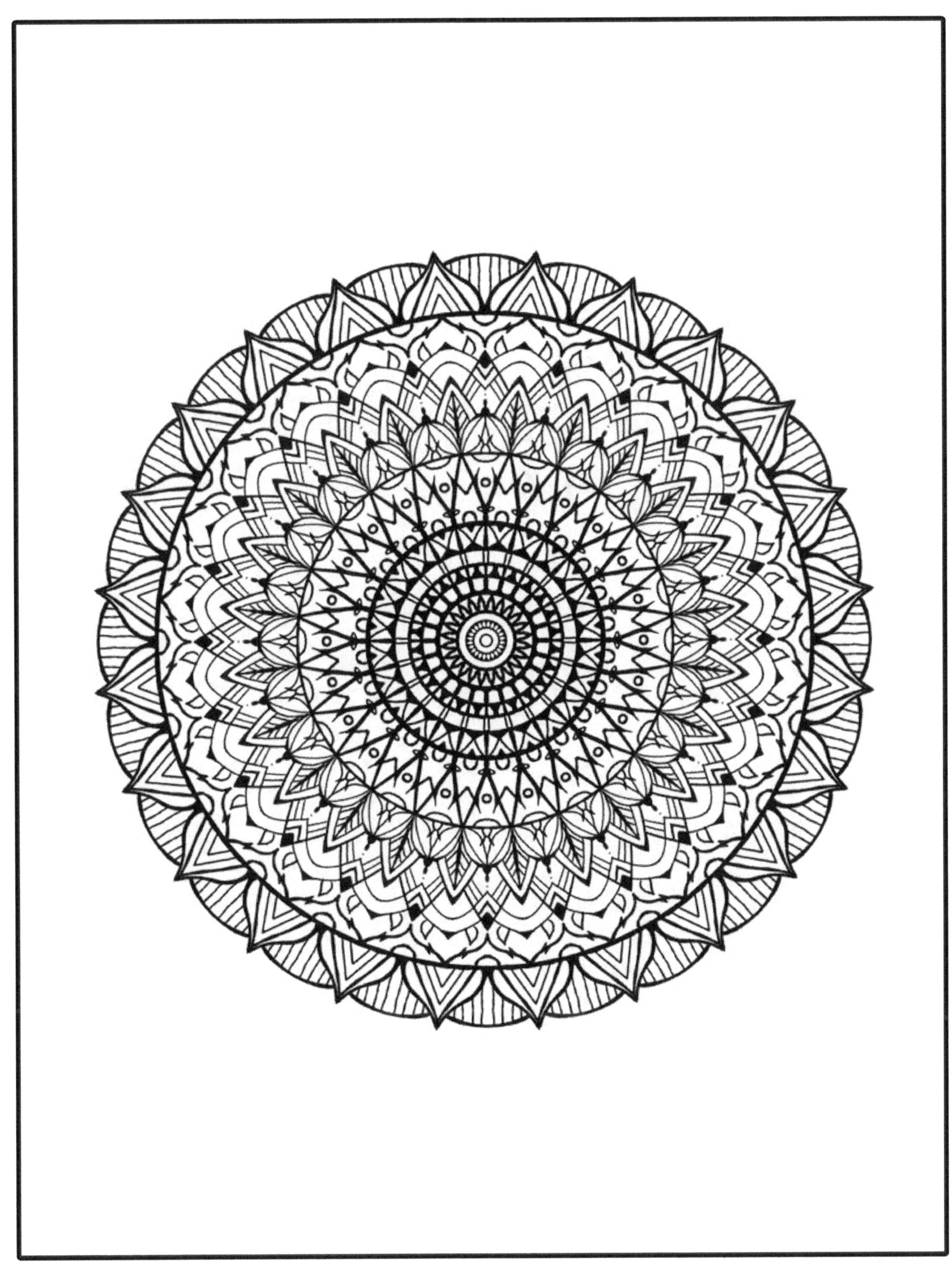

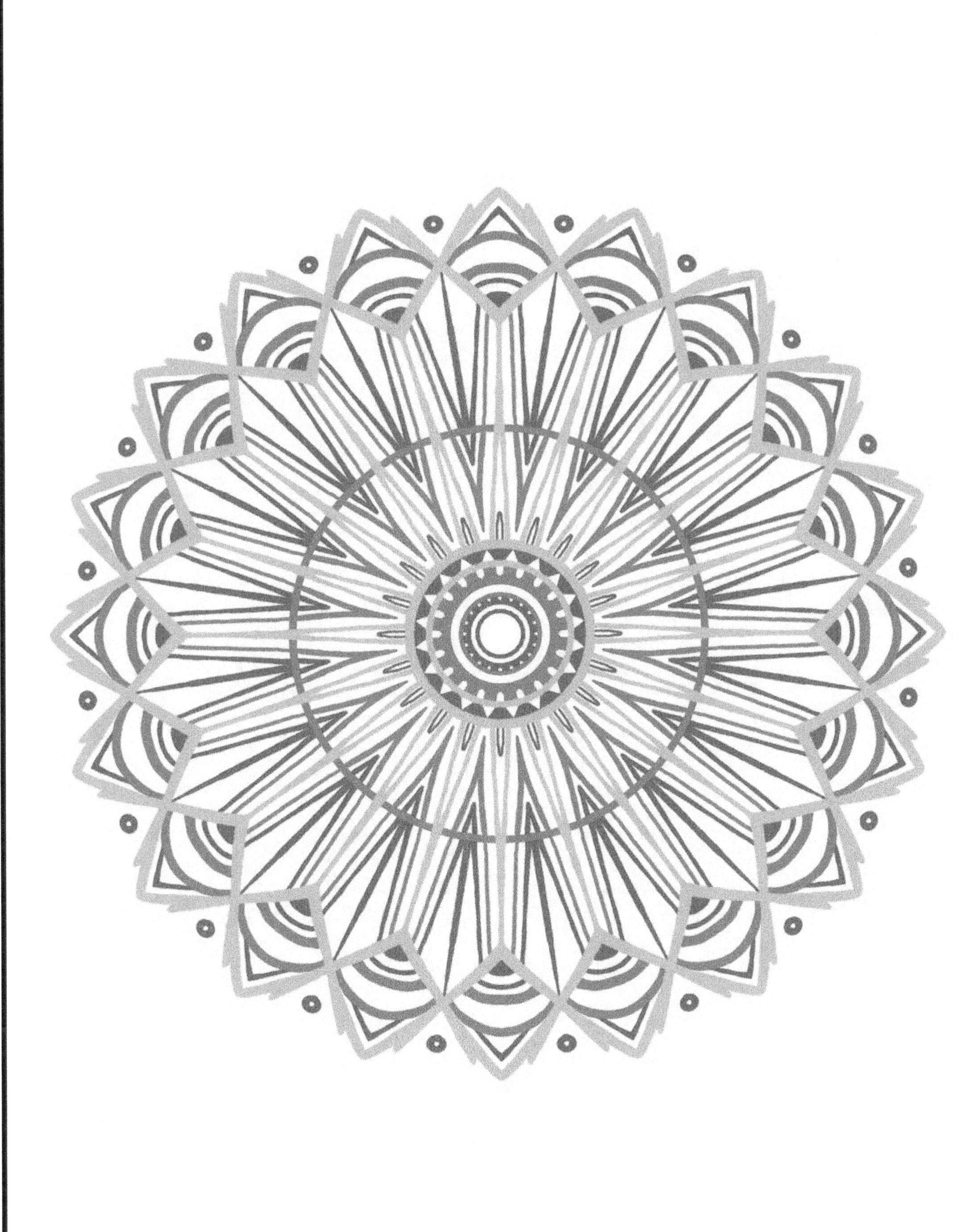

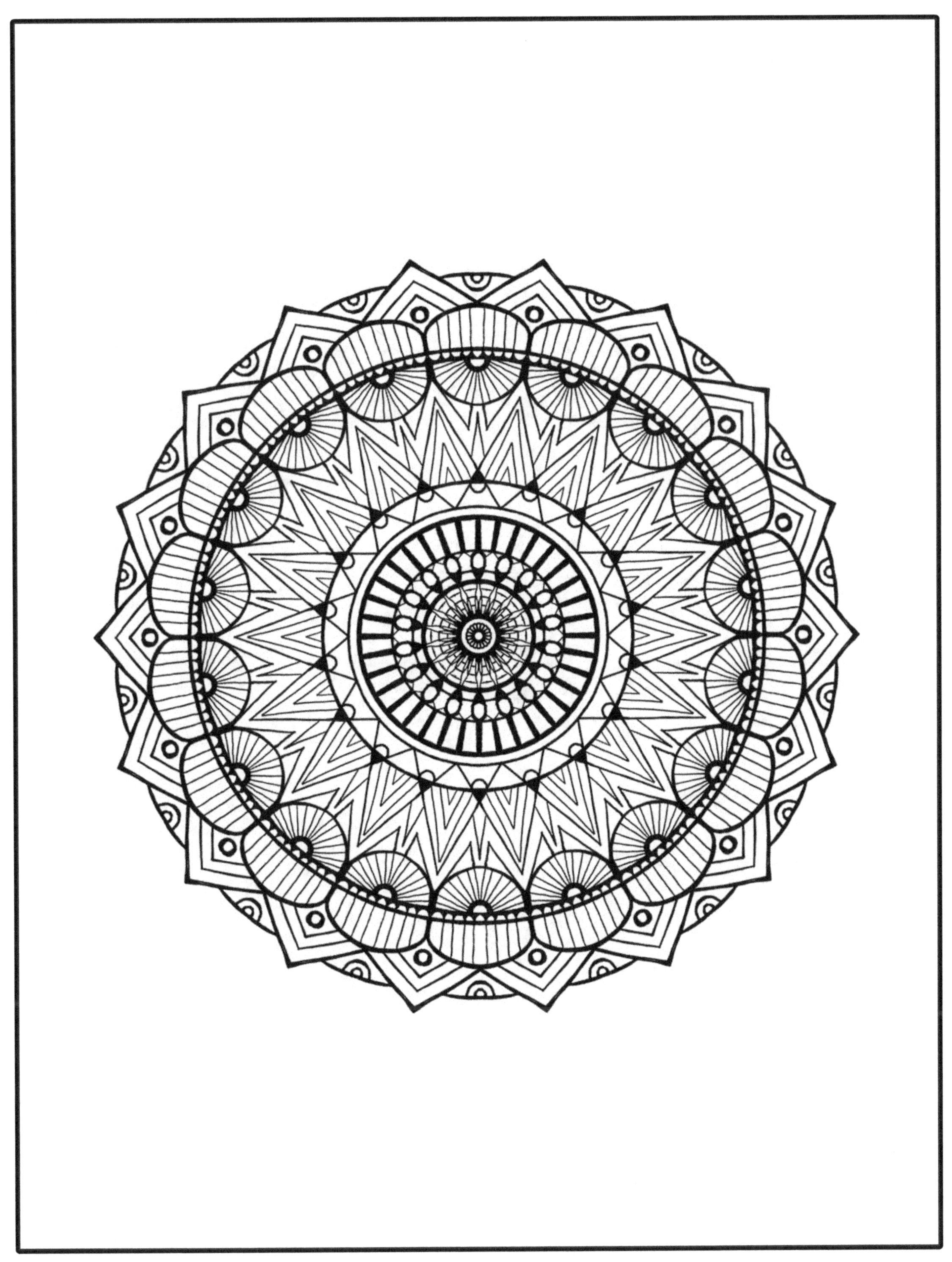

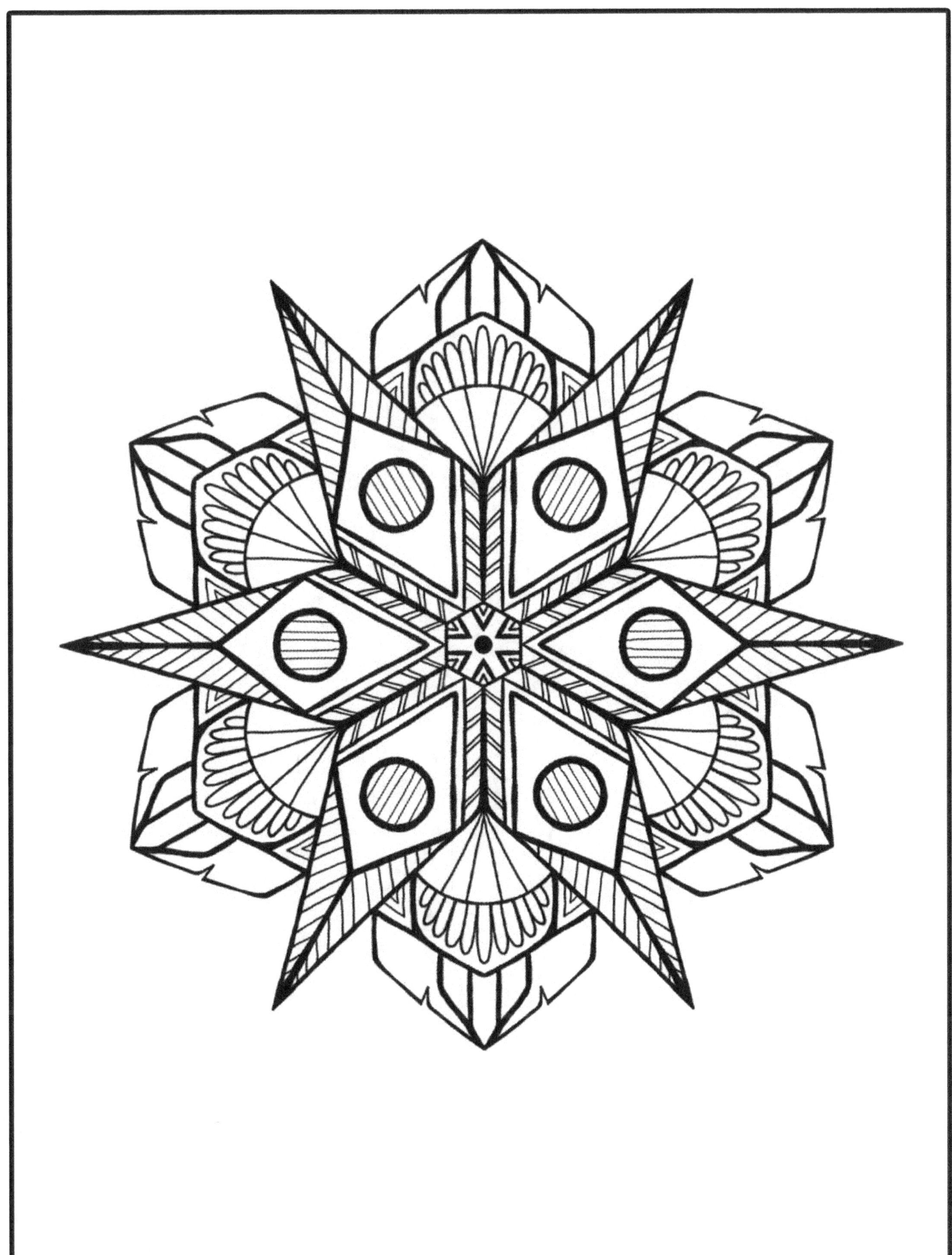

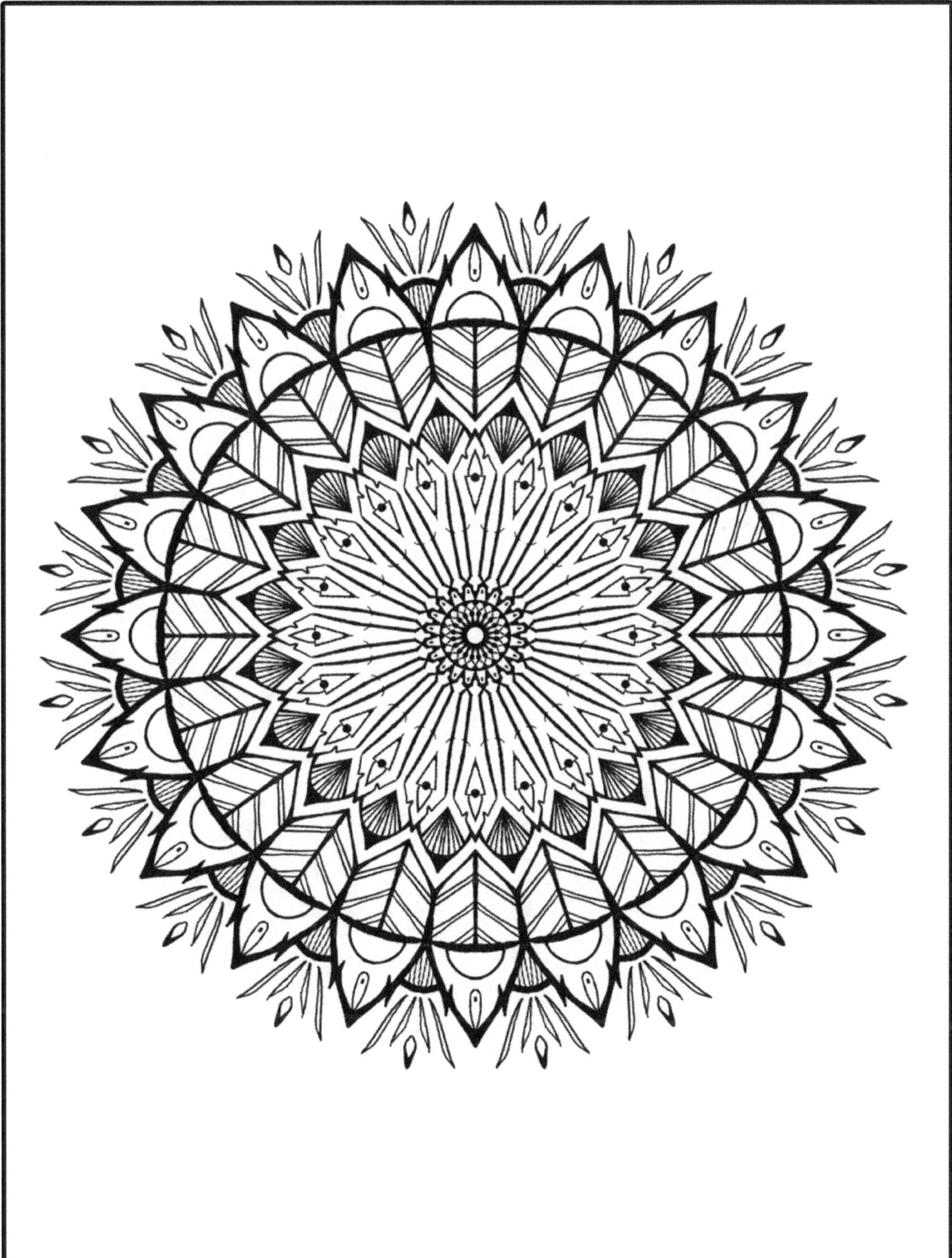

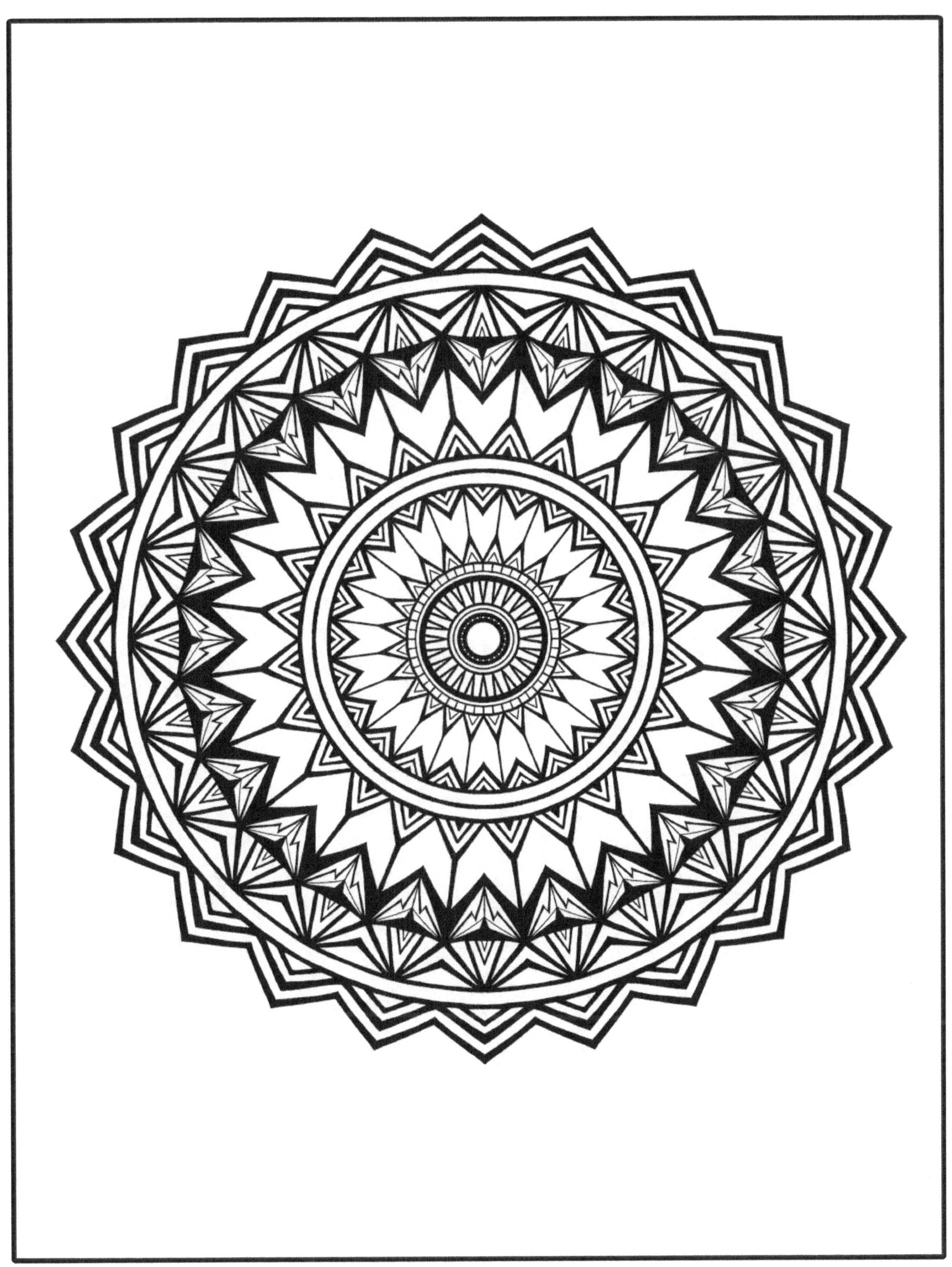

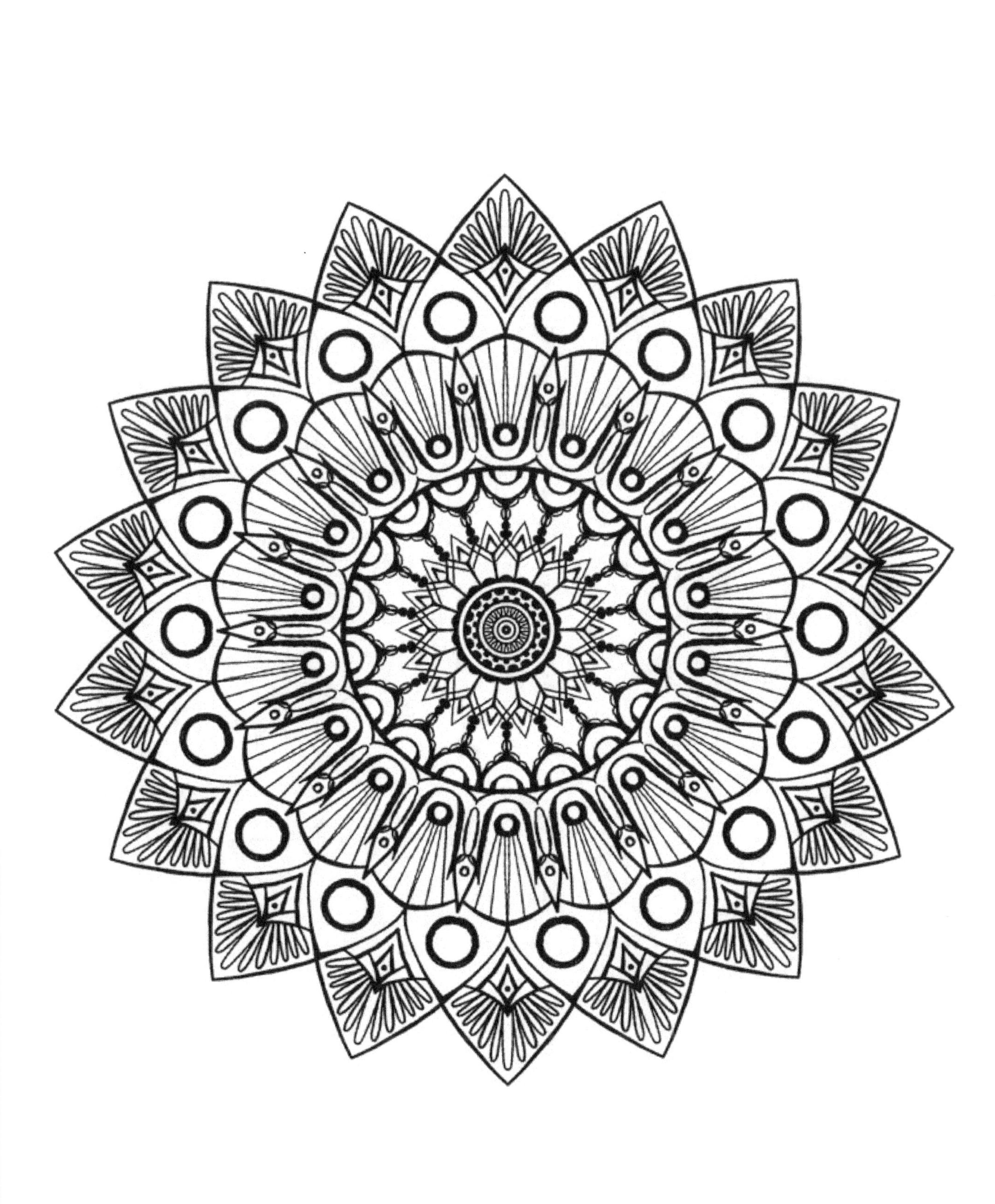

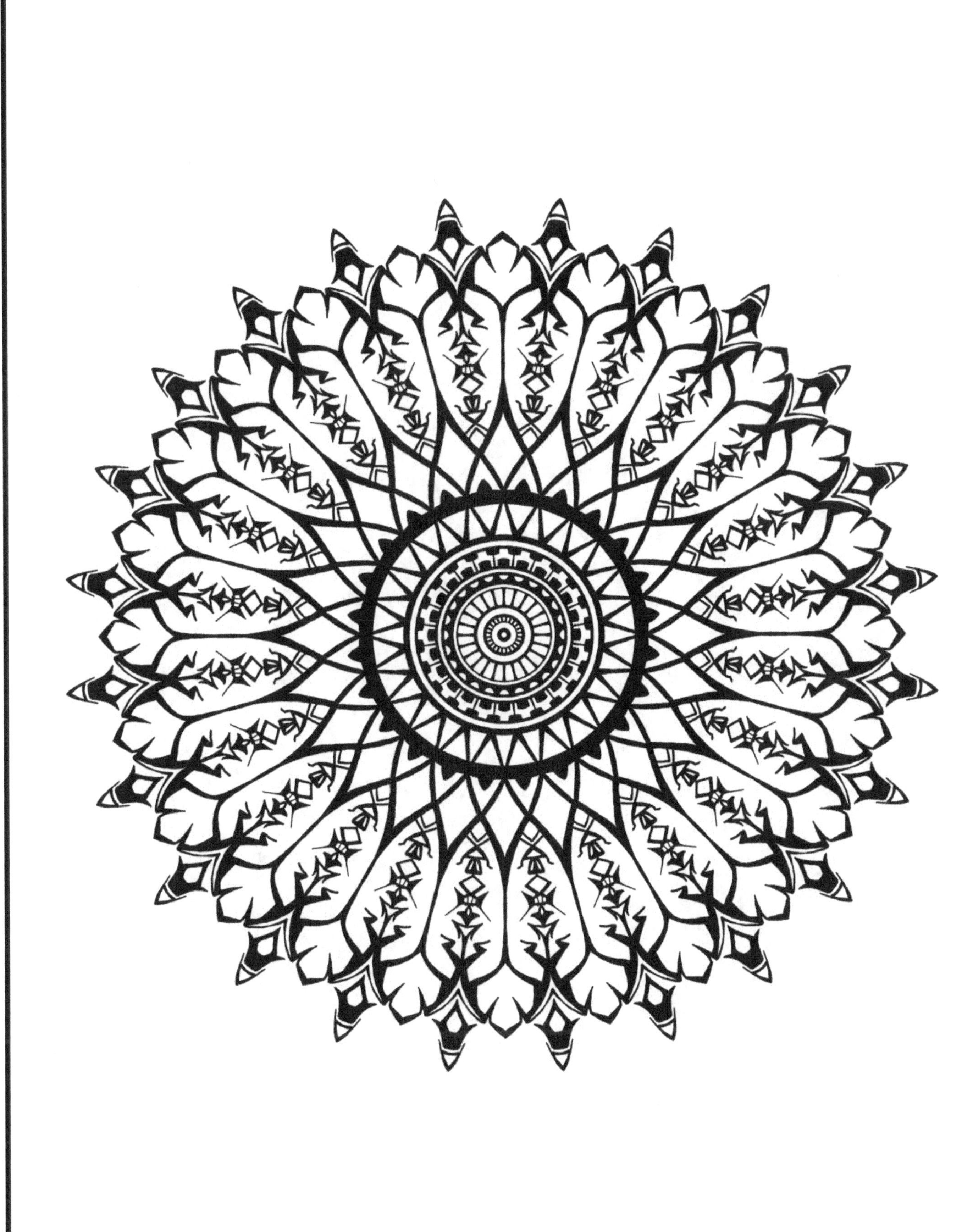

COLOR TEST PAGE

COLOR TEST PAGE